WHY THEY THINK I'M CRAZY

Except When They Really Think About It

Cover Art by: Dino Valdez, Jr.
www.undesigned.nu

Why They Think I'm Crazy

© 2010 by Carlespie Mary Alice McKinney. All rights reserved.

Published by Folklore Entertainment, LLC

No part of this book may be used or reproduced in any manner whatsoever without the written permission of the publisher, except in the case of brief quotations embodied in reviews.

Folklore Entertainment, LLC
500 River Place Drive
#5115
Detroit, MI 48207

folklore.entertainment@yahoo.com

Library of Congress Cataloging in Publication Data

McKinney, Carlespie M.A.

Why They Think I'm Crazy: Except When They Really Think About It

Carlespie Mary Alice McKinney

Includes Index.

ISBN: 0615336191

ISBN: 978-0-615-33619-0

1. Sociology – Modern Life.   2. Critical Thinking   3. Mary Alice

Printed and bound in the United States of America

WHY THEY THINK I'M CRAZY
Except When They Really Think About It

Carlespie Mary Alice McKinney

FolkLore Entertainment, LLC
folklore.entertainment@yahoo.com

TABLE OF CONTENTS

11 Turns Along My Twisted Path	i
Introduction	iii
Acknowledgements	v
Special Thanks	ix

Essay — **Page**

Scenes From The Human Drama

#	Title	Page
1	20 Things I Wish I Had Known When I Was 20	1
2	When The Student Wags The Teacher	4
3	How Sweet The Bitter Taste	6
4	Some Of The Facts Of Life On Prison Earth	7
5	The Kindest Cut Of All	10
6	Friendship (Part I)	12
7	A Tale Of Two Friends	14
8	They Said It Better Than I	16
9	Oranges Falling From An Apple Tree	18
10	A Few Things To Put On Your Mind	20
11	Served Without Notice	22
12	The Most Common Fool	23
13	The Most Important Ancestor	25
14	My Three Choices	28
15	I Doubt It	30
16	Self-Preservation – A Control Button	31
17	A Few Ends And Some Odds About Politics	33
18	The Infection Called "Stupiditis"	35
19	The Thick And Thin Of Blood And Water	37
20	Irony's Double Edge	39
21	What If (Part I)	41
22	How To Make The Best Movies About Your Life	43

Essay		Page
23	Character References – Revelation Versus Definition	45
24	Three Shades Of Motive	47
25	Beauty Me Or Beauty Thee	50
26	Four Random Thoughts	52
27	Blathering And Babbling On Planet Babel	55
28	The Mathematics Of Morality	59
29	Sanctity Of The Self	62
30	The Two Sisters: Timing And Consequences	65
31	The Unfair Fight: Truth Versus Opinion	66
32	Being "Right" Rather Than Being Right	67
33	The Locked Up Mind	69
34	Problem-Solving Jujitsu Style	72
35	Forgiveness? Walking And Chewing Gum At The Same Time	74
36	The Nature Of Power	76
37	Death By Punishment	78
38	Spanking The Butt Or Spanking The Mind	82
39	The Two-Headed Hypocrisy Of Abortion	84
40	Choosing Your Battles	87
41	Imagine	89
42	Ordinary Tragedy	91
43	Unconditional Love And Self-Hatred	93
44	Why The Owl Killed The Rooster	97
45	The Celebrity Of Self (Orbiting Your Own Star)	99
46	Heroes And Un-Heroes	101
47	Reality Is Perception?	105
48	Why Things Happen – The Real Reason	106
49	Where Is "Karma" When You Need Her?	109
50	Sugar-Tasty Poison	111

Essay		Page
51	Sex In The Real City	113
52	There, But For The Grace Of …	115
53	Yesterday's Brighter Sun	118
54	The Proof Is In The Pattern	120
55	You Don't Have To Kill The Lawyers	123
56	My Brother's Keeper … My Brother's Rival	125
57	Why 1+1 Is Less Than 2	128
58	Males Who Impersonate Men	132
59	The United States Of White America	135
60	Penciled In Thoughts On Paper Minds	138
61	Shades of Different Black	140
62	The Dark Side	143
63	Truth Lies In The Gray	145
64	The Word For Used Toilet Tissue	147
65	Three Sounds Of Stupid	153
66	A Sweetest Sound	155
67	Three Beautiful Words	157
68	Beware What You Believe	159
69	The Reason And The Obligations (Being Human)	163

Water And Oil … God And Religion

70	What I Believe About God (Part I)	169
71	What I Believe About God (Part II)	171
72	"God" In Quotation Marks	173
73	My Road To Deism	174
74	Ye With Too Much Faith	179
75	Explaining Imagine	184
76	Religion 101 (Introduction To Religion)	187

Essay		Page
77	What Religion Does Well	188
78	If I Were "God"	193
79	A Glass Of Power For The Thirsty	196
80	Religion: Reductio Ad Absurdum	199
81	Distinctions Without A Difference	201
82	Revelation Versus Evolution	203
83	Four More Said That Need To Be Things	205
84	Why "God" Never Says, "You're Welcome"	207
85	Out Of The Mouths Of Babes	209
86	Blessed	212
87	Holy Is As Holy Does	214
88	Coming To "God's" Defense	215
89	Maintaining "God's" Image	217
90	Playing "God" Or Being "God"	221
91	Questions I Have For "God"	223
92	*Est Is Totus Illic Est*	226

This Son And His Mother

93	Dear Mama	231
94	Helpless	232
95	4,654 Days	233
96	The Power Of Prayer	236
97	Pieces Of A Heart – Excerpts Of My Eulogy For Mama	237
98	Too Short The Time, Too Long The Pain	241
99	A Boy Knowing His Mother	242
100	Nothing New Under The Sun – The Murder Of My Mother	243
101	An Apple And An Orange From The Same Tree	244
102	Humpty Dumpty Or A Cracked Rubber Ball	246

Essay		Page
103	When I Was Put On Trial – The Innocence Of Guilt	248
104	To "Celemourn" My Mother	253
105	A Name Too Foul To Speak	254
106	Father In The Legal Sense … Son In The Illegitimate Sense	255
107	How My Mother Came To Name Me Carlespie	256
108	Why I Changed My Name	257
109	Stepping On My Own Face	261
110	As The Crow Soars	264
111	"Yestermorrow"	266
112	The Resurrection Of Mary Alice's First Child	268
113	… And I Am Better For It	272

The Finale

114	Humanity: Guilty Or Not Innocent	275
115	Dancing To The Songs In My Head … And Not The Ones …	278
116	A Dirge For Inamorata	280

About The Author	281
Suggested Reading	283
References	287
Index	291

Experience must be assessed and weighted within the context of a system of logic and reason.

11 Turns Along My Twisted Path

What a person believes or values is, to a great extent, a function of the time and place of his experiences and perhaps, to some relative degree, his DNA. Being idiotropic, I looked back over my life and determined there were 11 milestone events that altered my life and subsequently, my dominant personal *ethos*. This book reflects the impact of those experiences that formed the foundation of what I believe and how I have processed the information derived from those experiences.

To be sure, there were many other events that made their contribution to who I am, but none was as significant, at least up until now, as the following:

- Watching helplessly as my mother's husband beat her viciously and regularly throughout most of my childhood

- Witnessing my mother's murder at the hands of her husband

- Becoming one of Jehovah's Witnesses

- Earning an academic scholarship to Cranbrook High School

- Falling in love – getting married and having children

- The murder of a dear and precious friend at the hands of a robber/murderer

- Becoming an apostate by rejecting the beliefs of Jehovah's Witnesses

- Divorcing my wife

- Being transformed by a relationship that shredded my heart

- Searching to connect with "God(s)" only to become a deist

- Having an epiphany regarding my reactions to my mother's death

Given all the aforementioned, I also tried to make certain that my experiences have not skewed my perspective in such a way as to diminish my ability to see the broader scope of the human drama. Experience must be assessed and weighed within the context of a system of logic and reason that lies outside the person, hence my willingness to hold what I believe up to scrutiny and review by any who disagree because I alone am trapped inside this particular mind.

In the final analysis, I have no interest in persuading others to view the human drama through my lenses. I aspire only to share or incite thought and contemplation in others as well as in myself – thus this compilation of essays.

INTRODUCTION

Why did I want to use one of life's most precious and scarce resources to write and then collect, under one cover, dozens of essays which I wrote over a period of years? There are three preponderant reasons:

- I wanted my children and friends to know how my mind processes the realities of life on this planet. I wanted them to know the what and why of the who I am in one of the most expedient ways possible – by reading about it.

- I wanted to challenge, confirm or change what I believe about the realities of life on Prison Earth (because that is one of the prominent ways to engage our humanness).

- I wanted to honor the memory of my mother, Mary Alice.

Additionally, writing this book was part of the process of verifying to myself that I have, in a synergistic way, transcended my environmental, if not also my genetic, set points. I have become more than the combined effects of the various aspects of who I am – so I believe. Such an accomplishment would constitute a significant victory in my mission as a human.

As an observer of the human drama and condition, I have sought to pay attention and subsequently analyze and synthesize. Admittedly, being in the forest makes it difficult to see the forest as it actually is. Said another way, being a part of the human drama and subjected to its condition impede my ability to assess its state with pure and untainted objectivity, but I believe I have come close.

To elaborate, humanity is both self-destructive and self-actualized. Humanity is both cruel and compassionate. Humanity is both truculent and timorous. Thus, there is a case to be made for humanity, and there is a case to be made against humanity, hence a case "forgainst" humanity. What would be the verdict if a visitor were to judge? My verdict, as a visitor (for no one remains here forever) can be inferred from the essays contained herein.

This book also illustrates one of many salient issues regarding humanity: Life on this roller-go-round (i.e., roller coaster/merry-go-round) is best lived when it is scrutinized and cross-examined. Like a visitor, our stay on Prison Earth will end, and those who could have but did not live it thoughtfully with deliberation and reflection are guilty of wasting their primary resources – time and their humanness.

In different words, could it be that thinking for oneself, challenging belief systems and societal conventions are part of our responsibility of being human? Furthermore, could it be that not to do so is to squander one's humanity? I assert that many of humanity's woes and travails can be sourced to failing in this obligation.

To that end, I expect most readers will take exception to at least some of my views, and that would be fine provided their objections are cemented in reason and thoughtful consideration. What I hope to accomplish, however, is for the reader to share in my thought processes and to ultimately *understand* my views – not necessarily to accept them.

Also, I think it is important for the reader to know I did not intend to compose essays that were comprehensive and exhaustive. They are purposely short to best serve as a catalyst to initiate, not conclude, thought-provoking considerations.

Last of all, in honoring the memory of my mother, it was necessary to present a number of my childhood experiences. My experiences were not the worst ever and certainly not the best ever. Nonetheless, they were horrific and yet here I am – in all my "shame and glory." Perhaps my arrival, so to speak, can serve as a seed for others who have endured worse but wish to grow.

ACKNOWLEDGEMENTS

I believe most significant accomplishments are attained within the context of an exceptional support system of family and/or friends. There are relentless and ever-present internal and external forces which make it easier to do nothing but the mundane. A vibrant support system is more or less required to resist and counteract those forces and to subsequently equip one to achieve "flight." Also, painful or negative experiences can play a pivotal and integral role in providing a basis for achievement. Therefore, I wish to recognize those who made an impact on my most significant accomplishment to date – the making of the person I am.

Where The Love Began:

The foremost matter is that I dedicate this book to my mother, *Mary Alice*, (my Butterfly and Hummingbird), who never really had the chance to be the mother to me she so motherly sought to be. Though I wish I had been a braver son, I could not have loved her more.

Mama: *Though my eyes have long dried, my heart still bleeds tears for thee.*

My Four Songs:

I also wish to honor my children, *Ghislaine (BKA: "Baby Girl"), Matysse, DéToi and LeGé*. You have made life easier and something worth embracing by making me so proud of you. Your love and respect helped me to manage the insanity that would have otherwise decimated my life. I love you all preciously forever, and I thank you with all the love that beats in my heart.

My Five Senses:

James "Tommie" Thomas, Jr., Mama's youngest brother: You always believed in me more than I believed in myself. You have come to my rescue more times than my mind wants to count but not more than my heart remembers. You gave me my wings and made sure there was a net beneath me in case I fell. You are "family," not because of the DNA we share but because of the love we share.

Dwight G. Stackhouse, "Mon Cher": You are the definition of "Best Friend." You propped me up during some of my darkest days. I began to see who I was/am because you had the courage and love to turn on the light. We drank poison from the same cup. We fought dragons together with no more than a toothpick. No better friend could I have made. Without you in my space, how could I have ever become someone I respect? I am who I am because you are who you are. The love we have for each other plunges deep and soars high.

Millie McEady: You have loved and respected me with such affection and loyalty – even when I had nothing to give but a "thank you." You make being your friend easier than it is for me to breathe. You are my rainbow after the storm. I am a better self because you guard a place in your heart for me. It is how and why we love each other that will endure long after we both are gone.

Cynthia Taeug: You rescued me without the expectation of reciprocity. You are compassion in its purest form. You helped guide me to the quiet and safe place so I could blossom in a different light. I miss being part of your world but will always hold you dear in my heart, for I will never forget the friend you were.

Cheryl L. Neely: You are proof that brains and beauty are not like oil and water but can be like hand and glove. You demonstrate that brains are more beautiful than beauty. You are the melody to the song that is in me, and I sing of things that only we can. Why are there so few like you? I am indebted to your love and will love you until the day after forever.

To "Tommie," Dwight, Millie, Cynthia, and Cheryl to each of you – in the order in which you entered my orbit – I am better for being in your orbits. You are no less important to me than air and water. May I finish life on this planet before any of you do. But, it I am so mis-fortuned as not to, I will never allow another to stand in the sacred place I have created for each of you in my soul. I love you all with my all.

Teacher, Thy Student Has ... Into A Different Sort

Harold L. Flemings: I stood in awe of your encyclopedic knowledge and adroit use of logic. You gave me the tools to sharpen my mind. I saw the logic of "the Truth" – until I continued to use those same tools and began to see a different and brighter light; the student grew away from the teacher. Thank you. Thank you for opening my mind's eye. Though we are now at odds about "God" and "Truth," I am forever grateful because much of the way I think, I owe to thee. You will always hold a place of honor in my world, our differences notwithstanding.

Other Pieces of the Person I Am:

At the risk of committing the sin of omission, I also wish to acknowledge a host of others who either **helped** me or **hurt** me, or both, in such a way as to have *left their mark on my psyche* (a few of whom are now dead but not forgotten) to the extent that I owe who I am to them, albeit to a lesser or different degree than the persons mentioned above:

Elizabeth "Big Mama" Thomas, Helen R. Reed-Avery, George L. Bibbs, Delvin Walden, Frank & Claudia Askew, Trina S. Williams, Lois Arlene Leslie, Edward K. Lee, Cynthia C. Craft, Deborah D. Starr, Alma J. McKinney, Deborah Thompson, and others.

A Final Note: *Being acknowledged in this work does not, in any way, indicate an endorsement of my views or values – just as it does not imply that I endorse the views or values of those acknowledged.*

Special Thanks

I want to pay a special kind of thanks to C. J. Samuels, my Editor Extraordinaire. Your keen sense of the written word and your approach – precise without being pedantic, authoritative without being imperious – won my respect immediately. Your guidance and input proved to be insightful and enlightening. Thank you for deciding to add your magic to my work.

SCENES FROM THE HUMAN DRAMA

Never do either easily or without careful deliberation

20 Things I Wish I Had Known When I Was 20

- Most people are allergic to intelligence. Too many are even hostile toward it.

- Stupidity is highly infectious. Beware of its power and its masks.

- You can lead a fool to reason, but you can't make him think.

- Class: That combination of exceptional courtesy toward others surpassed only by an abiding respect toward self. Class: A function of one's character – not one's social class.

- If a straight line is the shortest distance between point "A" and point "B" then debating with a fool is the shortest distance between intelligence and stupidity.

- What two things of the following three are necessary for life on Prison Earth: Air, Food, Money? The one you did not choose reveals whether you look at life *as it really is* or as you merely *believe it is*.

- All other things being equal or near equal, which of the following persons would be your best choice for a friend?

    A.] The one who would not steal, lie, cheat, kill, and so forth because she believes those kinds of people will not get into heaven because "God" forbids those acts and expects love, honesty, kindness and respect

    or

B.] The one who would not steal, lie, cheat, kill, and so forth because she believes that society and its members are better served by love, honesty, kindness, respect and so forth.

The two are not the same. One is sugarcoated arsenic with a history of being sold by force and/or promises founded on fiction.

- One of the most effective ways to keep matters in their proper perspective is to remember that celebrities, political and religious leaders – the famous and the powerful – are all intimately familiar with toilet tissue. Need I say more?

- Religion or Evolution: Belief in one requires the suspension of one's faculties of reason; belief in the other requires the convoluted contortion of one's faculties of reason.

- When a physically beautiful woman enters a room, she alters time and space. When a charming woman enters a room, she alters all who are in it. When a physically beautiful and charming woman enters a room – the room, by definition, becomes a sublime and blissful reality.

- The glass is half-full or half-empty depending on what's in it.

- Having skin as black as a piece of coal or skin as brown as a paper bag? For too many African-Americans, they would rather there be several more options so that rejection of the first one would not seem so absolute.

- Is it that White Americans see where Black African-Americans once were compared to now – and believe all is well, or is it that Black African-Americans see where White Americans are now compared to themselves – and believe all is not well enough?

- Money, power and fame are aphrodisiacs; they seduce the body. Character, class and charm are aphrodisiacs; they seduce the mind. Seduce only the body and the mind can wander; seduce the mind and the body will follow.

- If women are "emotional" then men are no less so. For instance, a woman may cry when the hero of the movie dies. The hero of the movie was killed by a man who thought the hero was homosexual. Sympathy and misguided disdain are both emotions. The latter emotion has caused humanity more grief and agony than the former.

- Judge no side as so sacred and so right that you will not abandon it if it begins to sink in the face of a side that is more right.

- Hate, like love, is a precious emotion. Never do either easily or without careful deliberation.

- Beware of those who would do unto you as they would have you do unto them, for what others would have you do unto them should not be the light by which you should walk.

- Some proclaim that the United States was founded on Christian principles. Others say it was founded on a kind of capitalism based on the near genocide and denigration of one race and the brutal subjugation and exploitation of another. What is true, however, is that for many their consciences were assuaged by the former so they could perform the latter with not compunction.

- Many people can tell you why they believe what they believe, but most cannot tell you why they should not believe what they believe.

Lessons from experience often feed on themselves

When The Student Wags The Teacher

"Experience is the best teacher." This oft quoted line is usually embraced and repeated without much thought or contemplation. After pondering this adage, however, I assert that experience is a submissive teacher who does not determine the lesson; the student does.

During the late 1960s, one of my cousins recounted an experience in which he and another hellion attempted to beat up and rob an older man. Much to their surprise, the man was armed. As my cousin and his fellow miscreant fled, the would-be victim chased them quite a ways. Both assailants managed to escape being shot or captured. What I found more fascinating than his temerity to rob someone was the lesson the experience taught him. From that moment on, given that experience, he decided the best way to rob the next person would be to do so with a weapon.

It cannot be intelligently argued that he did not learn his lesson because his comments clearly evidenced learning. That is, he processed information and adapted accordingly. He changed his perception based on information obtained from the experience.

On the other side, however, when I was about seven or eight years old, I ate a pack of Kool-Aid I had stolen from a grocery store. When my mother asked me how did I get Kool-Aid all over my mouth (apparently I did not have enough sense to wipe away the evidence), I told a fantastical lie that only a complete fool would ever believe; she spanked me. I never stole anything again until I brought home a legal pad from work more than twenty years later.

Given the same experiences, many, if they dared to rob someone and barely escaped alive, would vow never to do anything like that again. Likewise, receiving a spanking for stealing would not have been a sufficient deterrent for many; they would steal again.

Lessons from experience often feed on themselves. The interpretations we make regarding an experience, be it ours or others we come to know about, are determined by our perceptions which, in turn, are based on the thickness and cut of the lenses through which we view life. Subsequently, the lenses through which we look at life can create or impact our experiences, thereby creating the need to interpret and so on. This circle can spiral effortlessly in many different directions – sometimes with invidious subtlety.

Experiences teach what we decide the lessons to be or not to be. We give the experiences meaning, power and value – or not. Given that point, experience, (as are many things in life), appears to be one thing, but is actually another. Rather than being the best or worst teacher, experience is a teacher that does the student's bidding; the tail wags the dog every time.

We expose ourselves to pain; in fact, we invite it.

How Sweet The Bitter Taste

A man lies in bed dying from an affliction for which there seemed to be no cure. He mumbled to himself that he would give anything to be cured. Suddenly, an old woman appeared and offered a solution to his predicament. She handed him an elixir that he had to take every day for the rest of his life. The potion would cure the ailment, and he would live an otherwise long and healthy life. There was one caveat, however.

Each time he took the potion, it would cause pain, and there was no way to avoid it. Sometimes the pain would be very brief or barely perceptible; at other times, it would be much longer or excruciating. The duration and severity would vary depending on the circumstances. But, he would be alive and otherwise healthy. If he stopped taking it, he would definitely suffer, wither and die an arduous death.

The man agreed to swallow the potion but just before he did, he asked the old woman what was the potion. She replied, "Love."

So goes it. Life is best lived if we love, whether we love a child, a sibling, a parent, a spouse or friend. We are genetically structured so that loving someone is what we need to do to be fully human – to express the meritorious side of our humanity. Loving someone, however, comes with a price. We expose ourselves to pain; in fact, we invite it. Pain caused by the one we love scraping her knee as a child or failing to be put in the high school homecoming game. Pain caused by the one we love being mistreated or being disappointed. Pain caused by a loved one's broken heart or unrequited love. Not to speak of the pain caused by the one we love being sick or dying.

We love; therefore, we feel for – we empathize with – the people we love. It is almost as if we feel what they feel – sometimes even more painfully. But to stop loving is to stop living (though not necessarily to stop existing). So, we drink the potion completely knowing we will suffer pain, later or sooner. So, we drink the potion and choose the pain of loving over the pain of not loving.

... sacrifice it in favor of standing even closer to the truth.

Some Of The Facts Of Life On Prison Earth

... I hope my small gift will serve as an expression of my best wishes for your future. Keep in mind, however, graduating from high school merits praise in only a small way because life demands so much more.

Having given you such a gift provides me with an excuse to finish this missive with a few rules to keep in mind. You will find we older people are often eager to give advice (or to pontificate) at the drop of a hat even though we did not embrace that same advice when we were your current age.

In any event, I present 16 plus 1 ideas for your consideration. Accept or reject them at your discretion and at your own risk:

1. Having your own money is great; having your own mind is even better.

2. Choose your friends carefully and with great caution; former friends make the worst enemies.

3. Think for yourself. Challenge what most people often accept without question. You will find it to be one of the most difficult things to do – but one of the most rewarding.

4. Never forget: If a person enters your space – he or she wants something; otherwise, there would be no reason to spend the time. Sometimes what the person wants is mutually advantageous, but too often it is not. The sooner you discover which it is, the better it will be for you.

5. I guarantee that people will disappoint you. I guarantee that you will disappoint others. Try hard not to disappoint yourself.

6. You are Black and you are female. Forget you are either one at your own peril. Do not boast of it; do not be ashamed of it. Simply remember it, for if you do not

– the world will unceremoniously remind you that you are.

7. Think long term; do not forget tomorrow. If you live long enough, you will pay tomorrow for what you do today. The stupid remain stupid because they fail to appreciate the connection between now and later.

8. Let people be who they are just as you want people to allow you to be who you are. Let them pay the consequences for who they are – you certainly will pay for who you are.

9. You can be beautiful in two ways. Your happiness and success are linked to which of the two you esteem most.

10. Physical beauty without charm is glitter because beauty is the sparkle, but charm is the diamond.

11. The world is full of "dogs" – many are male, and many are female. The difference is this: Many are male. Many are female. Both bark and have fleas. (Although it is true that one will bite far more often and viciously than the other – nonetheless, remain wary of both because a dog is still a dog.)

12. It is easy to blame others when the blame lies with you. Resist that temptation because it is the nature of the weak to take credit and reject blame when they should do the opposite. One of the keys to growth is to willingly accept your part in the matter and learn from it. In the final analysis, you are whom you -- and no one else -- have decided to be. Don't blame others for who you are – not your mother, not your father, not the way you were raised – not anyone but yourself.

13. Never forget: Words tell lies but actions tell the truth. Do not ignore the truth no matter how lofty and sincere the words.

14. Enjoy this trip as best you can. Watch out for the dips and curves and the obstacles in the road. Yes, the trip will be shorter than you may have thought but since you are doing the driving odds are you will end up where you deserve.

15. It is true that I am gluteophilic (I love the callipygian aspect of the female body), but speaking metaphorically, there are times when you have to kiss ass and there are times when you must kick ass. The key is to know when to use your lips and not your foot – and vice versa.

16. Do not believe the fairy tale: No lover is so unique that he or she has no equivalent on the planet. At any given time, there are at least *thousands* who could love you as much and in the way you desire – and vice versa. There is no such thing as a "one and only" out of the billions on the earth; if you love one, you can love another – unless you choose to be lost in the fairy tale.

Nonetheless, knowing there are thousands who can seize your heart (and you, theirs), in no way should diminish your fidelity to the one you have because this truism is solid: the faithful lover in your heart is already worth any two in the room.

Finally, you carry with you a bag of ideas and beliefs. Do not be afraid or even hesitant to challenge each one, especially those that impact how you live this life. To that end, I enjoin you to at least consider my basic credo:

There is no idea or belief I so dearly cherish so as to shield it from rigorous scrutiny or thoughtful challenge. There is no idea or belief I esteem so highly that I will not alter it or abandon it – sacrifice it in favor of standing even closer to the truth.

They do not want their views to be challenged

The Kindest Cut Of All

Years ago, I was riding in a vehicle with my best friend as I was condemning and ranting about what someone had reportedly done. I cited the news article as I berated and assailed this person. I asked how could someone do such a thing. My best friend, without skipping a beat, very casually reminded me that some years ago, I seriously contemplated doing exactly the same thing. I stopped. I literally shut up and thought. Finally, after a few seconds, I chuckled and admitted that he was right; he was completely right.

Genuine friendships are quite different from most other relationships. My friend could say what he said without fear of angering me. He would also say what he said in such a way to make it easy for me to actually "hear" him. I, for my part, could accept what he said without being defensive or seeking to justify when there is no basis for such. Friends can be that way because they know too much about each other to waste time trying to shield or prop up an ego or a misguided persona.

Would I have reacted the same way if someone other than a friend had said what he said? I would like to think so but certainly our being friends made it much easier. All too often, people state that they want someone who is honest and straightforward (yet tactful), but in many instances they really do not want that. They do not want their views to be challenged or their flaws revealed. Declaring they want such a friend sounds noble; actually appreciating such a person is quite a different animal.

There is much value in having a bona fide friend. Such a person keeps us honest and close to the "truth" of the situation. Authentic friends can disagree without undermining the core of what makes them friends. When friends talk or actually disagree they do not try to be "right" as much as try to be "understood." Friends will grab our hand and pull us in front of the mirror so we can see ourselves as we are and not as we imagine ourselves or wish ourselves to be. And, as a friend, we are grateful for being placed in front of such a mirror.

The "how" something is stated can be equally as important. A friend knows how to clearly and in no uncertain terms, say what needs to be said but in a manner that reveals respect. He or she can be direct, honest, but without the jagged edges of a critic or without the blinders that all too often accompany love for another. Furthermore, with a friend, words speak as loudly as actions, and actions say the same thing as words.

A friend, by the above definition, is as difficult to find as it is to be. Suffice it to say, however, most often, the word "friend" is a misnomer. It is a convenient or polite term used to describe regular informal interactions with another. The term is often used as opposed to the somewhat stark and formal (but more accurate) terms – "associate" or "acquaintance." To that end, the word, "friend" is often more of a cliché than the more precise description presented in this essay.

In Shakespeare's play about Julius Caesar, the emperor is stabbed by several men, one of whom was his close "friend" Brutus. In recounting the event, Marcus Antonius referred to Brutus' act as "the most unkindest cut of all." (*Julius Caesar* Act 3, scene 2, pg.181-186) Nonetheless, the words of a loving friend can sometimes cut, but it can be the kindest "cut of all" if the means and intent are driven by loyalty to the friendship.

In any event, I suspect, finding such a friend is most possible after a careful look in the same mirror and deciding to be the kind of friend you need. Out of the mouth of a friend can come words that stand in homage and testimony to one of life's rarest gems.

... enough like you ... but different enough

Friendship
(Part I)

Definition

Friendship, like so many other aspects of human relationships, defies a succinct yet comprehensive definition. Nevertheless, the urge to frame a definition is irresistible.

A friend should be enough like you so that you enjoy each other, but different enough in certain critical ways, so that those particular differences foster the growth of both of you as human beings.

My definition, like others, can only withstand a superficial critique. With that in mind please note the following framework.

Too Much Alike?

All too often, people recite cute little "truisms" without much thought. For instance, many believe that being "too much alike" can undermine or disallow a productive friendship.

"They are too much alike. That's why they don't get along."

"Both of them are just stubborn (or arrogant, or...)."

In effect, this perspective treats similarities as things that preclude friendship rather than things that can nurture it. Two stubborn persons could be close friends. If both agree on a matter and are stubborn in that regard, there is no conflict; hence, no impediment to being friends. If they stubbornly embrace the *opposite* position on a matter, however, then the makings of a friendship could be challenging. Being too much alike is inimical if they are too much alike on the opposite sides of the same fence like the south poles of two magnets that always repel each other.

Case in point: A married couple may stubbornly oppose allowing pets into an apartment complex when asked to vote on the matter. Both are intransigent and un-yielding, yet may be happily married because despite being "too much alike," they are "alike" on the same side of issues that are important to them.

True, being too similar without sufficient and well-placed differences can be (but not always) akin to being intellectually and emotionally incestuous or boring. If one person in the relationship merely rubber stamps the other's decisions or co-signs the other's position on matters, then only one person can be said to be really thinking – the other one is essentially a door knob. Perhaps such a relationship can be colored as a friendship but only in the way that two people can be called a crowd.

Opposites Attract?

A goodie-two-shoe falls in love with a rogue or the extrovert befriends the introvert. People explain it by saying: "Opposites attract."

It all depends on how they are opposites. If two people are opposites with respect to their core personality elements, then there is volatile fuel for conflict. If they are opposites in ways that do not interfere with the free expression of who they each are, then a friendship could bloom. After all, people argue, disagree, or debate because they are "opposites" with respect to the issue at hand. By definition, arguing requires the adoption of opposite (or at least different) positions. Therefore, opposites might never mix – like oil and water – or they might attract – like the north and south poles of two magnets.

The Right Combination

An authentic friendship requires being both alike and opposite in a peculiar combination of ways specific to the relationship. That winning combination of being both alike and opposite is rare enough so that most people seldom have more than one or two genuine friends.

To be certain, there is more to having an authentic friendship than simply being opposites and alike in the most effective ways; other factors impact, and hence, define the nature of friendship. In fact, each particular friendship has its own DNA, the nature of which still holds enough mystery as to resist concise explication – my attempt notwithstanding.

does not stand in a vacuum but in a windy place

A Tale Of Two Friends

Two women, my age or a little older, who are dear friends of mine present two divergent reactions to our friendship.

Some time ago, I saw one of them with her husband – they did not see me and I chose not to approach them. The next day I called her and told her I saw them but elected not to approach. She said I did the right thing by staying away; I was hurt, all over again.

I met her and became friends – platonic – before she married her first husband. We remained friends even after she divorced him. Later, after her second (current) marriage, she used her clout and authority to give me a job when I was nearly destitute – even buying me a pair of shoes. All her acts of kindness were done in the name of our friendship. Her interest in me and my interest in her was and always has been one of respect and love – but never romantic love. We have never even kissed or held hands; we were buddies.

My second friend came into my life fifteen years after I met my first friend. My uncle and I attended a dance where I saw her sitting at a table with her friends. I asked her to dance, and I flirted with her; she was divorced at the time. We went on two, maybe three dates. At most, we may have kissed once but never had sex. On our last date, however, we mutually agreed to be platonic. She even gave me a key to her apartment – but we were never physically intimate. Again, during a period in my life where I was struggling financially and emotionally, she helped me. We became close friends. In fact, she is my closest female friend to this day; we love and respect each other dearly. She eventually married a second time also.

Two women – both with husbands who love them and whom they love, too. Both women loved me as a friend.

The husband of my first friend never believed his wife and I were only friends and nothing more. In fact, she told me he believed she and I had an affair. Because of that mistaken belief, she has, in effect, set our friendship aside. Once a year or so, we speak on the telephone – at her job; I initiate the call. (Though at this point it has been a few years since we have talked.) She states her husband does not like the idea of me at all, so she acquiesces, and now, we are more or less friends from afar. (Which is why I did not approach them when I saw them.) Nonetheless, I cannot forget her kindness and love; she will always be dear to me. I miss what we once had.

The husband of my second friend was initially suspicious of the idea of the friendship his wife and I had. Despite that, she stood her ground and refused to set me aside. She said we were friends before she married him and that we would remain friends and that he would have to trust that she loved him and that she and I were no more and no less than friends. As time went on, her husband began to see and understand that his wife and I were close friends – not lovers. For more than a decade, he has accepted me warmly and genuinely. I can call his home, speak to him briefly and ask to speak to his wife – my friend – for as long and often as I wish. She and I even go out to lunch with his blessing and sometimes he joins us! We often say our "good-bye's" with saying, "I love you" in front of him, because we do love each other – as friends – and he is comfortable and secure with our relationship.

At the risk of oversimplifying matters and without knowing all the private details, I can state my friendship with one was contingent on the approval of another party, whereas my friendship with the other was contingent on just the two of us.

Questions arise: Was my first friend really my friend? (Actually, I believe she was.) Should a spouse dictate whom his or her mate could have as a friend – especially of the opposite sex? Is my second friend a stronger person than the first? Is the husband of my first friend insecure, whereas the husband of my second friend not? Is the husband of the second one weaker than the husband of the first? … and so on.

I can only say my second friend refused to let anything diminish our friendship and for that, she will always stand in a place held sacred in my heart. As for the first friend, it hurts me deeply to know that our friendship has been dismissed based on a false belief and probably a deep-seated insecurity.

Friendship does not stand in a vacuum but in a windy place and both parties must hold on to each other lest they be blown apart.

In politics stupidity is not a handicap

They Said It Better Than I

I have often pondered the phenomenon of politics. I have listened to many political speeches, watched a myriad of interviews of politicians and endured a steady high-fat diet of political ads and articles. After several years of this kind of grueling masochism, it is obvious to me that the ruthless and pugnacious as well as the noble and intellectual have all keenly explicated the nature of politics and the associated masses.

Adolph Hitler and Adlai Stevenson (American Presidential candidate in the 1950's) understood a fundamental precept of politics and government. Hitler stated, "Make the lie big, make it simple, keep saying it and eventually they will believe it" (Brainy Quote). He is also credited with saying the following two things – which come to the same thing: "How fortunate for leaders that men do not think" (All Great Quotes) or stated another way, "What good fortune for governments that people do not think" (All Great Quotes).

Whereas, Adlai Stevenson (Governor of Illinois and later, Ambassador to the United Nations who was deemed to be witty, high-minded and elegant in speech) repeated what Hitler said – but in a much different way. (This scenario is actually in dispute. Nonetheless, whether it actually occurred or not, it illustrates the essence of my point.) It is said that a supporter once shouted, "Governor Stevenson, all thinking people are for you!" Adlai Stevenson is credited with replying, "That's not enough. I need a majority" (thinkexist.com).

History, distant and current, is replete with examples of how politicians exploit the mentally indolent masses with specious ideas designed to appeal to that part of them that does not require them to pause and ponder but merely respond like a Palovian dog. To reinforce this point, Adlai Stevenson also noted, "In America, anybody can be president. That's one of the risks you take" (Quotes And Poems). Yes, in fact, French Emperor, Napoleon Bonaparte, quipped, "In politics stupidity is not a handicap" (Quote DB). It appears that the politics of the early 21st century U.S. has vividly verified this nearly 200-year-old observation.

Napoleon also remarked, "The barbarous custom of having men beaten who are suspected of having important secrets to reveal must be abolished. It has always been recognized that this way of interrogating men, by putting them to torture, produces nothing worthwhile" (Bonaparte, 1798, p. 128). Again, I present the first few years of the 21st century in American history as proof that not all the lessons of history are remembered.

Furthermore, Otto Von Bismark declared, "People never lie so much as after a hunt, during a war or before an election" (Bismark). How supremely true those words are when one examines politics both on a macro and mirco level.

Finally, advice that is applicable to most facets of life but especially politics. Carl Sagan explained, "One of the saddest lessons of history is this: If we've been bamboozled long enough, we tend to reject any evidence of the bamboozle. We're no longer interested in finding out the truth. The bamboozle has captured us. It is simply too painful to acknowledge – even to ourselves – that we've been so credulous. So the old bamboozles tend to persist as the new bamboozles rise" (Sagan, 1987).

As we all would agree, charlatans come in all political persuasions.[1] What frightens me, however, are the sheep that appoint or elect, then follow and defend the wolves with alacrity. Of course, in defense of the sheep, often times the choice is between electing a wolf or a fox – but even then, that is no excuse to blindly embrace and fervently cling to the "bamboozle."

---

[1] Additional information and examples are provided in Shenkman's book, *Just how stupid are we?: Facing the truth about the American voter.*

too much credit... and not enough blame

Oranges Falling From An Apple Tree

Years ago while researching the psychological impact of family structure on siblings, a researcher interviewed a set of identical twins. The twins were raised together by their mother. As adults, these twins were diametrically opposite with regard to their housekeeping habits. One twin was a man who could have been the poster child for being utterly sloppy and disorganized. The other was extremely neat, clean and organized.

The researcher asked the sloppy twin why was he such a slob. He answered, "I guess it's because my mother was a slob; it was the way I grew up." The interviewer asked the other twin why he was such a "neat-freak." He replied, "Because my mother was a slob; I can't stand clutter and dirt."

When I was about eleven years old, the family pet delivered her puppies inside the house. My siblings' father asked which one of the four oldest of us let the dog in the house. I denied it and so did my three siblings. So, their father made the four of us strip to our underwear and one by one, over and over, all night long, he beat us with an old-fashioned thick ironing cord – in the order of our birth. (He also forbade us to even holler or scream during the beatings) Finally, my brother confessed.

As an adult, my ex-wife and I had four children. One day, one of them broke something. No one confessed, and there was no way to prove who broke the item. As a child, I swore I would never punish all to ensure punishing the guilty even if it meant the guilty would escape punishment by lying. So none of my children were punished for that incident. My view of "Crime and Punishment": Justice should always favor the innocent – even if it sometimes favors the guilty.

The point is this: Children do not always follow the examples, positive or negative, of their caregivers. Consciously or otherwise, they pick and choose what beliefs and behaviors they will embrace or reject. Typically, it is far easier and comfortable to emulate one's parents – especially if the model is negative. To that end, parents often accept too much credit for positive outcomes and not enough blame for the negative ones.

This phenomenon does not lift the burden from parents to establish positive standards for their children, but as parents, we should realize our influence has its limits. Whether the lesson set by one's caregiver(s) is negative or positive (or neutral), it is always intriguing to observe how those under their care often adopt differing courses of action from each other with regard to the examples set by the caregiver(s).

People have often declared when talking about how children imitate their parents – "An apple never falls far from its tree." I agree for the most part except that often enough, the specific spot it falls on is slanted away from the tree and with the help of gravity (or some other equally powerful force), it stops at a place far enough from the tree to wonder how could he or she have even fallen from that particular tree. There are even times when the apple falls so far away, it actually becomes an orange; an orange can fall from an apple tree.

the same advice goes for loving someone.

A Few Things To Put On Your Mind

- Most people afflicted with "stupiditis" refuse to submit to a "stupidectomy" precisely because of their "stupiditis."

- Cognitive dissonance is one of the most feared phenomena in the human drama and most humans prefer the certainty of the lie rather than the discomfort of the truth.

- By the time you become good at being a parent, your children may have already grown up.

- Do not be deceived. Revenge is called, "Smith"; justice is called, "**Mr.** Smith."

- As a Black African American, I am vexed whenever I hear another Black person speak on what percentage American Indian or European they are – with a tone that reveals a bit of pride. No matter the percentage, however, they are predominately African. Their pride is misplaced and it represents a type of self-disrespect because they cite the least part as if the major part has less merit. To them, they may be 25% White or American Indian, or so forth; to me they are 75% African and 100% disgraceful.

- In the absence of defending himself from death or great bodily harm, why would a man beat his significant other or intimate: To force her to comply with his edicts and decrees? To prop up his feeble or artificial sense of self? To vent against someone who cannot fight back and win?

  Because he fails to appreciate that humanhood trumps manhood and humanhood cannot accommodate such behavior? Because he fails to see that his cruelty identifies him as person who is morally anemic? Because society either feeds this sense of entitlement or at least fails to starve it? Because he has defined himself using a broken and distorted model of what a man should be? No matter the reason, such men disgust me in the same way a six-foot high pile of slimy pigeon shit would.

- The center of gravity for many people lies outside themselves. I present the phenomenon of the obsequious and the sycophantic who apotheosize or deify the famous as proof. These people eagerly fight to and are proud to glue their lips to the asses of the famous.

- How much of Black women's obsession with weaves and perms in their hair is due to Black men's adoration of that kind of hair? Could it be that if more Black men admired that which makes Black women distinct from White women - physically (e.g., the texture of their hair) more Black women would treat their hair differently?

- Too often, too many people don't pay attention when they talk. If they did, we would never know how stupid they are.

- Whenever someone you love dies, removing her name and phone number ... has a dolorous note of finality. That simple act cries "good-bye" as painfully as any other.

- The most selfish, cruel or vile person was once a cuddly, soft little baby. Look at any group of children playing in a schoolyard. Some of them may grow up to be drug addicts, community leaders, rapists, judges, killers, mechanics and so forth (including combinations thereof). In short, whenever I see a group of very young humans, I do not see what is, but what will probably be.

- Billions are spent searching for life (intelligent or otherwise) or the conditions that would make it possible, on other planets in the universe. Imagine if humans spent money, time and effort in search of intelligent life on this planet (Prison Earth) and, upon finding it, study and honor it.

- Religious institutions almost always frame "modest" attire in terms of what women wear. That constitutes a tacit admission that men want women to be responsible for controlling the libido of men. (And women are suppose to be the weaker sex.)

- Never swim farther than you can swim back; the same advice goes for loving someone.

Such is part of the fabric of life on Prison Earth

Served Without Notice

Years ago I briefly dated an ambitious young lady; however, we soon parted ways amicably. Two years later, we ran into each other on a college campus. We were happy to see each other and, with words unspoken, we decided to revive what we had started years earlier. Later that week, I mailed her a letter. In the letter, I expressed how good it was to see her, and I wished her well and hoped that her ambitions and dreams would become a reality. The next night, however, while walking to her car, she was struck and killed by a drunk driver. Given that she worked at the college as well as attended classes there at night, I do not believe she ever got the chance to read my letter. Sadness struck me.

Years before that tragedy, an intimate friend of mine had returned from a trip. On the day of her return, she and I spoke on the phone on three different occasions. Later that day, she and her brother went to retrieve her baggage from the train station. While there she decided to use the restroom as her brother waited outside. When she entered the restroom, a man entered behind her. He tried to rape her. She resisted. He stabbed her at least 19 times and fled the restroom with her purse. When told about it, my heart burst into ineffable grief.

Dying suddenly, painlessly or not, robs the person of the chance to not only set her affairs in order, but to contemplate her mortality in the most poignant of terms. (Living each day as if it were to be your last is a mindless and borderline stupid idea – to do so would approach the impractical if not the impossible.) Knowing that death is nearly imminent, allows a person to wrap her mind around the thought in a way that cannot be accomplished by any other means.

Nonetheless, death comes when it does – usually irrespective of one's preference. I wish both ladies had had more time. I especially wish my friend could have remained – to laugh and otherwise live life. Some die too soon; too many, not soon enough. Some die without notice and others with notice. Despite the fact that death can strike at a time and place of its own choosing, there is something more than starkly distressing about being served without notice. Such is part of the fabric of life on Prison Earth.

... it requires guilty knowledge and deliberate effort

The Most Common Fool

Most of you are familiar with the adage: "Fool me once shame on you. Fool me twice shame on me." Maybe so, but I would like to add: "Fool myself, really shame on me." It can, depending on the circumstances, be no cause for shame when someone fools you more than once, but it is always a cause for shame when we fool ourselves.

The ability to deceive ourselves is both easy and pernicious. This is especially true when, in order not to, would require a modicum of ability to think independently and the fortitude to see the painful truth of a matter. In fact, not only is the easiest lie to tell the lie you tell yourself, but also the easiest person to fool is yourself.

Sometimes humans build or at least reinforce a framework of self-deception that is impervious to logic and/or to the obvious. When Harriet Tubman was asked how she successfully freed hundreds of Black slaves via the Underground Railroad during the US Civil War, she is said to have bitterly replied, "If I could have convinced more slaves that they were slaves, I could have freed thousands more" (Brainy Quote). Thus, it was a kind of deliberate ignorance or a comfort with the status quo even if that status quo was oppressive and dehumanizing; too many slaves fooled their own selves.

She could not convince some Black Americans they were slaves for a complex series of reasons not the least two of which were their complacency and how they defined their plight. More specifically, they had made sense of their plight and refused to lift the veil of self-deception from their eyes. Fooling themselves simply required they resist the cogent examination of their situation. So successful was this self-deception, not even a former slave could help them see their own reality.

African-American slaves were and are not the only ones who have mastered the act of fooling themselves. Almost everyone has managed to successfully fool himself. Politics provide a common example of such. Scott McClellan, former White House Spokesman for President George W. Bush, describes the President as unwilling "to admit mistakes ... believe in his own spin" and as a person who lacks inquisitiveness and indulges in "self-deception that may be psychologically necessary to justify the tactics needed to win the political game." He "convinces himself to believe what suits his needs at the moment" (McClellan, 2008). Do you believe President George W. Bush to be the first and last politician to fit McClellan's description? There are far more humans of the George Bush ilk than of the Harriet Tubman type.

Fooling oneself is deleterious and self-destructive, at least, but more often it is also baleful to anyone within reach of the fool's influence. What is also almost fascinating about self-deception is that it requires guilty knowledge and deliberate effort; in the heart of hearts of the person lying to himself, he knows the lie is a lie. To be mistaken or misled is one thing, but to lie to oneself is not a mistake but a premeditated act to maintain the comfort found in self-deception. Too often humans strive to know the truth about someone else but prefer the lie they tell themselves about themselves.

Thus, if someone fools you twice, you may or may not be the fool, but if you fool yourself – even once -- you are always the fool.

At best, they find a fractured facsimile of those things

The Most Important Ancestor

Much has been made about the value of knowing one's personal ancestry or genealogy. Often times a person will comment, "You can't know who you are or where you're going unless you know where you came from." Such a statement appears to be sensible and potent but, as do many such dicta, it has the sound of wisdom, but not necessarily the essence.

To make my point, I choose the British "royal" family. Members of that family can trace their ancestry back for several generations, if not more. Despite having the supposed advantages of such knowledge, they suffer from the same emotional and psychological foibles as others who are not of "blue blood." Such knowledge has not spared them from the same pains of divorce, deceit, drugs, and other human excesses that have plagued those who can barely trace their ancestry beyond their great-grand parents.

I question the pragmatic and relevant value, as an African-American Black – or any race or ethnicity for that matter – of connecting self-respect to knowing one's history. History can be important, but knowledge of it should not be the basis for engendering self-respect or pride. This is not to say one's history is completely irrelevant; it is to say, its importance is limited. After all, there are millions of people in prison or homeless drug addicts who could cite the historical accomplishments of their race or even of their specific ancestry. On the other hand, there are as many who do not know their personal history or even much about the history of their race, but who have accomplished much in this life.

Many African-American Blacks, especially during Black History month, will cite examples of historical examples of feats and accomplishments of Black people – but, as a race, we remain at the *dirt end of the totem pole.* Knowing our history has done little to advance us beyond that position. Showcasing our historical accomplishments is as important as the history of other races and peoples; it is also a specious source of confidence and pride no matter the race or ethnicity.

Parents do well to assist their children to become successful citizens by facilitating their success in school and by otherwise helping them to be productive human beings – irrespective of their personal history or ancestry. Pointing to one's ancestry as a source of pride and self-esteem may have some merit, but it is more often than not overrated. Just because a person's ancestors may have been kings or queens, famous or infamous does not relieve one of the responsibility of being a productive person today, no more than if ones ancestors were peasants, drunks, or simply stupid. Each person is who he is and is therefore charged with being the best he can be, his ancestry notwithstanding.

Pointing to history to procure self-esteem (usually unconsciously) by saying, "Look at what my ancestors did," does little to address the more pressing issue: What have you done? One's father, grandmother or great grand uncle/aunt may be been a person(s) of significant accomplishment, but that fact does little to answer the question, "What have you done?" Too many humans use the feats of their ancestors or relatives as a crutch; they achieve self-respect vicariously. Such self-respect, however, is shallow and spurious.

There are those who would argue that becoming acquainted with the accomplishments of one's ancestors could serve as an inspiration for those who do not have any current role models. I would argue that a young White girl could find inspiration in the life of Harriet Tubman and a young Black girl, if the matter is presented in "human" terms, could find inspiration in the accomplishments of Amelia Earhart. Notice, I used the word "inspiration" – something very different from self-identity or self-respect or a sense of self-worth. Those who look outside themselves for identity, respect or worth never find it. At best, they find a fractured facsimile of those things.

An ordinary woman cites her pedigree as cause for merit; a great woman cites her own accomplishments as cause for merit. Any person that diminishes or hides the accomplishments of another race is a painfully small person. Any person that boasts of what her ancestors did is equally as small.

This is not to minimize the importance of one's lineage in matters of medical and health concerns. It is to minimize the importance of ones lineage in matters of self-perception or identity. After all, who on this planet does not have ancestors, some of whom were fools or thinkers, miscreants or law-abiding? For the most part, the best thing we can speak about one's ancestry, pedigree or genealogy is that we are here because of it. Otherwise, the best ancestor should be the one you become – not the one you have.

... vanilla cookies, strawberry ice cream and Pepsi

My Three Choices

Many of us have been asked the question, "Who, living or dead, would you like most to meet?" My answer could not be reduced to only one; it simply could not. I would choose three (actually four, but I won't push it).

First Choice

I would choose to be with my mother. My first words would be that I did not know, did not have a clue, that her husband was going to kill her. I would cry to her that, "I ache knowing I panicked and fled rather than standing between him and you – dying with you if necessary." I would tell her that I am forever sorry that I did not grow up soon enough to stop him from battering her. I would tearfully explain, I wish I had been a braver son. I would curl up, burying my head in her lap like a baby and weep. I would hold her and not let go. I would tell her that I grieve and suffer – missing her so much. Then I would spend our final moments together sharing crème-filled vanilla cookies, strawberry ice cream and drinking Pepsi.

Third Choice

I would convene with all the founders of the world's major religions. I would show them proof of their legacy. The massacres, the rapes, the injustices, the wars, the subjugations and horrific cruelties all done in the name of their religions. Having done that, I would ask, "Would all of you do it all again?" I would ask, "Do you feel any shame or guilt for giving birth to a system that has spread ignorance, inhumanity and moral filth?" I would demand proof that some "divine" Being spoke to them or inspired them. If their answers to my questions were no better than what their present-day followers spout, I would have them arrested, chained to each other and locked up in a continuous loop where they could forever live through the pain and suffering their religions have caused – as fitting punishment for their "crimes against humanity."

Second Choice

I would like an audience with the Ultimate Intelligence(s) – better known as "God." I would beg to know what this Being(s) knows. My main questions would center around finding out why humans exist and what happens after we die. I would also want to know the rhyme and reason of human cruelty and suffering.

After procuring the answer to those questions, I would want to know *everything* else ranging from the nature of sub-atomic particles, to how barks of trees differ from distant nebulae, to what is the fundamental essence of the universe and all its component parts.

I would not be interested in power – only knowledge and understanding (I am aware of the cliché that "knowledge is power" but the two are distinct in the purest sense of their definitions). I would want my insatiable curiosity about every single damn thing to be quenched in a way that only a "God" could do it.

... for how else can there be light.

I Doubt It

A century ago, the French scientist Gustav Le Bon pointed to the smaller brains of women – "closer in size to... gorillas'," he said. He also said this explained the "fickleness, inconstancy, absence of thought and logic, and incapacity to reason" in women (Le Bon, 1879, p. 60-61).

There are a multitude of instances wherein scientists have been completely wrong (Youngson, 1998). These "learned" human beings are subject to the same misguided and inane mentalities as the rest of human beings. Noted French philosopher, Voltaire stated, "Doubt is not a pleasant condition, but certainty is absurd" (The Quotation Page). This kind of absurdity is often a function of deciding what is true (i.e., certain) and then searching for the confirmation – even if the confirmation is bogus or nugatory. Gustav Le Bon failed to question the prevailing notion about women; he failed to doubt what many in society believed about women. He was absurdly certain of his position and then searched for support of that belief by citing the size of women's brains as proof. In short, he took the ass-backward approach, which is the most popular approach when doubt is absent from the equation.

Well-placed doubt is borne out of skepticism, as opposed to its cousin, cynicism. Doubt can also be a function of the need to thoroughly understand how all the parts of a matter fit together. Humans are typically uncomfortable with doubt as they are also with ambiguity. They long for certainty, and in order to attain it, they will claim it whether the basis for such certainty is valid or not. Doubt acts as the necessary counterbalance to certainty. If certainty is fed by doubt, then the certainty is honest and valid; if it is not, then it is nocuous at worst and dubious at best.

It is the admirable and rare human being that can navigate through certainty using doubt as the rudder. They believe doubt is healthy and should only morph into certainty when all the available means of honest, dispassionate critique have been exhausted. These humans despise the ignorance of the dark and do not fear what the light will reveal.

Let there be doubt, for how else can there be "light."

The fear or the drive remains; only the objective changes.

Self-Preservation – A Control Button

As a young man, I heard many people parrot the principle, "Self-preservation is the first law of nature." That statement is much more true than not; most humans will cling to life no matter the circumstances. They would rather subsist in a "hell" than die – even if the "hell" is barely tolerable. Even if the odds of survival are small humans will most often pursue self-preservation. It is this aspect of humanity that goes to the following point: Fear of dying or the drive to live trumps the desire to sacrifice for the good of the group. This explains several things.

A group of 50 people can be held at bay by one man with a handgun that holds only 11 bullets. No one wants to be one of the 11 so that the other 39 can overwhelm the assailant. Imagine if such a mentality were not the case. What if people were of such a nature they would rather die than comply? Assailants count on this fear of dying or the drive to live to control their victims.

This sense of self-preservation accounts for why most Africans who were captured accepted their dire and horrific plight instead of jumping overboard the slave ships to their death or instead of refusing to eat and drink. Being alive as a slave and being treated as less than human was preferable to dying. Slave masters and other captors relied on this fear of dying or the drive to live to control their victims.

Another example: What if the people of country "X," which is ruled by a dictator, decided to rebel. If every non-military person decided they would rather die than to remain under such a regime, the dictator would, if he commanded the military, have to kill all of the rebellious citizens and be ruler of a country with almost no subjects. A dictator without subjects? No dictator can afford to kill *everybody*. As a dictator, he, by definition must have a critical mass of followers who will comply rather than die. Fortunately for dictators, self-preservation has worked in their favor so that *everybody* does not have to be killed – killing a relative few is usually sufficient to maintain power.

Of course this phenomenon is not as obvious when the goal is genocide or "ethnic cleansing." The oppressors want to kill everyone rather than to control everyone. But where the objective is to control, the fear of dying or the drive to live works in favor of the assailant/oppressor. Where the objective is genocide then the fear of dying or the drive to live works against the oppressor. In either event, the fear or the drive remains; only the objective of the oppressor changes.

I do not know if self-preservation is really the first law of nature, (parents or those who love deeply have been known to give their lives for their children or loved ones) but it is a law that is easily exploited, and it addresses why misery and sufferings define a significant portion of the human drama.

... the difference between a prostitute and a whore

A Few Ends And Some Odds About Politics

Politics is more about power than service ... except perhaps to service those in power. It can also be truthfully stated that most politicians have 10 objectives after they are voted into power: The first nine objectives are to do almost *anything* to remain in power; the 10th objective is do something that appears to serve society. The first nine objectives and the 10th objective are often mutually exclusive. So the 10th objective is often gutted or muted.

As an extension of those 10 objectives, if one political party found a way to bring peace to the world, the opposing party would accuse it of making peace the new weapon of war. If one party found a way to raise the dead, the opposing party would accuse it of not letting the dead rest in peace. This is the essence of bi-partisanship: working together so long as neither party gains the edge. Losing the edge places one's party in jeopardy of losing *power.*

In American politics, who has more power – the woman who goes into the voting booth with her vote or the corporation that goes into the politician's office with a bag full of dollars? In fact, it can be proven that it is that corporate dollar that influences the woman's vote and buys the politician's loyalty.

Republican politicians are proudly married to Corporate America and demonstrate their fidelity in a myriad of ways. Democratic politicians are married to the middle and lower class in America but they cheat on their spouse by having a torrid affair with Corporate America. Sometimes Corporate America even seduces his wife and mistress to participate in a *ménage à trois.*

When I was a teenager, we believed the difference between a prostitute and a whore was that a prostitute would let men have their way with her for money; a whore would let any man do so for free. Much of the American voting electorate is a whore. They bend over and let their politicians have their way with them without demanding anything in return. (True ... the pot is calling the kettle black.)

Most politicians understand that the American electorate consists primarily of the intellectually inert and the cerebrally jejune. These politicians have all dutifully studied and implemented the information in the immensely popular book, *How to get stupid people to vote for you: Because the majority of people are stupid.*[1] They understand that that is the easiest and most expedient way to win an election – albeit, not the only way.

If I were White (or any race other than Black), I would not even bother to vote in political elections – for reasons stated in this essay and elsewhere. I vote as a matter of respect and honor for the many Blacks who suffered or died so I could exercise my constitutional right. I vote as a matter of principle and not as an attempt to effect change. (Does going through the motions make me whorish?)

---

[1] For the record, I know of no such actual book but please read, Shenkman's book, *Just how stupid are we? Facing the truth about the American voter.*

The antidote is usually in short supply

The Infection Called "Stupiditis"

Albert Einstein is credited with asserting, "Only two things are infinite, the universe and human stupidity, and I'm not sure about the former" (Brainy Quotes) and Elbert Hubbard, an American writer and philosopher, observed, at an earlier time, "Genius may have its limitations, but stupidity is not thus handicapped" (The Quotation Page). Finally, one anonymous quote: "The sum of human intelligence is a constant; the population is growing."

I am bemused at why human beings have not managed to render themselves extinct, especially given that stupidity is one of the most infectious conditions known to humanity. The antidote is usually in short supply and profoundly difficult to procure.

Many humans are stupid, for the most part because, unlike lower forms of animal life, they have the option (free will?) to behave contrary to their best interest – and they often do. Stupidity is not the same as ignorance – unless the ignorance is by choice. Stupidity is not the same as human error – unless the warning signs or common sense are ignored. Humans are not instinctively intelligent or stupid. They have a choice in the matter and stupidity is often the course of less resistance or self-serving in the short term. For instance, believing the earth to be flat was ignorant; refusing to even consider that it was not flat or squashing any notion that it was round was stupid.

Based on the above statements and some of my own observations, I declare the following:

1. Stupidity accounts for as much tragedy as does malice.

2. Passion can make a stupid idea seem intelligent.

3. Passion can mute intellect more effectively than intellect can guide passion.

4. Opinions are often the most effective antidote for intelligence.

5. Parents (or their surrogates) are a common contagion of stupidity.

6. The difference between a stupid man and a stupid woman is the difference between death by cyanide or death by arsenic.

7. Stupidity is more contagious than intelligence.

8. For many humans, the official cause of death and the actual cause of death differ because stupidity is not considered an official medical term.

9. Stupidity alone can be dangerous; stupidity mixed with power is insanely lethal. It is one of life's most virulent combinations.

10. One of the most painful phenomena to witness is the sincere and deliberate efforts of some to be both ignorant and stupid. Worse, however, is when these same humans scorn, ridicule and sometimes, even stifle the efforts of those who choose not to be ignorant or stupid. Stupidity desperately craves company.

Being related is overrated

The Thick And Thin Of Blood And Water

As a child, I often heard grown-ups utter the words, "Blood is thicker than water." Finally, I asked my mother the meaning of those words, and she explained that it meant family/relatives are to be favored when a choice has to be made between relatives versus non-relatives; family first, others second. Since then, I have heard various renditions of that mantra, but my experience indicates that blood may be thicker than water but that often times thickness has little to do with what is important.

If you were to ask most people who their best friend is, they would point to someone not related to them. True, there are some people whose best friend(s) is a relative, but more often than not a best friend is not a sibling, parent, cousin, *et cetera*; membership in the family of relatives or the family of friends is not mutually exclusive, however. In other words, some humans enjoy the best of both worlds. Nonetheless, could it be that love, respect and loyalty are more a function of friendship as opposed to one's bloodline?

Many people are uncomfortable with this notion that the family of relatives may not be as fulfilling as the family of friends. History is filled with stories of murder, thievery, rape, deceit and all the ugly sides of human nature within the family of relatives. Sharing the same DNA is no more of a guarantee of love, honesty or self-sacrifice than any other relationship. In the absence of being related, some people would never even speak to each other.

Early in life most of us survive and/or thrive because of relatives – what is commonly known as family – but as we grow older and develop our own personalities (and powers of observation) including values and beliefs, we discover the realities of family: ***being related is overrated***.

We realize that mother, brother, sister, father, *et al* can be no better or worse than others outside the family of relatives. We come to know family members lie, steal, cheat, support, give or sacrifice just as those outside the sphere of the family of relatives. (Think the Cain and Able in contrast to David and Jonathan.)

The family of relatives is an institution best suited to have and raise children with no assurance, however, that those with blood ties will love or respect its members more than non-members. On the whole, blood may be thicker than water but if the blood is bad what difference does thickness make – except, perhaps, to vampires?

Imagine the irony

Irony's Double Edge

Every few years, Father's Day falls on the same day the man who claimed to be my father and the man I will forever loathe murdered my mother. The year 2007 was another such year. Imagine the irony.

My mother's husband would often tell my siblings and me that we should always stick together; we should always share with and help each other. ("If one got a piece of bread, you all got a piece of bread.") When he murdered our mother, I was separated from my six siblings and eventually they all were split up into different foster homes and/or otherwise institutionalized. To this day, we are not a close family. The very man who preached family unity was the very man who destroyed it. Imagine the irony.

When I was a teenager, I met a man who had a profound impact on how I think. In fact, I was so impressed with his logical thinking that I was more than convinced that the religion we both embraced was indeed, "The Truth." Nonetheless, years later, as I continued to ponder and contemplate this "Truth," I rejected it and was subsequently labeled an "apostate." The same tools he gave me to build my "faith" eventually became the same tools I used to reject it. Imagine the irony.

My ex-wife and I raised our children in that same religion. Years later, while my children were still young, I rejected that religion – as per the above paragraph and eventually became a deist – and thus was officially considered an "apostate." Fifteen years later, my daughter, "Baby Girl," still a member of that religion that I had dismissed, later married a man who was also a believer. As such, I was not allowed to participate in their wedding (i.e., walk her down the aisle or attend their wedding reception) since I was still considered an apostate. I raised her to be a member of that religion, and as life would have it, she could not allow me to celebrate her wedding because of that religion. I wept in pain on her wedding day. Imagine the irony.

I once loved a young lady dearly; she loved herself even more so; two people loving the same person. I loved her at my expense and she loved herself at my expense. Subsequently, she betrayed me.

Love is among the best things in life that are supposed to be free – but apparently at a cost. This "free" thing almost cost me everything of value. Imagine the irony.

... it is nearly impossible to achieve anything productive without being taught

What If?
(Part I)

What if we lived in a society in which someone being able to dribble a ball and throw it through a hoop would impress almost no one?

What if we lived in a society in which people asked for teachers' autographs and asked professional athletes directions to the restroom?

What if we lived in a society in which playing competitive sports was seen merely as part of staying healthy or learning how to be part of a team – but nothing worthy of earning more than a licensed plumber, a gardener or a gourmet chef?

What if we lived in a society in which teenagers hung pictures of their favorite teachers on the wall rather than someone who could skate and slap a puck through a net?

What if we lived in a society in which young people were more interested in learning how to multiply by seven than in learning how to tackle someone holding a football? Or being able to read a science book and write a cogent critique of the subject matter.

What if we lived in a society in which young people would find it difficult to imagine earning a living hitting a ball into a small hole in the ground?

As it stands, we don't. Thus, ...

What if those who oppose affirmative action acknowledged their hypocrisy? Athletic scholarships are often the twin brother to its twin sister, race-based affirmative action programs. A Black man who can tackle can generate millions for a college; a Black man who can become a doctor, lawyer or business chief can cost a college thousands (but could save society millions). The math is straightforward. Short-term thinking and hypocrisy prevail again – all for the almighty dollar.

P.S.
It would be an egregious error to conclude that I disdain professional athletes (they earn an honest living). It would be most correct to conclude that I wish young people and their

parents esteemed formal education and critical thinking more than they value being able to hit a ball hurled at 90 miles an hour.

P.P.S
I chose the profession of teaching not because I have been a teacher but because it is nearly impossible to achieve anything productive without being *taught*.

Either of these failures assures one's life will probably be a bad movie

How To Make The Best Movies About Your Life

In the movie-making business, after a day's filming, the film is shipped to a lab, processed and shipped back to the director by the next day. The processed film of the previous day is known as "dailies." (Actually, the process is a little different and more immediate now, but the concept is the same.) The director and a select few will then study the dailies. This allows the director to determine whether a scene needs to be re-shot or otherwise revised. For any actor who is allowed to view the dailies, this is usually uncomfortable at best and horrifying at worst. Some actors choose not to even view the dailies, and others who do, may see their performance differently from the director.

Using this movie metaphor, questioning one's motives and reviewing one's words and actions may, on occasion, require the objective eyes of another because our review may be honest but inaccurate. In the movie business the director examines the performance of others – the actors typically do not grade their own performance.

Thus, do we need a "director" to view our "dailies"? The answer is more "Yes" than "No." (In this instance, the "director" is a companion who assesses one's performance – not a person who actually directs one's performance.) If so, who? Preferably a friend who possesses a relentless passion for self-knowledge and honesty would be a superior choice.

Nonetheless, the paramount (no pun intended) matter is to engage oneself in the exercise of self-scrutiny; to probe and not accept the first answer we give ourselves as we dig for the truth about who and what we were the previous day, so to speak. To further complicate the matter, can a person's assessment of her "performance" be trusted? It depends. The reliability of one's self assessment is in direct proportion to one's courage and thirst – courage to face nasty or unpleasant truths about one's self and the degree of one's thirst for self-knowledge.

In the real world, as opposed to the reel world (pun intended), most people never view the "dailies" of their lives. Regular or periodic introspection or self-examination can be too disconcerting or too difficult so many avoid it or never give it a thought. Most people will live out their lives never looking at their "dailies." The easiest person to lie to is our self, and the easiest person to ignore is the person we are at our core. Routine examination of how we navigated the events of the previous day (or period) requires an uncommon type of discipline, and it is best when viewed with a critical and painfully honest eye.

A most effective way to develop one's humanity is to examine one's performance through eyes willing to acknowledge that one's past performance may have been other than the best for self and/or others.

The final aspect of reviewing one's "dailies" is to find the impetus to adjust, correct, desist or initiate specific behaviors based on the review. Therein lies part of the explanation of why humans have successfully managed to repeatedly shoot themselves in the ass: They do not study their "dailies," and if they do, they do not make the appropriate adjustments. Either of these failures assures one's life will probably be a bad movie with less than the best possible ending.

why a person does something goes beyond revelation

Character References - Revelation Versus Definition

Sometimes deeds are the shadow, and motives are the substance – even if the deeds are magnanimous. A person's actions may be revealing, but why a person does something goes beyond revelation.

A person finds a wallet with identification and money in it. He makes exhaustive efforts to return it, intact, to its rightful owner. A person with little money finds a ten-dollar bill on the ground at the entrance of a small store. He picks it up and returns it to the person he saw drop it. Another person, with little funds, offers to give another less fortunate person money. (The persons in each of the above examples performed these deeds expecting at least nothing or at most a, "Thank you.")

These examples of unselfish acts of kindness were greeted with, "God will bless you" or "What goes around will come around" or some other mantra that indicates the good deed will not go unnoticed or un-rewarded. In other words, people want to believe that good will be rewarded with good, and the non-good will be rewarded accordingly. The notion that good deeds can go un-rewarded is unpalatable for most.

How many people would decide to live a "good" life if there were no "heaven"? How many would avoid living a "bad" life if there were no "hell"? The same questions stand for those who believe that "what goes around comes around." To be sure, most of the time life does have a system of rewards and punishments (and everything in between); we call it the legal system or it can simply be how people respond to what others do to them – it is called reciprocity.

Oftentimes, however, the consequences of our actions – good or bad, kind or un-kind – are not evident and may never be rewarded or punished. For instance, letting someone take a parking space (in a crowded parking lot) closer to the entrance when you arrived at it a split second before would likely go un-rewarded, except maybe for the warm fuzzy feeling you might get.

What if a person is kind with no expectation of heavenly bliss, or the avoidance of endless hellish agony, or even to feel good about himself? What if a person is kind and caring as a way of simply expressing his humanity in ways that honor the humanity of others? What if a person also recognizes that "some good deeds will not go unpunished" in that those to whom he does good may betray him or may otherwise be unappreciative?

I submit that it is this type of person that is more honorable than the do-gooders who expect a reward from "God" or the "universe" or others (including themselves). Being kind, respectful and caring reveals character. The reasons for doing so are what define character.

Intrinsic motivation trumps extrinsic motivation every time

Three Shades Of Motive

Three women who lived in a state of penury stumbled across bank bags containing more than $150,000; the bags had fallen out of an armored vehicle. All three, without hesitation, agreed to return the treasure to the bank.

When queried by the press, each of them provided a very different reason for their apparent honesty:

The first lady, a devout worshipper of "God" and a practicing _____ (you, the reader, insert whatever religion you wish) stated she returned the funds because she loved and worshipped "God." "God" required all his worshippers to be honest – to speak and behave righteously.

The second lady, a law-abiding citizen who believed in the "rule of law," answered she returned the money because it would be illegal to keep the found money. She recognized that "finder's keepers" was not a legal justification for doing otherwise.

The third lady, a confirmed atheist, replied she returned the cash because her conscience, as developed by experiencing life, would not allow her to exploit the situation in which her gain would be someone else's unfair loss.

The honesty of each lady was driven by motives that were significantly different from the other; the underpinnings of their honesty were distinctly dissimilar. This presses the question: Who, of the three, was the most noble or honorable? Which of them would be the most trustworthy? Assuming each of their motives was authentic and not for show or praise from other humans, which one would make the best co-worker, the best neighbor or the best friend? (All other related matters being equal or near equal.)

With regard to the religious/spiritual woman, what if "God" proffered no reward for being "righteous" and no punishment for being "unrighteous"? What if "God" simply issued creeds and tenets for human behavior in which compliance was voluntary? What if these requests from "God" were provided within the context of there being no after-life?

I believe that people who are honest, kind, "good" for religious reasons are *extrinsically* motivated. They look outside themselves to find the motivation to pursue "good." On the other hand, those who examine themselves and ponder the realities of this life and thus, pursue "good" for reasons having nothing to do with the expectations of rewards or punishment in an after-life, are more apt to do so for *intrinsic* reasons. Thus, which of the two types is the more noble?

To be certain, motives can be part of a continuum that consists of two extremes with gradations in between or can be a mixture of the two – an overlapping of sorts, if you will. A religious/spiritual person may be intrinsically motivated as well as extrinsically. A non-religious/non-spiritual person (e.g., an atheist or a deist) will be intrinsically motivated but could also be motivated by the legal structure of his or her society.

But for those for whom religion is the primary motivation and for those for whom it is no motivation at all, the question can be stated otherwise: If I am "good" because "God" promises me a reward (or for other religious reasons) or if I am "good" because that is simply what I have grown to be as a consequence of deciding that to do so is best for society and myself (all other matters held to be equal or near equal and constant) – which is better?

For some, the question is at best academic and at worst otiose. In other words, they ask, "Does it matter why a person is "good," so long as he or she is? *The question is part of a larger issue, however.* If disbelief in "God" does not preclude kind and honorable behavior, what difference does it make to "God," in the final analysis, that the person is an agnostic, atheist or deist? If it does make a difference to "God" that two people are good, kind and loving yet one is a believer and the other not then why would such a difference be important? If beliefs are equally or more important than one's conduct, the questions that cry out are: Which beliefs? Which "God"? (There are a multitude of religions and varying beliefs even within those religions.) Why would belief or the acceptance of certain doctrine or dogma be relevant if the conduct of the believer is no different than the conduct of the non-believer?

On the other side, if it makes no difference in the final analysis then religion is as relevant, or not, as non-religion (with respect to how humans treat each other). Who is safer, the person who lives next to a believer who is honest and respectful or the person who lives next to the non-believer who is honest and respectful?

How fair would it be for the person who has honored and respected the humanity of others to be condemned to an "eternal burning hell" simply because she has not accepted "Christ as her personal savior" or has not submitted to the will of "Allah"?

So, with respect to the three ladies mentioned earlier, I believe intrinsic motivation trumps extrinsic motivation every time. For the first lady, all it would take to alter her behavior would be for a different interpretation of what "God" requires as per her priest, preacher, mullah or whatever. For the second lady, a change in the law would be sufficient or moving to a place where the law is different. For the third lady, a change in whom she is as a person would be required, and we all know that changing the person we are is one of the most intensely difficult things on earth to do. Hence, I would rather live next door to the third lady.

... can enchant the soul and make the heart forget how to beat

Beauty Me Or Beauty Thee

It appears the world has always placed a premium on physical looks, especially in women. In fact Diogenes Laertius (circa 200 A.D.) is reported as saying that Aristotle averred, "Personal beauty is better than any letter of introduction."

Quotations About Beauty

- *"Beauty pleases the eyes only; Sweetness of disposition charms the soul."* ~Voltaire (1694-1778)

- *"Beauty without grace is the hook without the bait."* ~Ralph Waldo Emerson (1803-1882)

- *"Rarely do great beauty and great virtue dwell together."* ~Petrarch (1304-1374)

- *"Charm multiplies the power of beauty."* ~Carlespie Mary Alice McKinney

The Power of Physical Beauty

All the above being so, Aristotle's point still stands. Being physically beautiful is an attention-grabbing introduction; it is difficult to ignore or set aside - initially. I have seen how men unravel in the presence of beauty. Furthermore, I have seen how women do nearly the same (though somewhat less overtly) in the presence of handsome men. When physical beauty steps into a space, that space is altered, if but for only a brief moment (as in the case of when the beautiful person opens her mouth and subsequently undermines her appearance).

Thus, just as talent and the required discipline to exploit it are a rare combination, so is physical beauty and a beautiful personality. Nevertheless, physical beauty has the power to cloud the otherwise good judgment of others. It can also empty the mind of common sense, turn the soft into hard and the dry into wet. A physically beautiful person can enchant the soul and make the heart forget how to beat.

A Hypothetical Question

The hypothetical question, therefore, I wish to present is this: Assuming a beautiful personality is present in both parties, which scenario would you prefer?

- You are average-looking, but your mate/partner is distractingly and profoundly good-looking, or

- You are distractingly and profoundly good-looking but your mate/partner is average-looking

I would select the former.

I would rather gaze upon beauty than to be beauty. Now, some who would choose that same option might do so because of how others would envy them for having a beautiful partner; the envy of others would actually feed his or her ego. I, however, could not care less about the reaction of others in this regard. I would rather be with a beautiful woman than to be a beautiful/handsome man because I enjoy, I relish, I delight in watching beauty in a woman. It alters my state of being by seducing my vision.

I also disagree with George Bernard Shaw (1856 -1950) who once stated, "Beauty is all very well at first sight; but who ever looks at it when it has been in the house three days?" I have been with beautiful-looking women for many months, or a few years – in the same house, job, *et cetera*, and yet never tired of soaking up the sight of their beauty.

I fully recognize that if I were profoundly handsome, many privileges would accrue to me. My presence would attract attention and advantage. Nonetheless, given the above-two options, my being deeply handsome would preclude me the pleasure of pleasing my eyes in a way that only a beautiful woman can. Obviously, if I could be very handsome *and* could have a beautiful woman, that would be the best of both worlds, but that was not one of the options. So, if forced to choose between the two, I choose beauty thee rather than beauty me.

1, 3, 4 And 2

Four Random Thoughts

Random Thought #1

Most humans, on most occasions, desire others to believe and feel as they do with respect to opinions or ideas they hold – ideas that may range from the trivial to the sacrosanct. Who has not witnessed a lively or passionate discussion about who is the most beautiful celebrity or the most talented athlete? Or, which is the best tasting beer or the best way to discipline an unruly child? In each of the above instances, each person had an opinion that he considered important enough to expend time and energy to convince another to agree – even if, by convincing the other party to see matters as he does, neither of their lives is altered in any meaningful way.

No matter the belief or idea, most humans find a kind of discomfort with opposing views and thus, strive to allay that discomfort by trying to persuade the other party to see things her way. This pursuit of what amounts to external validation of beliefs or opinions is fundamental to most humans. "If she believes what I believe then what I believe is right or OK," is the gauge many people use to assess the value of their own *ethos* or views.

True, some people eschew disagreements, especially with respect to religion and politics. Nonetheless, almost all humans have at many times or others engaged in a verbal jousting with one or more persons with the expressed intent of persuading them to see something the same way they do.

What is fascinating is that humans often argue as if there is something to lose rather than something to gain. They fail to see that disagreements are often opportunities to not only exchange ideas but to actually learn or understand a different viewpoint. Viewing opposing ideas as a call to compete – hence one wins, loses or draws – is shortsighted and sometimes, stupid. In most instances, perhaps the best approach is to debate with the intent of providing *and* receiving understanding rather than "winning" (i.e., convincing the other to see things your way as if your way is the only one with veracity or stubbornly holding to your view even in the face of a potent opposing perspective).

Random Thought #3

"Live each day as if it were your last," is advice that has been repeated for years. That advice, however, lacks the intellectual weight one should expect from words to live by. Imagine if you just found out you had, for an absolute certainty, twenty-four hours to live. Would you still sign up for that Pilates or yoga class as you had planned a week ago? Would you still fill that prescription as you had planned (even though you still have a two day supply)? Would you still refrain from eating the ice cream you had heretofore not eaten because of your diet?

For most people, knowing they have less than twenty-four hours to live would prompt them to make drastic changes. Most would not perform the mundane tasks that life requires. If a person would live each day as if it were her last, she would not make any plans that would require her presence beyond the next twenty-four hours.

Like many maxims, this advice is fallacious and borders on stupid after the most elementary of examinations.

Random Thought #4

It is quite popular for politicians in this country to end their speeches with, "God bless you, and God bless America." For the sake of argument, let us assume that part of what "God" does is to bless. I would then ask on what basis does "God" bless persons or nations? Why should "God" bless any nation? Has "God" actually blessed any nation? If so, which ones? What proof is there that "God" has blessed a nation? (For every positive point one can make about a nation, there are also equally negative elements.) If, for instance, the Iraq war of 2003 was immoral and illegal – resulting in the deaths of many thousands of innocents – as many Americans believe, would/should "God" still bless America? If the Iraq war was not immoral, then why would "God" bless a nation that is certainly responsible for the deaths of many thousands of innocents?

It seems that political leaders of all stripes, shapes and colors like to believe that "God" favors them and their decisions. Adolph Hitler is reported as stating during a speech in 1933: "We are all proud that through God's powerful aid, we have become once more true Germans." "Who says I am not under the special protection of God?" is another statement Hitler is reported as making after winning an election in Germany in 1933 (All Great Quotes). So the questions posed above still remain: Does "God" bless all nations; if not, why not? If so, then why – especially given that at any one moment, any number of nations are either fighting each other or subjugating their own populace?

Is using the words, "God bless …" actually a mindless filler – something people fill in a perceived empty space at the end of a speech? Or do they repeat those words because they are expected to do so? So again, is the request for "God" to bless, a mindless empty expression or is it a meaningful and relevant one? Perhaps the politicians hope that by uttering those words, maybe "God" might actually do some blessing. In any event, "God bless" **any nation** bears all the earmarks of mindless wishful thinking on the part of the one speaking the words and those who like the sound of them.

Random Thought #2

Before discussing or debating an important issue it is best to know why the other party wishes to. If she wishes to honestly understand your views – and nothing more – then indulge her with alacrity. If she wishes to compare your views with hers in hopes of sincerely determining which is the more correct (because she seeks truth even if it means dismissing her own cherished beliefs), then engage her for you may become the one whose views might be adjusted to move even closer to being more correct. But if she wishes to convince you she is correct and you are not, or she wishes to persuade you to accept matters as she does, or she wants to change your mind to match hers, then proceed with caution – if at all.

One of them always stands alone while the other two can sometimes be found together. The challenge is know which of the three is in play for all too often the most reckless one is the most common one. (All too often the speaker may not even realize which of the three intents are driving her at that instance.) As for the other two, you will rarely encounter them so cherish the moments whenever you do.

This makes communication efficient but not necessarily effective

Blathering And Babbling On Planet Babel

One of the more interesting accounts in the Bible is the one revealed in the book of Genesis. It takes place after the "Noachian Flood." The story implies that up until that time, all humans spoke one language. Furthermore they wanted to congregate in one location and build a huge tower rather than spread out over the earth. According to the Bible account, "God" wanted humans to spread out and populate the globe. In order to facilitate the dispersing of humanity and to thwart their plans to build that tower, "God" is said to have suddenly caused different people to speak different languages thereby impeding their ability to communicate (subsequently making it nearly impossible to coordinate the building of the Tower of Babel). People who spoke the same language found each other and traveled to other parts of the planet. Thus, the origin of different languages and the reason why people can be found in almost every part of the planet – according to the Bible.

Whether that account is correct or not, I assert that with respect to verbal (spoken) communication, speaking the same language only solves part of the problem of communication. Effective spoken communication qualifies as a "miracle" given who and what humans are. Considering all the variables at play during communications between two or more human beings, it is most noteworthy that people are able to do so successfully as often as they do. Even when all parties involved desire to communicate effectively, successful communication can sometimes be a near monumental feat.

In this piece, I am defining communication (effective, successful communication – efficient or not) as the act of conveying spoken information/ideas from a source to a receiver so that that source and receiver both understand the information (the source and receiver need not agree, but at least they have reached **the same** understanding of the communication).

Several years ago, I had the following conversation with a friend:

"Wow, my leather coat is in the cleaners, and I have to leave it in until I get the money."

"How much will it cost to get it cleaned?"

"It's already cleaned."

"But how much will it cost to get it cleaned?"

"It's in the cleaners; it's already cleaned."

Exasperated, she admonished, "You're not hearing me. How much will it cost to get it cleaned? You said your coat is in the cleaners, and you said you need money to get it out."

"You're asking how much will it cost to get it cleaned; it is in the cleaners, and so it's already cleaned. Do you mean how much will it cost to get it out?"

"Yes."

"But you didn't say get it out. You said get it cleaned."

"You know what I meant."

"I thought I did. That's why I said what I said …"

Some days afterwards I thought about that conversation. (I was actually fascinated.) How could I not understand what she meant and how could she not understand what I meant? I was not being mindlessly exacting or difficult. I was sincere and so was she! What caused me dismay was her becoming exasperated. I really thought I was responding properly. It did not occur to me that she was not really saying what she meant, and it did not occur to me, at first, what she really meant.

I have observed very similar conversations in boardrooms and restrooms. I have heard friends and enemies complain of the same phenomenon.

We often do not say what we actually mean, and even when we do, we still risk not being understood. Clarity can be elusive because we often speak in ways that require certain matters to be understood whether spoken or not. We often speak in a kind of shorthand when we assume that the listener already knows what we are not saying. This makes communication efficient but not necessarily effective or successful. In most instances, it is safe to assume that the listener understands the background issue; all too often, however, such an assumption leads to an abysmal failure to effectively communicate.

Communication is complicated. To be sure, we are products of our own values, perceptions and environment – all of which impact our communication. Furthermore, context is a key ingredient because it often determines the definition of the words we speak and do not speak. Additionally, often times our own thoughts are not clear to ourselves so that when we speak, effective communication becomes subject to chance.

The communication matrix has several moving parts. These are:

- What I actually said
- What I thought I said
- What I actually meant

Too often, those three things are not all the same. To exacerbate matters, two other component parts of the matrix must be considered:

- What you thought I said
- What you thought I meant

As with the first three, those two things do not necessarily match each other either. It may appear that words get in the way of thoughts, but actually it is the reverse; thoughts get in the way of words.

Engineers state that the fewer moving parts in a machine, the fewer chances there are for a machine failure. Communication is no different. In addition to the potential five components (as noted above), there are six additional component parts to any spoken communication. These additional elements also pertain to the psyche of the sender and the receiver of spoken word. This is best explained by what is reported as having happened to the French critic and satirist, Francois Marie Arouet (AKA: Voltaire).

History tells us that an acquaintance wanted to debate the great Voltaire. Voltaire refused. When the young man queried him as to why, Voltaire is reported to have said that if such a debate occurred, there would be six people in the conversation.

The young man was at a loss because he and Voltaire were quite alone.

Voltaire replied, "There is the man you think you are, the man I think you are and the man you really are – and the same holds true the other way around."

This is most evident when strangers or persons who are less than close friends argue or disagree. When close friends disagree, there usually is not the posturing and saving of face, and the façade or false persona. Thus, when six instead of two are communicating, this can make for miscommunications or ineffective communications.

With all these moving parts (at least five, sometimes 11) in most spoken communication matrix, it is worthy to note that there are not more instances of failed communications. I suspect if "God" had simply let human nature take its course, communication would have undone the prospective "Tower of Babel" without the introduction of a myriad of different languages.

a self-serving reason is often more compelling a reason to ...

THE MATHEMATICS OF MORALITY
(DOES THE END JUSTIFY THE MOTIVE?)

Many times people do the "right" thing for reasons having nothing to do with the intrinsic "rightness" of the thing. In fact, a self-serving reason is often more compelling a reason to "do the right thing" than to do the right thing as an expression of genuine rectitude. To speak it another way, moral decisions are not exempt from the utility of mathematics but are often driven by it.

Most people perform a self-serving cost-benefit analysis[1] in significant matters of ethics or morality. Namely, they weigh the cost versus the benefits to themselves of a particular moral decision. *It is from these cost-benefit calculations that their motives spring* and hence, moral decisions are made. Rather than deciding a particular course is either *"malem in se,"* that is, *"evil in and of itself"* or that an act is inherently or intrinsically "good," their moral decision flows from a "mathematically" derived motive.

The matter of slavery in America is an example that cuts to the heart of this subject. President Abraham Lincoln, when commenting on the issue of slavery in a letter to Horace Greeley, stated he would do whatever it took to preserve the Union. He declared that if retaining slavery would preserve it, he would retain slavery, or if freeing some slaves and keeping others enslaved would preserve the Union he would do that, and if freeing all the slaves would preserve the Union, then he would free all the slaves. The preservation of the Union was preponderant; the issue of slavery had to find its place within that framework (Letter to Horace Greeley, 1862).

Playing the "What If" game: What if he had freed all slaves to the irreparable division of the Union (i.e., a permanent split between the North and South)? Would Lincoln have been hailed as seizing

---

[1] Nevertheless, in the absence of moral absolutes (and the consensus to embrace them), we experience problems because we do not all use the same algorithms to perform these cost-benefit analyses. Moral absolutism, however, brings with it, its own set of conundrums and dilemmas.

the high moral ground at the expense of the Union? On the other end, if he had preserved the institution of slavery to preserve the Union of North and South, would he had been deemed immoral yet pragmatic? In any event, should Lincoln be *praised* for proscribing slavery (via the Emancipation Proclamation) or simply *credited* for proscribing it? In effect, could it be that President Lincoln did the right thing but for the wrong motive? ("Wrong" in that it was for political and not moral reasons. If so, he should be credited but not praised.)

The 21st century continues to provide more examples for cogitation. What if the Pope and his cardinals had believed that denouncing priests who sexually abused children would cause severe structural upheaval in the church and undermine its authority? Did the Pope and his cardinals condemn sexual abuse by American priests because it is morally repugnant or because the political fall out was becoming untenable?

Or consider another instance: Did Congress enact potent legislation against "cooking the company books" because doing so is simply fraudulent and deceptive or because the fiscal integrity of our economy (as reflected by Wall Street) was in jeopardy? Asking both questions another way: If the political cost to the Church were minimal, would the Pope and his cardinals have taken a bold stand against sexual abuse by priests? If "cooking the company books" had little or inconsequential impact on the American economy) but merely on the working poor], would Congress have enacted the most wide-sweeping business legislation since the 1930's (The Sarbanes-Oxley Act of 2002)?

The question to ponder is this: How important are motives if the end of the matter is "good"?[2] After all, if someone returned your lost money-filled wallet only because she found it while with a group of her mosque, synagogue, church, temple-going friends who saw her pick it up, you would still have your wallet and all would be well, her motive notwithstanding. If the end justifies the motive then why a person performs a good deed is essentially academic. Doing good for self-serving reasons having nothing to do with the intrinsic rightness of the deed renders doing good as something conditional or motive-dependent and not something

---

[2] The definition of what is "good" is subject to debate and extensive philosophical musing, but for the sake of this work, "good" is a universally self-defined term and, hence, understood.

more firmly directed as in a true compass whose needle always indicates one's position relative to North.

To illustrate, a high school bully was about to mercilessly pummel a frail but well-dressed young girl just because it was Tuesday and the weather was cloudy. Another girl intervened and chased the bully away. Ever so thankful, the frail young girl asked her savior why she came to her aid.

"I didn't want her to rip your sweater. My younger sister wants to ask you can she wear it tomorrow."

Motives can be very relevant, whether they spring from a sense of intrinsic morality or a self-serving, cost-benefit calculus. (Imagine if the girl's sister did not like the sweater.) The mathematics of morality that gives rise to motive may enhance or diminish the value of a good or moral act; it almost never negates it, however.

Furthermore, motives and their subsequent moral expression may shift from time to time and from circumstance to circumstance. Morally corrupt people have been known to occasionally display sublime moral awareness when faced with moral dilemmas. At the other end, morally responsible people have behaved immorally on occasion. Those instances are exceptions, however; people generally follow their moral center (which is near-immutable) when confronted with dilemmas of the ethical sort.

It is these species of moral dilemmas that betray who and what we are at our core. Moral issues identified by major or costly effects force the authentic moral self to emerge. *What a person does tells you what a person does. Why a person does tells you, who a person is.* To the extent that the difference between the "What" and the "Why" is relevant or of magnitude, then so is motive and hence, the mathematics of the person's morality. Finally, as a corollary comment, where the difference is worthy of note, the end might still justify the motive.

Many captured Africans who jumped off the slave ships ... to their deaths

Sanctity Of The Self

In Latin, the word *sui* refers to "self" and *cide* means to cut or kill — hence the word "suicide." The subject of suicide has exploded into two camps. Those who believe it to be illegal at best and immoral at worst constitute one camp. The other camp is composed of those who believe suicide is illegal only and simply because it is proscribed by society, but that it is not inherently immoral because it is an act of mastery over one's destiny — hence, it is an inalienable right.

To be sure, suicide has not always been viewed as illegal. History reveals many societies where suicide was considered an act of saving face or a dignified alternative to being executed (Samurai warriors or Roman patricians who participated in a failed plot against the emperor just to name a couple).

What is also interesting about suicide is that it is the only **attempted** "cide" — homicide, fratricide, infanticide, *et cetera* — that is not punishable by incarceration in a penal institution (mental perhaps, but not penal). For the most part, the prevalent attitude about suicide in many societies is that the person is not of sound mind — at least temporarily.

It should also be noted, most of the advocates for the right to suicide narrowly define this right to situations where there is a terminal and painful illness. These advocates do not support suicide based on other reasons such as saving face or to avoid embarrassment.

Nonetheless, those who oppose suicide, even where there is a painful terminal illness, cite a moral construct. They declare life to be sacred, and there is no right for anyone to end it before nature does. They also mention the "slippery slope" concept meaning that if the terminally ill are allowed to opt out of living, then other categories of people will want to claim the right to terminate their lives pre-maturely or friends and relatives may coerce them to.

The reasons put forth by those who oppose suicide for the terminally ill create several questions related to consistency and logic.

There is life, as in *existence*, and there is the *quality* of that life. For some, this is the distinction upon which arguments for or against suicide by the terminally ill rest. There is also the issue of what is "sacred." What is the meaning of sacred? Is life sacred, but not its quality? Are both things sacred? Are there circumstances under which the quality of life is more sacred than life in and of itself? Does being sacred in either way preclude deliberate termination?

What is interesting to note is that many of those who declare life to be sacred are those who believe the life itself is sacred, but not its quality. Thus, if the quality is not sacred, or at least held in high esteem, then it is easy to ignore or minimize quality of life issues, especially those related to others, such as the poor or economically disadvantaged. As I see it, if the quality of life were not sacred then the early American colonists would not have rebelled against the English monarchy and coined the phrase "inalienable rights" in the Declaration of Independence. After all, just being alive would have been sufficient – but because the quality of life is sacred – as much as life itself, they revolted. Patrick Henry's declaration, "Give me liberty or give me death," places the quality of life as more sacred than life itself.

It should be noted that many captured Africans who jumped off the slave ships in the middle of the Atlantic ocean to their deaths rather than be slaves have been hailed as honorable – who would dare call them immoral?

Furthermore, why is suicide considered heroic if one commits it to save another's life? There have been instances where a soldier threw himself onto a grenade to save his fellow soldiers. Many will describe such an act as honorable, but in reality it is suicide, no matter how you slice it. Thus, if life is so sacred, why not protest such an act rather than posthumously award the soldier a metal? Is it acceptable to commit suicide to save another but not to stop your own intolerable suffering? One can argue that war is different. In war, you can do what would be considered murder under any other condition. One can also argue that intolerable suffering is different just as is war.

There is also the situation under which one can instruct physicians and other healthcare providers **not to resuscitate** (DNR). That is interesting because omission is tantamount to commission – suicide by direct action or benign neglect – suicide just the same. Additionally, one has a legal right to refuse medical treatment (if one is an adult), an act that is essentially suicidal – at least in many instances.

The conclusion is that the quality of life is often considered as sacred as life itself, if not more so. Thus, if the quality is absent then life itself can be construed to be too futile to perpetuate. It can be argued that life is only as sacred as (under certain circumstances) its quality, and if its quality were diminished then life's purpose would be null and void.

With respect to the slippery slope argument, many issues have a slippery slope aspect. Some could posit drinking alcohol can slip into driving drunk, complimenting a student with a hug can slip into molestation, allowing gay marriage would slip into people marrying their furniture, holding hands can slip into promiscuous conduct and so forth. Slippery slopes exist, but many of them are closed off because of logic, good laws and good sense prevailing. Assisted suicide can also be regulated and framed so as to limit its use. The slippery slope argument is a classic case of mis-direction.

So, is it immoral (legality is merely a technicality that can be reversed or parsed at the pleasure of a legislative body) for a person who is not mentally ill or not depressed but who is terminally ill to commit suicide? The reasons for suicide lie along a continuum with mental illness or depression on one end and painful terminal illness with minimal quality of life (from the perspective of a person who believes life should be one of dignity) on the other.

Many humans strive to attain a life filled with meaning and purpose and not just one of existence. Existence is a means to an end, and if that end can no longer be achieved then it fails to be worth fighting for. Just as a sane person can refuse medical treatment or issue instructions not to resuscitate – such a person should be able to not merely omit but commit. Some people would want to cling to life no matter how painful or debilitating – no matter how long. Others would see such a life as not life but mere existence. To them, mere existence is not sufficient; existence outside the context of a minimal quality of life is not worth the pain or agony.

therein lies an invidious source of many of humanity's problems

The Two Sisters: Timing And Consequences

One of the positive or negative things about consequences is their timing. Sometimes consequences are immediate but in many other instances, they are not immediate (or sometimes not at all). Therein lies an invidious source of many of humanity's problems. It has often been declared, "Timing is everything." Few, however, have applied that idea to consequences.

Humans continue to smoke because cancer or emphysema is not an immediate consequence but whatever pleasure is derived (physical or psychological) is. Humans rape, steal, murder and commit all types of other atrocities because justice, as a consequence, is often experienced long afterward (if at all) but the gratification is often immediate. The same can be said of adultery, procrastinating, eating too much and so forth.

Admittedly, the sword cuts both ways. The consequences of a hungry man eating a wholesome meal are both immediate, and if he continues, there is a long-term positive payoff also. Furthermore, locking a door or hanging a stoplight can also have an immediate positive impact whereas the positive consequences of studying night after night to earn a degree are often not immediate.

How different the world would be if the consequences of inimical and nocent behavior were not only painfully flushed back on the perpetrator but were immediate or at least near immediate. All too often, however, the consequences of ugly acts never come back to haunt the perpetrator and if so, they are muted due to the timing. The timing associated with the consequences of negative acts serves to be a timid deterrent; the gain is immediate, but the costs are deferred if not avoided. In other words, timing really is everything – almost everything that is wrong with Prison Earth.[1]

---

[1] See essay 78

Humans often find this task to be daunting and demanding

The Unfair Fight: Truth Versus Opinion

Truth and opinion are constantly battling each other for acceptance and the battle is often fought within the context of a zero-sum game. Former New York Senator Moynihan once quipped that we can all have our own opinions, but we can't all have our own facts. The problem is most humans confuse the one for the other. In fact it is that phenomenon that is the source of much of human misery. Voltaire, the French philosopher once stated, "Opinion has caused more trouble on this little earth than plagues or earthquakes" (Brainy Quote).

Truth moves in tandem with fact, but opinion is the one that often masquerades as either. Truth and fact can be elusive, even evasive. Thus, the valid is often difficult to identify or acknowledge and so when presented with an issue, one must sort out, collate and present as is – in all its naked glory – what is fact or truth and what is opinion. Humans often find this task to be daunting and demanding.

As a matter of course, humans prefer opinion over fact or truth because opinion often does not tax the mind but rather sedates it. Fact and truth are exacting taskmasters whereas opinion often requires mindless compliance, which is the course of least resistance. Once opinion is introduced into the equation, the answers are often the same: Wrong! This is starkly evident in science, religion, politics and all the other realms of the human experience. Opinion has the advantage over truth because humans, as a matter of course, have demonstrated a proclivity for choosing the shiny rock rather than the diamond in the rough.

Truth and fact are worthy of relentless pursuit, and sometimes they may even take on a fugitive-like stature, but opinion should be slaughtered at every turn – except where it is openly acknowledged that opinion and not fact or truth is at play. When the man called Jesus spoke of truth to Pontius Pilate, Pilate quipped, "What is truth?" He was never given an answer. The philosopher, Diogenes is said to have walked the streets in broad daylight while holding a lantern. When asked why, he is reported to have said he was searching for an honest man. May we all do likewise – searching for facts or truth, and along the way, give no more power to opinion than what it deserves so as to ensure that the fight between the two is fair.

Everything I believe remains on the altar of truth

Being "Right" Rather Than Being Right

The only thing worse than being wrong is stubbornly refusing to accept it when in your heart of hearts, you know you are or might be.

Everything I believe remains on the altar of truth – ready to be sacrificed, if necessary, as part of my constant and relentless pursuit of truth or accuracy. It is this pursuit of truth that moves me to engage in discussion/debate. Stated again, I have little interest in persuading or converting another to my position or belief; I argue merely to test or construct what I believe – not what someone else believes. I willingly expose what I believe to ridicule, question or review because my ego demands that I throw out the incorrect and save the correct. In fact, I detest being wrong so much, that I am not afraid to learn that I am so that I can stop being wrong. (See Bonaparte quote on page 161.)

I aver that most people embrace beliefs as did the man who went to the psychiatrist and proclaimed to the psychiatrist that he himself was dead. The psychiatrist told the patient that dead people could not talk. The patient disagreed and cited his ability to talk as proof-positive that the dead could talk. Finally, the psychiatrist got the patient to agree that dead people do not bleed. The psychiatrist rose and cut the man. Blood oozed from the small cut. The patient exclaimed, "Wow, I didn't know that dead people could bleed!"

In short, most humans, when confronted with evidence that contradicts their cherished beliefs, simply re-interpret the evidence just to preserve their beliefs. Few would react by stating they might be wrong and that they need some time to ponder the new evidence and perhaps reconsider their current belief. For most, the possibility of being incorrect is worse than the possibility of having a terminal disease. They would rather be "right" – in their own eyes – rather than actually being right. This is especially so when the subject is politics, religion – even science or other sacred dogs.

Of course, I have not defined what "truth" is. For my purposes, I define it as that which coincides with fact or reality. (Even so, there are philosophers who would then pose the question, "What is fact or what is reality?" – that discussion is beyond the scope of this essay.) Having defined it as such, I agree some truths can be elusive, unknowable. Also, some truths can be described as absolute and others as relative. Furthermore, some phenomena may not fit into the category of true or untrue, right or wrong, logical or illogical. For example, a man is either six feet tall or he is not, but whether he is nice or not can be a subject of endless and futile debate.

The fundamental point, however, is that no idea or belief should be unassailable or beyond scrutiny. To behave otherwise would amount to simply believing for reasons having more to do with feelings than with reason.

There is no idea or belief I so dearly cherish so as to shield it from rigorous scrutiny or thoughtful challenge. There is no idea or belief I esteem so highly that I will not alter it or abandon it – sacrifice it in favor of standing even closer to the truth.

Few people value truth and follow it no matter where it leads.

The Locked Up Mind

An article published on June 12, 2003, in the *Detroit Free Press* entitled *DNA tests exonerate man* illustrates how justice can be distorted by pre-conceived notions. It presented how justice can be immolated in the unspoken name of expediency and flabby thinking.

Kenneth Wyniemko was sentenced to 60 years for repeatedly raping a 28-year-old woman for four hours in April 1994. After being imprisoned nearly ten years, a group known as the Innocence Project initiated DNA testing conducted by the Michigan State Police, which proved that someone other than Kenneth Wyniemko left traces of biological evidence in the Clinton Township home of the rape victim.

The injustice of this case is particularly interesting because racism was not a factor but something far more pervasive and equally as insidious was. Humans often fail to challenge what they believe; they loath to consider the opposite position. It is easier, less taxing, to adopt a position whose form appears to be more familiar than correct; it is easier not to peel back the layers and examine the substance.

Also, as stated in the above article, "At the time, Clinton Township Police were confident that Wyniemko was the rapist, even though the far less sophisticated scientific testing of the time – mostly blood, semen and hair tests – ***ruled him out as a suspect*** ... Police said their case, though circumstantial, was strong based on the victim's identification and the fact that Wyniemko could not explain how he had come into nearly $3,000 – almost $4,000 was stolen from the victim" (Author's emphasis).

The article continues: "Clinton Township Police Chief Al Ernst said his detectives did the best job they could with the technology of the time." But the technology of the time ***"ruled him out as a suspect"*** (Author's emphasis). How much sense did that make?

The Police Chief also stated, "It's easy to criticize the police. But I will stand by the job that our people did. And if you look at it almost 10 years later, the evidence our people collected is what came to really save this guy."

Evidence is what the police were not inclined to examine but merely ignore until forced to do so again.

Further stated in the article, "Out of nearly 50 pieces of evidence, the unknown person's DNA was present in saliva on a cigarette butt, on nylons stuffed in the victim's mouth and in blood and skin scraped from beneath her fingernails. We went through all of the possibilities if there were any that could still be consistent with Wyniemko's guilt, and we could not come up with any rational conclusions." Therefore, now they had to let him go, at last.

The police thought their case was strong despite hard evidence that ruled him out. They convinced themselves the circumstantial evidence was strong and the weight of the forensic evidence was marginalized. Furthermore, it does not matter how many eyes looked at the evidence. No doubt, more than one police officer reviewed the report as well as people in the district attorney's office. The same can be said of the judge and jury. *Hard forensic evidence "ruled him out as a suspect." Circumstantial evidence prevailed over the hard evidence that ruled him out!*

Human beings are obscenely notorious for resisting, refusing, repudiating any evidence that undermines or flat-out contradicts what they want to believe. Accepting that one might be wrong or mistaken is an arduous challenge for most humans. The police thought the man was guilty and made sure he was considered as such no matter the evidence to the contrary.

Cognitive dissonance is often too painful for people to handle, so they revert to a comfortable place that disallows the discomfort of having to change what they believe. It is almost natural (as are several other odious things about humans) for people to filter out what is classified as not matching the "colors" they have already picked. If it cannot be filtered out or ignored then the contrary evidence is bent, twisted, or painted to match what is already believed.

This human tendency has been seen in politics, religion, business, the military, families, personal relationships, *et cetera* – any place where humans are. It is simply difficult for humans to reject what they once believed. Most humans do not have a thirst or longing for truth. Few people value truth and follow it no matter where it leads. *Admittedly, sometimes, truth is difficult or impossible to know.* But sometimes, however, truth slaps us upside the head with the force of a club wielded by a giant, and still, we humans resist it. A forceful illustration of this kind of thinking was seen when Louis Pasteur discovered that microscopic organisms caused diseases. "The causes which provoked opposition to Pasteur vary in the case of each of the discoveries ... Pasteur made these enemies not entirely because his discoveries stepped on the toes of old theories and beliefs" (Stern, 1927, p. 71). The scientists and clerics of his day scorned and derided him. There are many more examples in history of such behavior. Hence, much of the horrors and sufferings we humans perpetrate against each other can be traced to our fighting, resisting and otherwise squelching the known truth of a matter.

A more current example occurred in the closing years of the 20th century as experienced by a young astronomer, Stacy McGaugh. "McGaugh has taken so much flak in defense of MOND he should be issued with a Kevlar jacket. If the way the dark matter problem was overlooked for forty years taught Vera Rubin how dumb scientists could be, McGaugh, who used to be one of her graduate students, taught her something else: just how resistant science is to change" (Brooks, 2009, p. 29).

A mind may be a "terrible thing to waste," but a mind that is already made up (locked up) can be a terrible thing.

Humans are naturally selfish

Problem-Solving Jujitsu Style

The mother of two feisty boys intervened when the boys began arguing with each other about how to divide the last piece of cake. They each feared that whoever cut the cake would cut the bigger piece for himself. The mother decided that one would cut the cake and then the other would have first choice in selecting which piece would be his. Obviously, the one who did the cutting would be certain to cut that cake as evenly as possible. The mother mitigated the human tendency to seek our own unfair advantage at the expense of others. She employed a kind of jujitsu by using the likely selfishness of the boy who would cut the cake against himself just as a jujitsu fighter uses the weight and strength of an opponent against himself. How resourceful!

She could have intervened and cut the cake herself, but the better way was to simply establish the ground rules. Problem-solving jujitsu style manipulates the innate human selfishness in one person to the advantage of the other person, thus muting the incentive to be selfish. This is one way to achieve equity and parity between two or more humans.

Legend tells of a time in an ancient kingdom in which there were a king and his two daughters. In this kingdom the heir to the throne would be the winner in a horserace between the two. On the day of the race, the king learned that someone administered a drug to one of the horses to make it run faster without fail. Not knowing which horse was given the concoction or which daughter was behind the scheme, he decided to alter the rules of the race. He declared that the winner would be the owner of the horse that came in second.

To ensure that both of the women would not purposely "lose" by coming in second, he also stated that the daughters would not ride her own horse but the horse of the other. (This would guarantee that each daughter would earnestly try to win the race so that her own horse, ridden by the other, would come in second – and thus ensure ascendancy to the throne.) The king used the deceit of the schemer against herself. How clever!

It appears, however, most of life's problems and issues do not lend themselves to these kinds of innovative solutions – or do they? Humans are naturally selfish often to the detriment of others. One way to minimize or neutralize the impact of such a natural tendency is to erect a framework in which selfishness is contrary one's own interest or one's self-interest is best served by at least placing the interest of others on par with your own. Of course, this solution convicts me of idealism because the nature of selfishness more often than not defies a jujitsu solution; unfortunately a right cross or left hook to the head tends to be the only solution.

It will vary as does whom we love or not.

Forgiveness?
Walking And Chewing Gum At The Same Time

Alexander Pope, an English poet and satirist, asserted in his work, *An Essay on Criticism*: "To err is human, to forgive divine." Furthermore, Christians have been advised (Matthew 6:14) to forgive others in order to be forgiven themselves. Accepting these words as words to live by has led some to even forgive rapists, murderers and other brutal perpetrators. For most Christians, however, they seek to implement Jesus' words in their everyday lives by forgiving those who commit lesser offenses. They believe that forgiving those who offend frees them of the so-called burden of hating or resenting. For others, they believe forgiveness is part of the growth process.

Whether for religious or "New Age" reasons, forgiveness has been touted as a necessary aspect of evolving into a better person. Proponents of forgiveness declare failure to forgive locks one into a continuous loop that disallows one to move on to a better life. They believe that not forgiving and reaching one's full potential are mutually exclusive. Those who believe such are mistaken.

Who is to say that a person cannot achieve his pursuits while still harboring hatred and hostility? The ability to do this requires one to adroitly compartmentalize. For some, if not many, this can be performed almost effortlessly, even matter-of-factly. It merely requires one to be the master of himself.

It is true, forgiveness has its merit – its place. In fact, forgiveness is more often than not the course to pursue. There are, however, events or people that are unforgivable. Who decides what the unforgivable is? You do. What about "God"? If "God" wants to forgive or not is a matter for "God" but in the interim, the decision to forgive or not is yours. This is especially so since there is no empirical proof (merely a belief) of "God" doing any forgiving or not.

Be that as it may, I will provide you with an example that is not unique. I have hated my mother's husband since 1963 even though he has been dead since the mid 1970s. I decided what he did from 1951 to 1963 was unforgivable. Since 1963, my hatred has not impeded my ability to function as a productive human, and it has not compromised my ability to grow beyond my natural set point and reach a state of synergism.[1] My un-dying hatred for that man has not been debilitating; it has its place, and I keep it there. I refuse to dishonor the memory of my mother and to minimize the enormity of what her husband did by forgiving him. My hatred for him is visceral; forgiveness is simply unimaginable.

Each of us must decide who and what to forgive or not. It will vary as does whom we love or not. No doubt, there are many on this planet who refuse to forgive but also refuse to let that decision to interfere with their humanity – be they otherwise synergistic humans or not. Just as most people can walk and chew gum at the same time, humans can choose not to forgive and choose to function well at the same time.

---

[1] See essay entitled: The Reason And The Obligations

Much of life is both mundane and complex

The Nature Of Power

There are several kinds of power. This work is about power granted as a function of responsibility bestowed. It is this kind of power that Abraham Lincoln referenced when he stated, "Nearly all men can stand adversity, but if you want to test a man's character, give him power" (Think Exist). It is this kind of power that R.G.H. Siu spoke about when he said, "Cruelty is only a tantrum of frustrated power," especially power welded by petty people. Power and the petty is a noxious mix (Siu, 1979, p.7).

Power can intoxicate, blind, seduce and mislead; it is the stuff of horrors and tragedies. Of all the good power can do, it can do even more harm and is most dangerous in the hands of those who are tubby of spirit or mind – those whose perception of themselves exceeds the reality of themselves.

Much of life is both mundane and complex. Life for many is essentially bland with an occasional sparkle of the sapid and colorful. Humans strive to feel needed; they want to feel important enough to merit attention and respect. The routine of living entails complying and submitting, following and accepting – with few, if any, other viable or tolerable options. Power, however, alters the mix -- it changes the game. And like a child with a gun or a drunk with an automobile, power can seduce and delude – much to the detriment of others, including the one who wields it.

Note the clerk at the desk. Even though he may be a low-wage earner, he has the power to obstruct or facilitate the needs of those who seek his services. He can serve or rule. He can do so without technically violating company policy or if he does, he can do so with near impunity. All because he has power – power to delay, lose, destroy, or expedite. Or note the high-ranking executive who has the power to hire, fire, transfer, demote, ruin or make other decisions that are capricious, arbitrary or self-serving – all for reasons that are legitimate or fabricated, depending on her agenda.

Conclusions
Power is best exercised by those who would *sip* it from the glass and who drink it as part of the meal. Power is exercised at worst by those who would ***gulp*** it from the goblet as the meal itself. For

some, power strokes the ego, for others it masturbates the ego, but for the few who are truly worthy, it subdues the ego. In short, the fool who exercises power grabs the sword by the blade. The not-so-foolish who exercises power grabs the sword by the handle, but the wise one who exercises power first grabs the sheath for she knows power, like the sword, need not always be drawn.

Can the sanctity of life be a function of character?

Death By Punishment

One person, living in a particular state, kills another person. He is tried and convicted of first-degree murder. In the same year, another person, living in the same state, also kills another person under circumstances and conditions similar to that of the other murder. He, too, is tried and convicted of first-degree murder. One of the convicted murderers is sentenced to life imprisonment without the possibility of parole while the other is sentenced to death. Both men had very similar criminal backgrounds.

Race, gender, age, social status, and so forth, of the perpetrator and the victim as well as the composition of the jury, the defense, the prosecution and whoever the judge is – all of these impact the decision to imprison for life or to execute. The same wrong often results in a different solution. Thus, my fundamental criticism of capital punishment: it is not invoked in an even-handed, consistent way and it is also influenced by the superfluous.

No legal system is perfect, however, ours starves for improvement. One suggestion is to establish a universal standard for which crimes must carry with it the death penalty – no exceptions. But, if such a standard were adopted, then plea-bargaining and/or not-guilty verdicts would become more prevalent – blatantly in favor of the privileged or dominant group in society.

What I am proposing is the ideal, but given that it will never be achieved because the rich and/or the dominant group in society will always find a way to circumvent "justice," it will be the poor and disenfranchised who will be *disproportionately* over-represented on death row (as they are now). Said another way, I support the death penalty but not in this world because this world simply does not know how to be sufficiently fair to use it. That being said, I do not accept the other reasons opponents of capital punishment present.

For instance, capital punishment has been assailed as "legalized murder." If that characterization is valid then the confiscation of contraband could be classified as "legalized theft" and arrests as "legalized kidnapping." In other words, societies grant their governments power to commit acts that are otherwise forbidden for the individual member of that society to do – society legalizes what would otherwise be illegal for its members.

The most prominent reason set forth by opponents of capital punishment is that there is the ever-present possibility of executing an innocent person. To that argument, I present two counterpoints:

- The innocent are subject to be executed because capital punishment is not invoked consistently without bias; justice is sacrificed in favor of expediency and pedantic legal procedure. Therefore, this form of punishment should be available only under the most stringent circumstances. Death by punishment is appropriate when the evidence is empirical, unambiguous and dispassionate (as opposed to being primarily circumstantial) and when eyewitness accounts are supported by objective and concrete evidence. Anything less than these criteria should at best warrant life imprisonment – not death.

- It is interesting how some who oppose capital punishment do not oppose war. That being so, it is well documented that in almost each and every war, innocent civilians are killed. Not necessarily deliberately (though there are notable exceptions such as the bombing of Hiroshima and Nagasaki), but nonetheless it does occur, and the sanitized term "collateral damage" is uttered to describe this phenomenon. The point is that some consider the killing of innocent civilians as the unavoidable cost of conducting a war; a cost they are willing to live with because of the "greater good." When it comes to the possibility of executing an innocent person convicted of a crime, however, some consider it more egregious than the killing of innocent persons in the fog of war. Apparently not all innocents are "created equal."

There are those who proclaim capital punishment fails to deter crime. Again, I respond with another counterpoint:

- Such a claim may be more correct than not but apparently sending people to prison also fails to deter crime – at least for many – as evidenced by the recidivism rate. I reject the premise that capital punishment was intended to be a deterrent or should be considered as an attempt to do so. Capital punishment should not be viewed as a tool to deter crime. Of course, there may be instances in which a person decides not to commit a capital crime out of fear of being executed but the number of such occurrences is next to impossible to know and such an occurrences may be a positive aspect of the law of unintended consequences.

Lastly, other people reject capital punishment because they assert life is sacred and thus should not be taken. This assertion raises several questions. How do we know if life is really sacred or not? Does sanctity simply mean that life should not be taken, or does it imply other things as well? Is sanctity even relevant? If so, is life sacred under all circumstances? Is this sacredness absolute or relative? Furthermore, is it that life in and of itself is sacred, thereby making the life of a Hitler, a Pol Pot, a Stalin (or many others I could cite but for the lack of time and space) as sacred as the kindest and most loving person you know?

Or can character diminish or enhance the sanctity of life? Do time, place and circumstance impact the sanctity of human life? Does life being sacred preclude it from being rightfully or justly taken? Suppose that character impacts sanctity in such a way that it determines its nature or structure. In short, can the sanctity of life be a function of character? Those who believe life is sacred have to answer these questions if they wish to adhere to their position.

If it is argued that every human – at birth – is endowed with the right to life, it can also be argued that such a right brings with it responsibilities, and the violations of certain responsibilities should precipitate the forfeiture of those rights. We have the right to live as long as we do not violate certain other rights such as the right of another to live (under most circumstances because there are a few circumstances under which killing another human being is justifiable).

As I declared earlier, I support the principle and idea of capital punishment; I am vehemently against its current application because our legal system is not designed to ferret out biases and inconsistencies. One prominent reason for this failure is that justice and fairness are not always the same – too often justice (legal formalities, *et cetera*) supplants basic fairness. (The definitions of which are admittedly debatable.)

Capital punishment should be reserved for the crimes of treason, certain homicides and the first-degree criminal sexual assault of the pre-pubescent. I believe a country has the right to expect its citizens not to betray it, and I believe first-degree criminal sexual assault of a pre-pubescent is so heinous as to be beneath disgust.

In short, there are some crimes so repulsive, so dastard and despicable (as in the above three) that it assaults our moral sensibilities. Those crimes should be addressed with nothing less than execution by the state provided, however, the state can be just and fair in using this power; *to date, however, the state lacks the facility to be what it should be with regard to capital punishment. To that end, capital punishment should not be sanctioned as a response to criminal conduct.*

"Cruelty is a tantrum of frustrated power"

Spanking The Butt Or Spanking The Mind

A productive debate requires, at least, the definition of terms. Otherwise two people can end up disagreeing about something about which they actually agree, or vice versa. Similarly, they could end up arguing about "A" and "B" thinking they are arguing about "C." The difficulty surrounding terms is exacerbated by synonyms as well as connotations. After all, Voltaire said, "If you wish to converse with me, define your terms" (Think Exist). That said, should a caregiver spank a child?

There are many expressions used interchangeably when talking about "spanking." Whopping, whipping, beating are all terms used with regard to punishing children. Corporal punishment is a continuum ranging from spanking to beating. Then there are degrees of intensity with respect to each element on the continuum. That is, a firm tap on the child's bottom with an open hand (spanking) to a blow to the body with a fist or an object (beating).

Having said this, there are those who believe parents should not administer corporal (physical) punishment at all. Those persons embrace the notion "Spare the rod," save the child. They also believe that spanking "teaches a child that violence is the way to resolve issues." On the opposing side, there are those who believe corporal punishment is a legitimate and effective component of discipline – up to and including beatings. "Spare the rod, spoil the child."

It is true that many parents beat their children often and impulsively; as stated by R.G.H. Siu, "Cruelty is a tantrum of frustrated power" (Siu, 1979, p. 7). Parents who want to control as opposed to teach will often feel frustrated by an unruly or disobedient child. To be sure, there are extremes on both sides. Parents who physically abuse their children – beating them with fists, sticks, or whatever and then there are those who do not administer any corporal punishment – they simply restrain or confine the child for long periods or withhold food, *et cetera*. Both extremes are reprehensible.

Any form of discipline can be pushed to an extreme. Nonetheless, being physical with a child does not necessarily teach violence as a solution to problems. It all depends on the context. For example, many parents will enroll their children in the martial arts – a violent activity – to teach them, of all things, discipline. To that end, does sending a child to her room as punishment for lying rather than letting her go to a party teach the child that isolation or confinement is a way to solve problems?

I submit, any form of punishment can be taken to an extreme if love and *respect* for the child are not part of the lesson.[1] Context is the deciding factor. The context could be one of abuse and mistreatment (without even resorting to physical punishment) or one of teaching and learning based on love and respect, even if spanking is included as one of the disciplinary methods.

Imagine the following: Love and *respect* the child. Then, if necessary, spank, not beat, a child as a last resort after talking or other forms of discipline, thereby making spanking a rare event. Spanking a child early, when appropriate, so that before too long, there is almost no need to ever to spank a child.

There is a point, however, when spanking a child would be an exercise in futility: he or she is just too old, and spanking would simply be ineffective and counterproductive. An example is the tone of voice – not just the words – you would use in talking to a two-year-old about being nice versus the tone of voice you would use in talking to an eight-year-old would be very different. So the methods of discipline should likewise be different – age appropriate.

As a parent, I spanked my four children on rare occasions, and before too long, I almost never had to. I would never spank them if I were angry, and when I did spank them, I explained why and then hugged and kissed them afterward. Spanking, like any other way of responding to a child's misbehavior, is only as effective as the context in which it is administered. A context of love and respect will produce a different effect than a context of hostility and anger. Context is everything whether you spank the butt and/or spank the mind.

---

[1] The love and respect is most evident by the kind of relationship the child has with the caregiver and not what the caregiver says.

Both sides bring their hypocrisy to the game

The Two-Headed Hypocrisy Of Abortion

Each civilization categorizes homicide (from the Latin word, "man," and "kill/cut" or to "kill a human"). There are justifiable homicide, first degree murder and second degree murder, voluntary and involuntary manslaughter, accidental homicide and so forth. Those categories are often a matter of intent and context, and the lines between them can be blurry and shifty. Then there are state-sanctioned executions and war, suicide bombings and honor killings – all are by definition homicides blessed by society or at least part of society. In short, not all homicides are "created equal" as evidenced by how society codifies them.

So where does abortion fit into this framework? Many people consider abortion to be murder because, as they believe, life begins at conception, and hence, an embryo is indeed a human being – a person. On the counter side, many people frame the issue to that of a woman's right to decide what happens to her body (i.e., a constitutional right to privacy). The latter side often challenges the notion of when life begins and what is the status of an embryo or a fetus.

Both sides bring their hypocrisy to the game.[1]

Pro-"Life"
War is as much a part of human existence as wet is part of water. Humans accept war as a persistent reality. They even have "rules of war" that govern whom and how to kill. In almost every war, however, innocent civilians are *guaranteed* to become casualties. Helpless men, women and children are knowingly killed – a reality considered unavoidable however tragic. Many anti-abortionists are supporters of military actions and those military actions bring with them, "collateral damage." How often do anti-abortionists gather to protest the deaths of the innocents in a war? How is supporting such military actions different from abortions? They both can be described – rationalized – as necessary actions for a greater good or cause. Is it acceptable to

---

[1] I use the term "game" not to marginalize the value of life or to trivialize the debate. I use the term because the hypocrisy of both sides effectively reduces the issue to a "game."

kill innocent children in the heat of battle as part of national security but immoral to terminate a pregnancy?

Furthermore, any who oppose abortion should also oppose the wishes of a next-of-kin who wishes the proverbial "plug" to be pulled in the event he or she is brain dead. Or such a person would not support a "Do Not Resuscitate" order, for how would that differ from an abortion given that it could be argued that one is an act of omission and the other an act of commission – both resulting in death? Hypocrisy stains the pro-life position.

Lastly, if abortion is "murder" then both the physician and the pregnant woman are also murderers. Some physicians who perform abortions have been murdered by anti-abortion zealots, but how many of the women who had abortions have been murdered by those zealots? None that I am aware. The hypocrisy extends further. Anti-abortionists preach that life is sacred, but they are often silent about that sanctity *after* that child is born.

"Pro-Choice"

Most societies grant humans the right to accept or refuse medical care. After all, it is their body. That being so, pro-choice advocates state a woman's right to privacy (as interpreted to be part of the 4th Amendment to the US Constitution) should also extend to her right to determine if she will carry a pregnancy to term.

But is that right absolute? Where is the boundary drawn? After all, if a woman has a right to say what happens to her body then why does this right not include the right to decide what goes into it such as marijuana or cocaine or heroin? Furthermore, why can't a woman decide to use her body as a cash-generating entity and not run the risk of being charged with prostitution? Given these matters, the right to decide what happens to one's body is not absolute (constitutional right to privacy, notwithstanding); by logical extension of the pro-abortion position, it should be, or at least almost, absolute. The same principle should hold for men also. They should have the right to determine what happens to their bodies also with respect to drugs or prostitution.

Many pro-abortionist, however, would not support the legalization of prostitution or substance abuse (or use). Hypocrisy also stains the pro-choice position.

A Different Frame

Pro abortionists object to the term "murder" because they object to the definition of an embryo or fetus as a person; anti-abortionists embrace the term because they believe the embryo to be a human being. Both sides present worthy arguments, but the worth of those arguments is limited by the glaring hypocrisy on both sides. The abortion issue should be framed differently by discarding the euphemisms, politics and the subsequent hypocrisy.

If I were a US Supreme Court Justice I would write an opinion that would include the following:

Pro-abortionists should accept the notion that an embryo is essentially a human being; there is more evidence than not to support that notion. Therefore abortion is a homicide. Anti-abortionists should accept the notion that certain homicides are legal as explained above and that abortions are legally codified as permissible homicides.

Humans kill. They always will. It is an ugly fact, and one of the things humans are clever at doing is to label homicides based on their context and intent. Both parties in the abortion debate creep around that fact and for that, they will always constitute an irresistible force running head on into an immovable object.

... you can learn a great deal about a person's character by observing ...

Choosing Your Battles

One of the most taxing challenges of being human is determining not only the time and place to "do battle" – physical, verbal, legal or otherwise – but choosing which battles are worth the fight. In fact, some believe you can learn a great deal about a person's character by observing which battles she chooses to fight and, subsequently, how she fights the battle. This power to choose is significant.

Several years ago, I went on a date with a former co-worker. We sat in a movie theatre, and suddenly three teenage boys sat behind us and began talking and laughing loudly during the trailers/previews. I suggested to her that we move to another area of the theatre. She instead turned around and told the boys to be quiet. They obliged.

After some introspection and after giving the circumstance some thought, I determined why her actions concerned me. If the young hellions had chosen to react belligerently, I would have engaged them to protect her (using tact and diplomacy or violence depending on the direction of the dynamics), but I would have been fighting a battle, verbal or otherwise, that *I* had not chosen – fighting a battle on terms her actions would have defined rather than my actions. Not only would *my* control of when, where, how, but *if* I wanted to do battle at all could have been jeopardized.

Yet, I could not cast her in a pejorative light because, again, at a different moment and space, I would have turned around and asked them, tactfully of course, to lower their voices. And, if they had reacted churlishly – but not dangerously – I would have moved to another seat or taken some other non-aggressive action. But in that instance, I, and not some other human, would have made the decision to do battle or not do battle.

We are all different. We choose to fight battles largely based on the circumstances and our disposition at the time. Thus, I cannot say my date was wrong for telling the boys to be quiet. I can only say, from my perspective, she was wrong for telling the boys to be quiet while she was with me – unless, for some reason, she was able, willing and ready to kick ass without my assistance.

Not every thing is worth arguing about, and not every argument is worth winning. Not every battle should be waged as not every battle should even be won. The battle you choose is as important as the one you do not choose – both decisions should be made with deliberation and foresight, not with impetuosity or temerity.

To illustrate: A famous and revered knight sat at a table with several other renowned warrior knights. He was being honored for having killed the most feared and dangerous dragon of them all. The other knights told tales of how many dragons they had slain – one had killed four, another boasted of killing seven, the others made similar claims. Finally, one of them asked the knight who was being honored how many had he slain.

"One," he calmly replied. All of them gasped with surprise.

"Only one?!"

"True," he responded.

"Why, when there are so many to kill? Why only one?"

"Well, I couldn't sneak past it like I did the many others. He was too clever. I couldn't trick him either. I had no other choice but to fight," the famous knight replied.

All but oldest of the men smirked and chuckled as the famous knight gazed out the window pensively, "He has lived longer than most of you ever will," the old man said.

"But I'd rather die young but brave than old and a coward," one of the others loudly retorted.

Silence grabbed the room. The famous knight turned to that knight and glared daringly into his eyes. He spoke quietly. "I may not be the best or bravest knight in the kingdom, but not even that person would dare challenge me."

Valor is more closely related to wisdom than bravery and the line between bravery and foolishness is wisdom. That is not to say a wise person cannot be bold and daring; it is to say, wisdom defines an act as either bravery or foolishness.

... who does not need a "hell" with which to punish

Imagine

Imagine a "God" who does not believe in the Bible, the Koran, the Torah, the Book of Mormon, the Veda, the te Ching or any other book as being "holy" or "divinely inspired" but rejects them as the product of the human imagination.

Imagine a "God" who is completely anti-religion.

Imagine a "God" who has nothing to do with our successes or our failures.

Imagine a "God" who does not want credit for catastrophes or blame for "miracles" (or even vice versa).

Imagine a "God" who does not need a Satan with whom to stand in contrast.

Imagine a "God" who does not need a "hell" with which to punish or a "heaven" with which to bribe.

Imagine a "God" who is something other than a "He" or a "She" (maybe an "It" or a "They" or something entirely different).

Imagine a "God" whose ego does not require or desire praise, adulation, sacrifice or worship from humans.

Imagine a "God" who does not need humans to kill or punish "in the name of God," because if such a "God" wanted to kill or punish, It or They would do it without any help or participation from humans.

Imagine a "God" who does not need prophets, priests, preachers, ministers, deacons, reverends, mullahs, monks, ayatollahs, elders, nuns, and so forth, to speak or teach the will of "God."

Imagine a "God" for whom how humans treat each other is infinitely more important than whether people believe someone did or did not die for their sins, or whether a particular place or day is "holy," or whether people should wear this and not that, et cetera, (the list extends much too far and wide).

In other words:

Imagine a "God" not made in the image of "Humans."[1]

---
[1] See essay 75

... ice is cold and water is wet

Ordinary Tragedy

It was indeed a grievous tragedy, for many, to suffer the loss of seven astronauts in February 2003. Many in the nation gathered to honor and extol the personal virtues of those lost during the return of the spacecraft, *Columbia*. The media, politicians and "ordinary folks" wept with the families and friends of the deceased. Once again, the "nation" was in mourning. On that same day, however, a child somewhere died from abuse and neglect, a woman was murdered by her husband, and a father died in an auto accident – millions of others around the world died – without recognition, buried with minimal ceremony with only a relative few to mourn their deaths.

Even in death, time and circumstance can trump who you are, and the death of few can be deemed more worthy of note than the death of the many. That is life on Prison Earth. Death is so common as to be attention-getting only when it is someone we know or someone famous – or there are multiple deaths from a single event. How else could we manage living if the death of everyone who died brought us to despair and grief? Nevertheless, there is something lachrymose about this fact.

I recall an occasion when I was hurrying to an appointment. I stopped at a red light, and when the light turned green, I still had to wait; a caravan of cars trailed behind a black vehicle carrying a casket. To those especially close to the deceased, this was a tragic time; to me and the rest of the world, however, it did not receive a second thought, not including that moment.

Those we love will die soon enough, and then it will be our turn to drive behind their casket – unless we happen to be in the casket. In any event, others will wish our funeral procession or the funeral procession of our loved one to hurry and pass.

Somehow, there is still something that creates cause for pause about deaths unnoticed by the many juxtaposed against similar deaths mourned by the few. Maybe it is because death happens to us all if we stick around long enough. Or maybe it is no more of a worthy phenomenon than birth – worthy of celebration by a few but ordinary to the many.

In the final analysis, under most circumstances, being born and then dying is of importance to the one it happens to, and you are lucky if it matters to someone else – even if it is just one. In some inexplicable way, that fact seems tragic, but I cannot imagine any other viable reaction. Maybe then it is no more tragic than it is to say, in the final analysis, that ice is cold and water is wet – everybody lives and then they die. What can be more ordinary than that?

The three sisters are Lust, Infatuation, and Love

Unconditional Love And Self Hatred

In recent years, the phrase "Unconditional Love" has come into vogue. It is spoken as if it is a superior form of love. To many people, to love is sublime, but to love unconditionally is divine.

This notion creates several questions: Does true and genuine love have to be unconditional? Is loving someone unconditionally better than loving someone deeply but not unconditionally? How is loving someone unconditionally different from loving someone blindly or obsessively?

The Oxford English Dictionary defines "Unconditional" as, "Not dependent on any condition ... Without condition or restriction or stipulation ... Not limited by conditions or circumstances."

Thus, unconditional love is love that is not contingent on or limited by or subject to conditions or circumstances or situations; it is unrestricted, without conditions. Logically then, unconditional love is not a function of reciprocity, and it does not have to be nurtured – otherwise it would not be unconditional. Stated another way, love can be conditional (e.g., subject to how you are treated) or it can be unconditional (not subject to anything).

Most discussions about love would be incomplete without defining it and her two sisters. The three sisters are Infatuation, Lust and Love. The first two often masquerade as love and sometimes love includes lust and/or springs from infatuation. While entire theses could be written about each of the three, the following concise definitions will be sufficient for this work. Lust is fundamentally a function of the libido, and it may or may not be accompanied by one of the other two. Infatuation often impersonates love; however, it often lacks the staying power and substance of love. Love is the genuine attraction to and the deep concern for the interest and well being of another. It is often demonstrated by self-sacrifice and other expressions of selflessness. Like any emotion, however, it can border on or become pathological.

There are two subsets of the human population that bear on the subject of unconditional love: Young children and the mentally disabled. The element those two have in common is that they are not fully responsible for their actions or words, yet they need the loving care and attention of those who are. Members of this group are natural candidates to receive "unconditional" love. They need to be loved, yet they cannot earn it in that they lack the wherewithal to incite it in others, except on a purely visceral level. That visceral level being the almost natural inclination to love members of that group because of their dependency or helplessness (physical and/or emotional-mental).

Society establishes exceptions for persons of this group as evidenced by laws which exempt them from the severe punishment that would be meted out if they were adults who had sufficient use of their emotional and mental faculties. We, and the law, for example, are more forgiving (loving?) when a toddler or young child steals money from our kitchen table than when an adult steals it. Most people understand the need to love infants, toddlers, young children and the mentally ill "unconditionally" and often do so with alacrity.

Nonetheless, somewhere, during (certainly after) adolescence, we hold humans responsible for their actions and words; they cannot claim exemption from the consequences of their behaviors. Do these persons deserve unconditional love, or should they be loved for as long as they are worthy (i.e., as long as there is sufficient and appropriate reciprocity)? In short, do those who posses the mental wherewithal have to earn love – or otherwise prove worthy of it – rather than to receive it without conditions? Especially given that most adults who are genuinely (not blindly) loved had to prove worthy of it – at least in the beginning.

For instance, imagine meeting a person for the first time. An attraction might simmer or flare up. If love follows, does it do so for no reason? Does one simply decide to "love" that person or does one "fall in love" or otherwise come to love the person for a reason(s)? Maybe love develops because of the kindness and similarity in tastes or ideas, *et cetera*. The elemental point is that love arises out of something, and that something(s) is the *reason*, and that reason is the *condition*.

In the absence of that "something," one would not fall in love or come to love. If the love arises out of the dynamics (social, emotional, mental and so forth) of the interactions of two persons then that love is *not* unconditional – it is, by definition, conditional. Otherwise, one can simply love a stranger in the same way one loves a long-time friend. To love unconditionally is to love without regard for the value or worth of love itself. Love is a precious experience and as such, should be earned; it should be a function of some sort of reciprocity. Friends, lovers and the like are such because they have done something in return and should continue to do so. Hence, to love unconditionally is to love obsessively or psychopathically.

To love conditionally, as opposed to unconditionally, does not preclude forgiveness. It does, however, preclude persistent unyielding forgiveness that remains in the face of blatant, reckless, disregard. Love must be nurtured and continually earned. Unconditional love does not require anything from the object of that love; he or she does not have to do anything to receive it. That is what love without a limit or unconditional love means.

To love unconditionally would mean to continue to love the scoundrel who was once the prince. The woman who marries a loving man who, over the years, becomes abusive and truculent has the right to stop loving him at her discretion. If she loved him unconditionally then she would love him even while he continues to demean and denigrate her. Can it not be said that he no longer deserved to be loved? Unconditional love means to love even if the person becomes someone you would not have loved in the first place if she were the person she is now.

Many people have fallen in love with the phrase, "unconditional love." It sounds superior to good old-fashioned love. Love is precious, however, and should not be squandered on the unworthy whether that person is a son, daughter, mother, father, *or whoever*. Love must continue to be nurtured by doing and saying that which fosters it; it must be earned in order to be deserved.

That does not mean that one does not treat persons for whom one has no love disrespectfully. To not love a person does not mean to mistreat or disrespect him. It simply means that one does not afford that person the same emotional prize one bestows on a worthy friend, worthy spouse, *et cetera*.

What about, "Love your enemies"? I do not advocate mistreating or even hating your enemies – for the most part. (There are some enemies, however, who deserve to be hated, but even then, not necessarily mistreated.) The question is, what did Jesus mean when he uttered those words? I agree that hate feeds on hate and that love is one way to short circuit hatred in a relationship. I also know, however, that love can take the form of the negative –

namely to not mistreat or to not disrespect. Whatever Jesus meant (for those who treasure his words as sacred) unconditional love remains an irrational, self-disrespecting act.

The popularity of using this term "unconditional love" is another example of people uttering sententious rhetoric without thinking about what it actually means. The person who loves unconditionally (except for loving those in the stipulated group) does not respect love but is enamored with a counterfeit notion of it. To love unconditionally reflects a self-hatred because to love and respect yourself, by definition, would demand that the other person be worthy to receive your love.

The world would still remain a dark and dangerous place

Why The Owl Killed The Rooster

A Simple Prayer that was overheard by a nephew:

Dear God:

> *I know you're really proud of me because, so far today, I have not used any profanity, insulted or screamed at anyone. I have not stolen or vandalized anything. I have not told any lies or deceived anybody. I have not guzzled down an entire bottle of wine in less than 10 minutes or had wild, nasty sex with my neighbor's spouse. In short, I've been really good.*

What comes to mind when hearing this prayer? Would you conclude this person has successfully resisted baleful urges and bad habits? Would you conclude this person has thus far won the "battle" after having struggled? Based on the information revealed in the above prayer, those conclusions would appear to be reasonable, especially if there is no bias or prejudice introduced into the thought processes. Conclusions, after all, are often a function of the amount and type of information available. Incomplete information, however, can often lead to erroneous conclusions.

Notice the final words of this prayer:

"But it's 7:00 AM, and I'm ready to get out of bed now and start my day – so I'll really need your help if you want me to be good the rest of the day."

– A prayer by Auntie Sara

As cute as this prayer may be, it illustrates an engaging point. The final words paint a more complete picture of the circumstance. The answers you may have given to the questions in the second paragraph would probably be different. The mere act of having more information can often cause a re-calibration of one's perspective. Acquiring more information often requires patience and diligence – two things for which humans are not particularly noted.

There are also times when humans draw short straight lines instead of long circuitous lines between two vastly remotely related ideas or they connect the wrong dots. Both are functions of incomplete information (and no doubt other phenomena also).

A thought-provoking example of how incomplete information can lead to seemingly valid but incorrect conclusions: The Sambian men of New Guinea believe that fellatio with a woman is necessary to prepare her for lactation and they believe that the semen she ingests converts to breast milk. To them, the connection between semen and breast milk is a short straight line or they connect the wrong dots. In either case, their information is woefully incorrect (The Sambia, n.d.).

Imagine if more people would seek as much information as is practical and identify and question assumptions before drawing conclusions. The world would still remain a dark and dangerous place but the positive impact of reaching correct conclusions would be enormous. Jealousies and suspicions, misconceptions and lies, arrests and convictions, revenge and betrayals, persecutions and even wars – have all occurred because of drawing conclusions based on incomplete or partially examined information.

Reaching conclusions based on incomplete information explains why the rooster thought the sun rose to hear him crow and why the owl killed the rooster thinking it would stop the sun from rising.

I am my own knight in brilliant armor, for who could be a better champion for me then I?

The Celebrity Of Self
(Orbiting Your Own Star)

After Alexander the Great had conquered much of the world that he knew and as he basked in all the glory of such greatness, he found himself being entertained and lauded in some of the most obsequious ways. Politicians, philosophers and others of note came to truckle and flatter. Alexander noticed, however, that one man, a noted philosopher, had not come to see him; he, therefore, decided to pay that man a visit.

Alexander and his entourage approached a man wearing only a loincloth lying face up, basking in the sun. The man looked at Alexander, and Alexander looked at him. Silence. Finally, Alexander greeted him with flattering words. Still, the man said nothing. After a long and uncomfortable silence, Alexander asked him what it is that he wanted and that whatever it was, Alexander would see that he got it.

The man looked at Alexander the Great and asked him, nonchalantly, to step aside because he was blocking the sun (apparently, that is all he wanted from Alexander). Alexander left, dejected and reduced. Members of his entourage tried to dismiss the man as crazy. Alexander objected and replied, *"If I were not Alexander, I would wish to be Diogenes"* (Diogenes).

The sunbather, Diogenes the Cynic, was the philosopher otherwise known for carrying a lighted lantern in broad daylight looking for an "honest" man. Not that one should espouse cynicism as a way of life or that one should treat others in a way that approximates rudeness, but there is something worthy to be gleaned from Diogenes' reaction to Alexander The Great.

Fans or admirers of the famous, the powerful or wealthy often apotheosize them (or even their relatives and friends). If a person possesses athletic prowess, or the talent to entertain, or millions in a bank account, or political power, or physical beauty, *et cetera*, it becomes sufficient cause for many to fawn, envy, stalk, imitate or otherwise elevate such persons onto the proverbial pedestal. The celebrity of others, no matter the size, often invokes adoration akin to something unctuous. All this, despite the fact that in every way, the wealthy, famous or powerful are as intimately familiar with the experience of flatulence as anyone else.

Imagine, however, having a vibrant and healthy sense of self. Imagine having a perspective of self that is a function of valuing your own peculiar and uncommon uniqueness and that such uniqueness, after all the important things are said and done, can stand along side whatever talent or skill another may have and not feel diminished.

Then it would be easy to respect, or even admire the talent or ability of others while not losing sight of the fact that those admirable assets remain subject to the same humanness that defines all of us. It then becomes easy to acknowledge a person's wealth or position in the same way you acknowledge a person being left-handed or right-handed because you understand the elements of humanity and subsequently, you value the celebrity of self, realizing it is worth no more and no less than the celebrity of other humans.

To that end, I am my own knight in brilliant armor, for who could be a better champion for me than I?

I look up to myself because no one stands taller than who I believe I am, my status as an obscure member of the working class, notwithstanding.

Diogenes may have been an incorrigible misanthrope and an insufferable cynic for reasons explained by his *ethos*, and Alexander The Great may have relished the treatment received from his many sycophants. Their encounter, however, provides the thinking person, famous or not famous, with knowledge that humanity should supplant celebrity every time.

To pose the question is not to diminish the value of the services

Heroes And Un-Heroes

Having heard the word "hero" used to describe persons in a variety of situations ranging from that which is just this side of the prosaic to the completely dangerous, I wonder what does it mean to be a hero? What must a person do to legitimately deserve that designation?

Several years ago, a local television news station in Detroit, Michigan reported two incidents in which two persons were described as "heroes." One man was described as a hero because he ran into a burning building and carried out an 83-year-old woman. He voluntarily put his life at risk when he could have simply remained on the outside wondering and worrying like many others would have. That same news program reported that another man, while driving on the expressway, suffered a stroke or heart attack and hit a semi-trailer/truck. A professional football player stopped, called 911 and otherwise provided assistance. The news personnel described the professional football player as a "hero." On another occasion, a 12-year-old boy suffering from leukemia was featured on the local news. He, too, was declared a "hero" by his classmates and the newscaster.

Bone marrow donors, Girl Scout cookie buyers/sellers, generous donors to a worthy cause, soldiers, police officers, teachers and so forth have all been crowned as "heroes" by one person(s) or another. It appears it does not take gargantuan efforts or Herculean acts to be crowned with that nomenclature. In short, almost anyone can become a hero by simply doing something a bit out of the ordinary – something just this side of what is expected or just this side of the mundane.

This phenomenon of calling almost anyone a hero is a function of the bastardization of the language. I clearly understand how language – its words – is/are dynamic and meanings change over time. Accordingly, the word "hero" could rightly be used to describe a healthy child who walks five blocks to school through a safe and pleasant neighborhood everyday rather than ride his bike to school. Or, the father who digs ditches during the day and plays video games with his children in the evening could, by the expanded definition, be deemed a hero.

Definitions are vital for effective communication and clarity of thought. I assert there are three fundamental categories of honorable behavior and hero is just one of them. There is the "hero," the "dutiful steward," and the "Good Samaritan." Admittedly, the lines of demarcation are blurry and wavy, but they exist nonetheless. And lest we confuse all three and lump them into the category of hero, we diminish the stature of real heroes and marginalize the value of the "dutiful steward" and the "Good Samaritan."

According to the *Carlespie Mary Alice English Dictionary (1st Edition)*, a hero is someone who unselfishly and without *obligation or duty* makes a profound personal sacrifice on behalf of another and, in doing so, places her safety or security at risk or in jeopardy. True, my definition is narrow, exclusionary and open to questions of what are "profound," "risk," "unselfishly," and so forth. Nonetheless, as you will see, it elevates the term to a place different from the person who buys $2,000 worth of cookies so the marching band of the local high school can attend a major competition in another state.

Using my definition of hero, the man who entered the burning building to rescue the 83-year-old woman could properly be called a hero. It was not his duty or obligation to do so, and by doing so, he placed his safety at risk. This situation, however, can become more complicated. What if the 83-year-old woman was the man's mother or other relative? Would he have had an obligation to rescue her? If so, would he rightfully be deemed a hero or not? If not, what would he be called (other than a good son)?

Now, what if the rescuer were a firefighter? Would he or she be correctly called a hero? I say not. By saying, "not," however, I am in no way marginalizing the importance of the responsibility and value of the firefighter; I am simply defining the firefighter's actions as that of a "dutiful steward." This term is not pejorative or opprobrious. The firefighter, police officer or soldier has voluntarily accepted a job for which she is paid, and in exchange for that compensation, she has agreed to put herself in harm's way. It is her obligation and duty to run into a burning building or to raid a drug house or to invade a country by force. Doing what she has volunteered to do for compensation constitutes the behavior of what I call a "dutiful steward" and not a hero – except in the instance of performing her task **above and beyond the call of duty**. We call those actions worthy of a medal and hence, worthy of being called hero – in that instance.

After all, the issuance of medals for valor is an implicit statement that the recipient has performed in a way that exceeded her obligation. If it did not, she would simply collect another paycheck for doing what she was supposed to do. The "dutiful steward" is absolutely vital for the protection and welfare of our society, but by and large, they are not, by definition (albeit mine) heroes.[1]

As an aside, what of the volunteer firefighters as opposed to paid firefighters? Are they heroes? This is a distinction without a difference. These, like other public servants, have agreed in advance to put themselves in harm's way – not for compensation, *per se* – but for the sake of the community of which they are a part. They practice, train and otherwise prepare to perform dangerous tasks. Just as with the paid firefighters, they are doing their jobs – an honorable job, but a job nonetheless.

An extension of this notion of the "dutiful steward" (though not the same) is the person who may exhibit some sort of personal endurance in the face of pain and/or ill health. Struggling with the effects of a stroke or surviving cancer, or living through years of false imprisonment, and so on, are not the actions of a hero but of a strong and willful person. *Admirable, yes. Hero, no. Praiseworthy, yes. Hero, no. Tenacious and Optimistic, yes. Hero, no.* Trying to remain alive and in good health is not the mark of heroism as much as it is of self-preservation – the so-called first law of nature.

The final term is the "Good Samaritan." As the Bible story goes, it is someone who willingly and without obligation helps another in distress. There is no perceived risk to the helper; he or she does not place her security in jeopardy, as does the hero. Thus, the football player who stopped and helped the person who suffered a stroke on the highway was a "Good Samaritan." One could argue that in these perilous times, stopping to help someone *could* be placing your security at risk because it *could* be a trick. That is a special circumstance. There may or may not be a risk, but with regard to the hero, she knows there is a risk before taking action – the danger is apparent and obvious – there is no maybe as in the case of the "Good Samaritan."

---

[1] This matter of duty and obligation accepted by the "dutiful steward" is further made poignantly by the fact that firefighters and police officers in some communities can actually go on strike or a work stoppage. In short, what they do is first and foremost a job. If your accountant fights off a would-be rapist, he is a hero. If your police officer does it, he is doing his job as a "dutiful steward."

True, the primary difference between the hero and the Good Samaritan is one of risk or danger, but that is a difference worthy of note. Stopping to help a wounded man can be quite different from stopping a band of hoodlums from beating up that same man. The extent of danger is what constitutes the difference between the two (not to mention whether one has an obligation or duty to help in each case).

A hero or a "dutiful steward" or a "Good Samaritan" are all different but all honorable. A ruby or a pearl or an emerald are all different, but all are precious stones. Most of us will travel through life without performing any heroics, but being a "dutiful steward" or a "Good Samaritan" are noble things in and of themselves. A hero is not worth more than either of them. In fact, the world needs more of the other two than they need heroes.

In our culture, the term hero has been so casually spoken so as to lose much of its luster. Why is naming a person a hero preferable to calling her persistent, strong, kind, generous, reliable, good, honorable or whatever (except hero)? The overuse or misuse of the term hero minimizes the importance of the other two terms presented in this piece. In a world in which most people exist as faceless, nameless cogs, humans long for distinction and they look for it in names. How unfortunate that they believe the hero to be better than what they may actually be – a "Good Samaritan" or "dutiful steward."

I realize that for some people to question whether fire fighters or police officers who die in the line of duty are heroes as well as those who overcome near insurmountable challenges is sacrilege, but I believe that just as an ace of hearts should be called an ace of hearts and not an ace of diamonds, a hero should be called a hero, except when he is not.

These ideas force us to confront another question

Reality Is Perception?

It has often been asserted that "perception is reality," meaning that whether some phenomenon or belief is true or not is almost irrelevant; what is relevant is whether it is perceived to be true. If it is perceived to be true, people will act and think as if it is in reality, true, whether it actually is or not. William Isaac Thomas a noted sociologist (1863-1947) stated it more eloquently: "If men define situations as real, they are real in their consequences" (GAIA) As an example, if a person believes a bar of soap is laced with poison, he will behave as if it is whether it is or not; perception might as well be reality.

If "perception is reality," could the opposite also be true? Could reality be perception? Stated another way, if reality is a function of our perception, is our perception a function of our reality? A German novelist, essayist and Nobel Prize laureate, Paul Thomas Mann, stated an interesting perspective – "A great truth is a truth whose opposite is also a truth" (Brainy Quotes).

Reality, for the most part, is independent of perception (a cat is a cat whether you believe it to be a moose or parrot) and yet "perception is reality." Despite that, however, perception is often the opposite of reality. If the reality is that the bar of soap is not laced with poison and a person has no reason to believe that it is, she will behave accordingly. Given that same bar of soap, however, another person may perceive it to be laced with poison and will behave accordingly. For the first woman, reality is perception (reality creates her perception); for the other woman, perception is reality (perception creates her reality).

These ideas force us to confront another question: Is it possible for a reality to actually be different for two people, irrespective of their perception? Yes. A cat is a cat is a cat is a cat and not a moose, perception notwithstanding, but the sun is either rising or setting – at the same time – depending on where each observer is standing, perception notwithstanding.

Perception may define reality, but reality can return the favor.

Maybe it is as profoundly simple as that

Why Things Happen – The Real Reason

I was sitting in a restaurant, and once again I overheard someone pontificate that "Every thing happens for a reason." I sighed and shook my head. Such a statement bears the mark of both logic and a kind of comforting reassurance. But only if you fail to reflect on it logically.

What does that mean, "Every thing happens for a reason"? To most, it assures one that life is not a random mix of events, people and time, but that there is a force or entity that coordinates and manages all human affairs (no matter how grand or minute) with some ultimate purpose in mind for each of us. Sounds impressive and reassuring that our lives have purpose as decided by something or someone greater than us and that there is no such thing as mere coincidence or chance but every action/event is purposeful and is part of a grand scheme.

But on the other hand, maybe everything happens for a reason, and the reason is this: Life happens. Life happens according to the laws of nature and the laws of how humans behave within the context of the whims of "Lady Luck" and her twin sister, Random Chance. Maybe it is as profoundly simple as that. The reason for a thing can be found in or with the thing itself – nothing more, nothing less.

For instance, a woman wanted to plant a tree on the northwest corner of her front yard but her neighbor protested vehemently because there was a dispute about the property line. She relented. A few years later, it was determined she was correct and her neighbor was wrong about the property line, but she had already planted the tree on the other corner of her property (the northeast corner). As she lamented, her son comforted her with the assurance, "Everything happens for a reason, whether the reason is obvious or not."

Twenty-three years later, a group of teenagers died in a car that crashed into that tree. Family and friends of the dead grieved them and declared they now had a deeper appreciation for life.

Which makes more sense? The tree was planted on the northeast corner so that people who had not yet been born could crash into it and subsequently precipitate a deeper appreciation for life in those who survived them. Or, maybe the tree was planted on the northeast corner because of who and what the lady and her neighbor were within the context of time and place and that whatever happened after that (i.e., the auto accident) was no more a part of a larger plan than some other car crashing into some other structure.

I will say it another way. The driver of the car was speeding and lost control of the car at the exact spot that would result in a collision with the tree. Had he lost control of the car a few feet before or after, he would have crashed into something else or nothing, depending on what else was in his path.

Could it be that "Everything happens for a reason," and the reason can be traced to the laws of nature and the random confluence of the activities and behaviors of humans? Could it be that "Everything happens for a reason" has nothing to do with some ultimate guiding force manipulating human events to some grand purpose?

Of course, if a person wishes, he could present a divine "reason" why a man ties up a woman and sexually assaults her four-year old child. Or a person could opine there to be a cosmic "reason" why a police officer would shoot a man in the back who is handcuffed and lying faced down. Or a person could infer some spiritual "reason" why innocent children are killed during a bombing by an occupying army.

Not to be one-sided in this issue, a person could present a divine "reason" why a man with five children was hired rather than a man who had none. Or a person could opine there to be a cosmic "reason" why a woman could be stabbed several times by a rapist but survived to testify against him. Or a person could imply some spiritual "reason" why a group of refugees were discovered by a band of soldiers who happened to be traveling along a route in which they were not authorized.

Nonetheless, some will not give up their belief that there are no such things as coincidences but that there is an ever-present guiding hand in all human affairs no matter whether the "reason" is ever known or not. Given that notion, a human could postulate that the guiding hand could be "God," or Allah, or Shiva or some other deity depending on which religion she subscribes to. Does that make sense? If a plane full of Christians, Muslims, Jews and Hindus crashed and all survived, which "God" should deserve the credit? These questions are very significant given that each of those religions are, in many regards, at theological odds with each of the other. I submit that the laws of physics and random chance should be credited with the survival of the passengers. Otherwise, if a follower of the god, Koa Boo Boo was on board, she could claim that a mystical force emanating from pigeon droppings was responsible for her survival and what Christian, Muslim, Jew or Hindu could prove otherwise?

As disconcerting as the idea may be, we live on Prison Earth where life is a dynamic mixture of people, places, things and time and where random chance is a significant element. Everything does happen for a reason, just as the sun rises and sets for a reason, flowers bloom and wither for a reason, buildings shake and collapse for a reason, forest catch fire for a reason, people get hired and fired for a reason, cars run out of gas for a reason, cats climb trees for a reason, firefighters recue children trapped in a fire for a reason, men rob and murder for a reason, mothers abuse their children for a reason, people are falsely accused and convicted for a reason, racists stereotype others for a reason, we inhale and exhale for a reason, and we die for a reason.

Life happens. That's the damn reason!

Good things happen to bad people

Where Is "Karma" When You Need Her?

The adage, "You reap what you sow" is oft-repeated in New Age terms as "What goes around comes around" or summarized in one word, "Karma." It is a disconcerting thought to many to think there are times – perhaps many times – when humans may not reap what they sow. Sometimes in life, people actually get away with lying, theft, rape and other cruelties including murder. Sometimes what goes around may not come around, and karma is nothing more than a romantic notion that the universe will achieve balance by either righting wrongs or punishing them.

Of course, some humans may retort that if not in this life then the next. There is no proof there is a next life or if there is, there is no proof that any reaping occurs that is connected to the sowing one did in this life. There is no proof. There is, however, belief – belief no more or less correct or ludicrous than the belief in divine intervention by any number of "Gods" (Vishnu, Allah, Osiris, Jehovah, Zeus, and so forth).

That being said, I wish to speak on what we do know – **this life** – reaping and sowing in this life. History is overflowing with examples of where people have reaped what they did not sow or have reaped less than what they have sown – or maybe more. There are thousands of examples of humans escaping justice, thereby not reaping what they have sown. The lynching of Emmett Till is a prominent example.

In 1955, two men, Roy Bryant and J.W. Milam kidnapped, tortured – in medieval fashion – and murdered fourteen-year-old Emmitt Till for allegedly "offending the honor of Mr. Bryant's wife." The men admitted taking Emmett Till from his great-uncle's cabin but were still acquitted of kidnapping as well as murder. The trial lasted four days, and the jury deliberated 63 minutes before returning with a verdict of "not guilty."

The following month, both men sold their story to *Look Magazine* for $4000; they admitted their guilt with pride and in no uncertain terms. Thereafter, both men's efforts to operate their business and farm ... failed. Roy Bryant's store closed as a result of blacks boycotting it. Milam's farm failed (as did many others by the way). The Bryants later divorced – as many couples do –

and both men died natural deaths decades later – as do most people.

On one hand, a fourteen-year-old boy was tortured and murdered for committing a perceived slight or insult. On the other hand – Where was the "karma"? What "came around" given that his torture and murder "went around"? Where was the "reaping" of what was "sown"? A failed business, a failed farm, a divorce, and natural deaths hardly constitute reaping what was sown. And that is just one of no doubt millions of examples.

There is Joseph Stalin who was responsible for the deaths of 10 million of his own people, and Pol Pot was responsible for the deaths of over 1,000,000. Idi Amin killed over 300,000 of his citizens. "Lucky" Luciano, the murderous Mafia boss, murdered tens of others. My mother's husband brutalized her physically and verbally for 10 years before finally murdering her for leaving him. Stalin, Pot, Luciano and my mother's husband all died of natural causes with no evidence that their lives were subject to some "karmic" force – no more than anything or anyone else who had not committed any atrocities.

Less severely there are every-day instances of cruelties, injustices, wrongs as well as kindnesses, affections, sacrifices – all going unpunished or un-rewarded. True, sometimes humans reap what they sow, but it is largely a hit and miss phenomenon. Good things happen to bad people and bad things happen to good people and vice versa in both instances. Humans are uncomfortable or ill at ease with the notion that life on this planet may not be governed by some universal force or entity that keeps things in balance. Sometimes what comes around has nothing to do with what went around. Sometimes you reap and sow in ways that have nothing to do with what you reap and sow.

Thus, it can be correctly stated that at many times Karma is either on frequent bathroom breaks or is asleep at the switch – if not MIA altogether.

there is one kind of lie that is baneful

Sugar-Tasty Poison

Lying facilitates all manner of human evil. Pogroms, war, rape, domestic abuse, theft, deceit and all other related activities either require or are facilitated by the lie. Without lying, much of what makes life painful or miserable could not occur.

The following news article, Breaking Election Promise OK: Judge, provides an interesting perspective on the subject:

> "It's official: Politicians can break campaign promises with impunity. An Ontario Superior Court judge has absolved Ontario premier Dalton McGinty of breaking an elaborately signed contract that promised not to raise or create new taxes. Justice Paul Rouleau said anyone who believes a campaign promise is naive about the democratic system."
>
> (*Calgary Herald*, January 30, 2005)

What I find most interesting is that lying is treated as being an integral part of the political process – even in a democracy. True, some campaign promises are made in good faith and are subsequently "broken" due to forces beyond the control of the candidate. Nonetheless, many campaign promises have been made while the candidate knew he or she was lying. Such lying is viewed as a necessary component to procuring a win. Under any other circumstance, signing a contract and then breaching it would be considered grounds for the injured party to receive compensation for damages – but not if the breach was made in the context of a campaign promise. Perhaps the powers that be consider the prospect of not being re-elected as a kind of adjudication for lying.

To further illustrate the matter of lying, I have known women and men who have told me that whenever a person flirts with them or otherwise expresses interest, they believe at least half of what the person says is a lie. It is part of the game, the ritual. Often lying is done with an ease equal to that of a healthy person breathing.

Humans lie to protect themselves, enrich themselves, or inflate themselves. They lie to protect others, deceive others, or exploit others. Children learn very early the cost of telling the truth, and therein lies the issue: The lie is always told after, consciously or unconsciously, calculating the cost of telling the truth much like an investor calculates the return on two different investments. And like an investor who makes a bad decision, the liar eagerly seeks to justify or minimize the reality. Furthermore, lies are almost always presented as the truth (something almost implicit in the definition); the lie is the façade – the shadow posing as the substance. In short, the lie can never present itself as such or else its purpose would be defeated.

It is interesting that witnesses in legal or official matters are often required to swear or affirm to tell the truth. This does not ensure that they will but it provides the basis for prosecution in the event they do not. After all, if telling the truth were natural and expected, there would be no need to require a person to take an oath. Lying is so typically human that people are often required to promise not to do it. Despite that, they often still do. They take an oath not to lie, but they lie about the oath.

Lastly, in addition to those realities, there is one kind of lie that is baneful, potent and prevalent – the lies we tell ourselves. It is those lies that impact our beliefs and hence our behaviors. It is those kinds of lies that generate much of the malevolent psychology that identifies humanity.

Of all the poisons that humans serve each other, beware the one laced with the lie, for it is the lie that gives the poison such a sweet taste.

... salacious, silly and serious

Sex In The Real City

In our heterosexualistic-homophobic culture, the macho game of American football is the one occasion in which one man bends over while another man squats behind him and places his hands between the other man's legs – on a field with 20 other men and in front of thousands or even millions of viewers – and not be colored as being gay.

Also, in the American culture, a heterosexual woman can refer to her female friends as her "girlfriends" whereas if a heterosexual man referred to his male friends as his "boyfriends," he would be labeled as gay.[1]

What is also interesting is that if a man takes a woman he has never met to a hotel room and pays her to have sex with him, they have committed a crime in almost every place in the United States. If, however, she signs certain documents, has sex with him in front of a camera crew and receives money in exchange, it is considered pornography and not a crime.

Then there is the phenomenon of statutory rape and murder. A 14-year-old girl or boy is deemed unable to give legal consent to have sex and is, therefore, protected by law. Nonetheless, that same 14-year-old girl or boy can be tried as an adult if she or he commits murder (Age of Consent).

Speaking of the age of consent, actually, in some states in America, 14 is the age of consent whereas in other states, the age of consent ranges from 15 to 18 depending on the particular state. This disparity is interesting in that if parental consent is given, the minor can marry and then have sex. If a minor is too young to consent to sex, why isn't she or he too young to get married – especially since marriage is far more exacting than having sex? If parental consent is the fulcrum then why can't a parent just consent to his or her minor child having sex instead of

---

[1] Furthermore, in certain Arab countries, it is not altogether uncommon for two businessmen to hold hands while traipsing down the street – and not be considered gay. For two men to do that in any city of the United States would be seen as evidence of homosexuality.

getting married? If a parent can determine that her 14- or 15-year-old is suitable to get married, then isn't the minor ready to have sex? (Pregnancy is an irrelevant issue given that birth control is available). I am in no way advocating sex among teens; I am simply highlighting where the "con" in contradiction is.

Last of all, rape has been described as being about power, control and domination – not sex. Since rape, by definition, is not simply controlling or dominating another, but it entails sex, then the question arises: Is rape about power by means of sex, or is rape about sex by means of power? I suspect rape is about both.

Sex in the real city is salacious, silly and serious.

A rich man once looked at a haggard beggar and uttered...

There, But For The Grace Of ...

All of us are the combination of the random confluence of our genetics and the time and place of our living.

More specifically, consider the circumstances of your origin. If your parents would have had sex a few days or hours earlier or later (or even if they had sex in a different position) then a different sperm – one out of many millions of other eligible candidates – could have fertilized your mother's egg thereby giving life to someone other than you. A different egg or a different sperm would have resulted in a different you. In short, your parents having sex at the time they did as opposed to some other time made you be here and not someone else – you are the combination of a very specific egg and a uniquely specific sperm.

Furthermore, if your parents had moved to a different country, state or even city when you were very young (or if they had often moved from place to place) you also would likely be a person different from who you are now. The impact of environment can easily be illustrated: If you were born in New York City but at the age of two you were taken to and raised in the outback of Australia, would you be who you are today? Would your view of the world and this reality match your current perspective? Not likely. What if you were born in a small village in Iraq but raised in Los Angeles, would your values and *ethos* be as they are now? Not likely. What if you were born in the year 1537 or the year 1896 or even 10 years later or earlier than you were? (assuming the exact egg and sperm from which you were formed were the ones that we are talking about) You would be different with respect to your views and ideas.

To illustrate the point further, if you were born in a small village in Pakistan rather than in Mississippi, USA, more than likely you would have a different set of religious and moral ideals. Mohammed rather than Jesus would be the one whom people in the community would revere. The prevailing views about gender roles and family would impact your perspective on those issues. Or, if you were born in Virginia in 1813 and were of European descent, the prevailing beliefs about slaves would have exerted pressure on you to conform. Each generation, at a given time and place, is identified by the dominant beliefs and ideas – it is the rare person who adopts views that are heterodox because most people fall in line with the culture of their time and place. For most of us, most of the time, we only think about or consider what we are exposed to. What we are exposed to is a creation of the time and place of our living.

Depending on when and where you were born, your ideas and beliefs about the cause of disease and the existence of demons, the earth's shape, homosexuality and pedophilia, the role of men and women and their comparative worth, the idea of criminal justice, your view of Mohammed, Jesus, Shiva, Buddha, the Sun, the Moon, human sacrifice and so forth would all be a function of the culture and era of your existence.

Thus, it can be stated again, with more truth than not, all of us are the combination of the random confluence of our genetics (egg and sperm) and the time and place of our living. What we believe and think, and do, are often more of a function of elements into which we are born and/or by which we are surrounded. That being so, consider the ramifications of these facts especially when it comes to religion, politics and other matters.

Having said all this, now imagine a "God" that blesses you with "heaven" when the circumstances of your birth and life (of which you had little control) had as much if not more to do with your beliefs as your decision to be a Christian. The same applies to being raised as a Hindu or Shintoist or whatever. How fair is it to be condemned or blessed by virtue of the circumstances of ones birth? Is that how "God" does it?

A rich man once looked at a haggard beggar and uttered, "There, but for the grace of God go I." Did "God" have anything to do with his being born into a wealthy family – or however he attained his wealth? (Even the so-called self-made man cannot dismiss the elements of time and chance. A different turn, a chance encounter with a different cabbie or clerk, a stomach ache or the sight of a pretty girl who looked or did not look his way, could all have impacted the moment in time when things turned in favor of or against the self-made man so that he would have been not self-made but made by someone else.)

If he were a recipient of "God's" grace then was the poor man a recipient of "God's" animosity or something other than grace? Why would "God" do such a thing – bestow grace upon some and not others? Or, could it be that time and chance are the factors and not "God's" grace (or lack thereof)?

One could argue that "God's" grace with respect to the beggar was present but not evident. If so, then the statement, "There but for the grace of God, go I" is meaningless and misleading.

Instead of "God" there are the "Grand Three" – *an unholy trinity: Chance, the Agenda of Others and Our* Own Doings. Thus, more cogently, "There but for the grace of "God"...? No! There but for those three go I and everyone else.

The lenses of the rear-view mirror...are distorted

Yesterday's Brighter Sun

I have had quite a few happy times in my life but only two extended periods of un-tainted joy and happiness. Those periods were the summer of 1961 and my junior high school (now known as middle school) years. In both instances, my mother's husband was not present to create a state of fear and terror. In the first instance, he left for California in preparation for our subsequent arrival and in the second instance, he was in prison for murdering my mother. (As painful as it is to admit, the relief of not living with him practically negated any grief I felt regarding the loss of my mother – until decades later.)

Over the years, I have collected more than 11,000 songs to enjoy on my iPod™ and of that number, nearly 1000 are songs that were popular during my much younger years. Those songs spark memories of a fleeting youth as they allow me to temporarily escape the present and soak into memories of both pleasant and not so pleasant moments. Those particular songs have the power to seduce me into reminiscing – longing wistfully for what I boyishly perceive to be brighter times as today no doubt is for many.

Why is it that yesterday's sun seems brighter and its moonlight more enchanting? Why do humans reminisce about the "good ole days"?

For me there are two reasons:

- My youth was a period in which my responsibilities were minimal and less consequential than those I shoulder as an adult. As a child, there were no bills to pay, no lover to adjust to, no job that stood between financial ruin and me.

- Most importantly, however, as a youth, I had not yet made the mistakes for which I had to pay and for some, still am paying.

There is also the fact that oftentimes when we look back, the lenses of the rear-view mirror we use are distorted. Somehow the pain and angst are minimized or even forgotten and the happy moments are magnified. To be sure, much of life is mundane and un-remarkable and whenever we are grieving or lamenting the present, we allow our minds to escape to another time that we believe was better than the present. Yesterday's pains are more or less behind us but today's pains glare at us right in our face.

Most certainly, however, life for many is better now than it was in the past. That would be true for me also except for the two periods I referenced earlier. Nonetheless, life now is more grievous than not because I have no answers to the questions that choke me.

In any event, our minds are most adroit at contaminating our faculty of recollection so that the rose had no thorns and the orangutan somehow looked like the beauty and not the beast.

... it has morphed from the overt to the crafty

The Proof Is In The Pattern
(Racism: The Dirty Face Behind The Mask)

On 16 July 2009 two men locked horns in Cambridge, Massachusetts with each drawing the incident with a different color paint. President Obama stepped into the fray and inadvertently pushed the matter to the center stage of America's race relations and subsequently set off another challenge to Whites and Blacks in America to talk openly and honestly about race. Henry Louis Gates, Jr., director of Harvard's W.E.B. Du Bois Institute for African and African American Research, accused James Crowley, a sergeant in the Cambridge police department, of racial profiling; Sergeant Crowley arrested Professor Gates for disorderly conduct.[1]

After having read several newspaper accounts and listening to a radio host read the entire police report filed by Sergeant Crowley, it appears that both men tripped over their own egos. One man ranting about racial profiling and alluding to his stature by retorting, "You don't know who you are messing with" instead of tamping done the bravado and blustering. The other man electing to flex his authority instead of ignoring the ravings of man who posed no real threat (perhaps to teach him a lesson in how to respect police authority).

In that situation, outside the courtroom, Professor Gates was the egg and Sergeant Crowley was the rock (Crowley had the power to arrest at his own volition) and when the two collided, one man ended up in handcuffs, and the Cambridge police was described as "acting stupidly." Later, the charges of disorderly conduct[2] were dropped.

The question still stands, however. Was Sergeant Crowley guilty of racial profiling? The only person who knows is Sergeant Crowley. In the absence of an admission of racism or his making any racist comment, no one else can know except if there were an individual ***pattern of behavior*** one could cite.

---

[1] Disorderly conduct is sufficiently loosely defined as to be subject to the officer's interpretation.

To be sure, the United States of White America has a long and horrific history of racism, particularly against Blacks. From slavery, to Jim Crow laws (and the tacit sanctioning of lynchings and forced labor) to the passage of the 1964 Civil Rights Act, racism had openly thrived. In recent decades it has morphed from the obvious and overt to the subtle and crafty because legislation has forced racism to adapt thereby making it more challenging to identify in the absence of a pattern. Instead of hanging a sign, "No Coloreds Allowed," Blacks are allowed in with Whites, but they simply are not "chosen." They are not chosen for any number of ostensibly legitimate reasons, but the actual reason has often been racist. And therein lies the problem.

Government and university studies show (by identifying a pattern) that racism with respect to housing, employment, sentencing, healthcare and so forth, is still vibrant but crafty. So crafty that it is best identified when there is a pattern of behavior. A single event is typically not sufficient unless that single event entails the hurling of racial epithets or something equally as unambiguous.

Therefore, a clerk may provide me with incorrect information because she is a racist or because she did not like how I presented myself or because she did not know the information she provided was incorrect (or some combination thereof). The employer may not promote me because he is a racist or because I am not the best candidate for the position or because I failed to invite him to my grandson's pool party (or some combination thereof). The judge may reduce my settlement amount in a suit because he is a racist or because he is in the pocket of the defendant or because he simply believes the settlement amount was excessive (or some combination thereof).

In other words, who can know, except the person himself, if his behavior/decision is tainted with racism? Other than confessing that his attitude and behavior is based on a racist perspective, one can only infer a racist attitude if there is a pattern because in most instances the proof is in the pattern. That is to say, a single incident is not sufficient to make an inference; only a pattern can provide a basis for making an inference.

Racism has a dirty face, and in the United States of White America, that face is often hidden snugly behind a mask of some "legitimate" explanation. This ugly face with its pretty mask is how racism operates in America.[2] To complicate the matter even more so, the question arises: How many acts or decisions constitute a pattern? For sure, it has to be more than one, but beyond that, it can be a challenge to call out racism.

My final perspective about these matters is that because racism is such a pernicious component of our society any accusation should be well-founded. The accusation should be made with caution and deliberation because racism is indeed a filthy face behind a clean mask of fairness and honesty. Otherwise, we Blacks would be seen as always "crying wolf" and seeing every act or every word of a White person as a Black and White issue – even when it is not. Unsubstantiated accusations would also serve to mitigate the grievousness of racism in the eyes of White Americans; it also makes for needless defensiveness on their part. In the end, we Black Americans cannot afford the issue of racism to be viewed as anything other than the revolting and repugnant reality it is and it is best confronted and challenged in the face of proof.

---

[2] This statement does not in any manner minimize the significant strides America has made in reducing racism. But I am not so obtuse as to believe racism is no longer a threat to a better America.

Words evoke images and ideas; they can alter perception

You Don't Have To Kill The Lawyers

A government agency bugging its citizens' phone lines can call it, "verifying the audio integrity of communications." Stealing is "re-distribution" and starting a war can be called, "defensive aggression." Telling a lie can be described as "embellishing the truth" and racial profiling becomes "selective identification." In fact, a turd can be called a "non-utilitarian by-product of a life-sustaining activity."

Every effective political, religious, business and community leader understands this phenomenon and most are fairly agile at renaming an issue to their advantage. Words evoke images and ideas; they can alter perception and hence reality (i.e., its perception, at least). The above examples illustrate the use of euphemisms but another method is to simply re-name to thing.

What you call a thing can be more important than what the thing is. This reality is often the way of power – the way to control or the way to empower. Power is most effectively projected when first using this key. Renaming a thing creates a new frame or context; create a new context, and you create a new reality or perspective.

"What's in a name? That which we call a rose, by any other name would smell as sweet." (*Romeo and Juliet* 2. 2. 1-2). So wrote William Shakespeare. On the surface, the truth of those words may seem indisputable. Flipping it around however, by calling a turd a rose, it would probably smell as foul nonetheless. But by calling a turd a rose would allow one to view and treat it differently – at least persuade others to do so. Thus, the power of what you call a thing.

Euphemisms and re-naming are both very effective communication tools. (As the above examples about "turds" reveals.) The advantage of both is that euphemisms sugar coat but re-naming deflects. Politicians are especially good at both.

In Shakespeare's play, *Henry VI* (4.2), there was a plot to start a revolution. In order to facilitate such a plot, it was suggested, "The first thing we do, let's kill all the lawyers." Yes, despite the reputation lawyers have today, their importance in maintaining a civil society was once well known and valued. Today, however, instead of killing all the lawyers, in order to disrupt civil society, all a leader has to do is to change what a thing is called or sugar coat it. Do either – and announce it repeatedly. Enough humans will swallow it and they will follow like dumb sheep on drugs.

Which is better ...

My Brother's Keeper ... My Brother's Rival

The polar opposites – individualism and collectivism on their continuum combined with the polar opposites of homogeneity and heterogeneity (i.e, diversity) on their continuum, all define the structure of a society and subsequently produce disparate outcomes.

Individualism

Individualism, a mind-set that elevates independence, self-reliance and the favoring of individual action over that of the collective or the group has long been lauded as a major impetus that catapulted the United States to its status as an economic powerhouse. Rugged individualism as espoused by the pull-yourself-up-by-your-own-bootstraps *credo* has been venerated as the American Way. There is little doubt that the spirit of individualism has fostered many advantages that cannot be discounted or dismissed, but like almost all human traits, there is a point at which its exercise can be counterproductive or marred with a host of painful consequences.

A pronounced spirit of individualism can engender the notion of "every man for himself" which can be contrary to, if not an anathema to, the concept of being "your brother's keeper." There is a natural tension between exercising individualism and submitting to the will of the group. It is said that individualism fosters risk-taking, creativity and innovation; it certainly can. Beyond a certain point, however, it can give rise to the notion that you are on your own if you fail or that something is wrong with you if you fail (never mind that success, to a substantial extent, is also a function of chance – individual ability or talent notwithstanding).

Yes, with individualism the proverbial sky may be the limit. We are seldom told, however, that many may fly but few will soar. We are seldom told there is a shortage of parachutes and the net has huge holes in it. The spirit of individualism does not promote helping the other as effectively as collectivism (except perhaps to help the person to achieved as an individual by means of individualism – so the circle reproduces itself).

But in societies or organizations where the good of the collective is deemed more important than the good of the individual, there may be less disparity in the distribution of resources and opportunity; hence, collectivism. Collectivism has its advantages. In fact, the military is a viable example of collectivism. A well-trained force relies on *unit cohesion* – something diametrically opposite rugged individualism. Indeed the military is rigidly structured and does not suffer individuality lightly. Nonetheless, most societies cannot be run like a military but the concept of collectivism has its merit. When people sacrifice a certain amount of individualism for the good of the group, the group is more likely to provide a safety net for the individual.

Nonetheless, collectivism can be an impediment to pushing outside the envelope to experience or discover the new and the improved. Change can be viewed as an infection to be resisted. If change does occur, it usually occurs slowly and methodically – which can be a positive or negative phenomenon. For collectivists, the *status quo* can be an end in itself and historic examples abound with the original or critical thinker (one of the core features of individualism) being ostracized or disdained because she does not march in step with the group.

Individualism and collectivism – opposite ends of the same continuum and like most things on Prison Earth, the crème is probably in the middle.

Diversity

Diversity is a pungent source of conflict. There cannot be diversity without conflict on some level; not all conflict is nocent, however. Diversity in a group, be it of the religious, cultural, gender, racial, or national type, provides a fertile ground for conflict. It can be the excuse for pogroms, discrimination, bigotry, divisions and all manner of foul human behavior. The presence of differences makes it easier to mistreat or stereotype.

Yet, heterogeneity (i.e., diversity) can promote fresh, innovative, and insightful solutions and experiences. It can broaden one's perspective and push one to grow. Without a diversity of ideas as a function of the diversity of the group, much of human advancement (positive or negative) would not have been achieved.

Homogeneity, on the other hand, induces compliance as well as a sense of oneness. It facilitates unity that could prove to be formidable in the face of external strife and other challenges. On the downside, the absence of diversity can stifle advancement and improvements. New ideas are less apt to be greeted with acceptance; the heterodox is often viewed with skepticism if not fear.

The Mix

Which is better, individualism or collectivism? Which is better, diversity or homogeneity? Which mixture of the two sets is optimal and which is not? Most organizations, societies or groups are a mixture of some sort. These questions are germane because they are part of the explanation why some nations or societies experience completely different outcomes with respect to productivity, happiness, and an array of other conditions that impact the quality of life.

Imagine these combinations: Individualism in a diverse environment and individualism in a homogenous environment; collectivism in a diverse environment and collectivism in a homogenous environment.

For all the reasons specified above, individualism in a diverse society can be a virulent mix of strife, angst and shattered dreams – or a fertile plot where new and rewarding ideas and advancements can be cultivated and harvested. Competition for resources can be fierce, and harmony is often sacrificed in favor of the self-serving. Out of that competition can come rewards enjoyed by the few and travails suffered by the many (though some of the fruits of those rewards can trickle down to those who were not so fortunate as to win).

Individualism in a homogenous environment is not as easily achieved and maintained because in a homogenous society collectivism is usually the norm and collectivism is less conducive to individualism. Thus, collectivism in a homogenous society can be a banal mix of the mundane yet less stressful (maybe even happier) because of the safety net of the group. It can be stifling with respect to the fresh and the unorthodox because there is less incentive to consider the different or the unusual.

To finalize, I agree these are generalizations and exceptions are frequent but not frequent enough to dismiss the observations and conclusions *in toto*. In any event, one of the above combinations is more apt to give rise to a cutthroat kind of sibling rivalry with its associated consequences than the other combination.

In the end, society created them, the privileged and the female

Why 1 + 1 Is Less Than 2

Humans are born into a society, no matter how small or large, that can shape and mold them into beings that can accept/believe virtually anything the society wishes. Societal norms, values, beliefs and attitudes are not genetically driven but are almost 100% imposed by the culture. Comparatively very little of what humans do is instinctive; they are primarily and fundamentally victims (or beneficiaries) of their culture.

This explains *seppuku* (ancient Samurai ritualistic suicide, aka, *harakiri*), honor killings, female genital mutilation, arranged marriages, homophobia, racism, killing children who are born with a physical disability, the subjugation and domination of females and an endless litany of other cultural elements. In short, a society can create almost any kind of person it deems correct and will pressure, punish, ostracize or kill the aberrant or the contrarian. Society is the framework, the structure within which every human functions; it is almost as much a necessity for existence as is oxygen.

To that end, imagine a society that has a fiercely rigid view of domestic spousal abuse – especially of the physical kind. In this imaginary society, striking a woman would bring so much shame and dishonor on the assailant that he would rather resort to suicide than face the disgrace. Furthermore, the thought of killing a woman (except in instances of legitimate self-defense) would be as repulsive as eating pigeon droppings. This is not to say that these men would be an emasculated segment of society; they would be as macho, strong, self-assured and aggressive as ever, but their respect for women would preclude perpetrating violence against them.

This would not be a chivalrous society where women are treated as dainty objects of adornment; they would be treated in an otherwise egalitarian manner. Furthermore, to ensure the perpetuation of this kind of belief system, part of the acculturation process would be to teach males, from the time of birth, that honor and respect for women is a basic requirement for citizenship and acceptance. Hitting a girl or woman would carry with it severe and painfully ugly consequences – more severe than if they struck a male. All young girls would also be taught never to strike a man as another way of facilitating the successful acceptance of this norm by the male population.

Lamentably, such a society does not exist. Domestic abuse is part of the fabric of most societies and its acceptance is as deeply entrenched as most any cultural norms. More specifically, spousal abuse, (almost always perpetrated by the male), has long dominated the family structure in almost every culture for millennia and is a function of a caste system in which females occupy the lower echelon. In some cultures, physical spousal abuse is sanctioned, explicitly or tacitly.

In other cultures, it is deemed illegal and subject to penalty – though unofficially sanctioned. This phenomenon is a function of a patriarchal system designed to subjugate one half of the human population and where this system is supposedly not "in play," there are enduring vestiges of it.

Given this reality, I will speak regarding countries where physical spousal abuse is declared to be illegal. (Where it is not illegal or for all practical purposes, viewed as a misdemeanor, I can only state that those societies or sub-cultures have a deeply ingrained, execrable view of women, and girls and spousal abuse is just one facet of it.) Men who perpetrate violence against their female intimates may do so as an expression of their need to exert power. The need to project power may be the nexus of the matter, but I believe two other factors are at work. (It does not elude my understanding that there are several other reasons for this phenomenon; the following two, however, are probably among the most common.)

One aspect is anger – anger that is a byproduct of living in a society that often strips the male of his dignity. (Of course there are other things about which a man can be angry. I am focusing on one of the primary drivers of this kind of anger.) The male may feel reduced to feeling like a feeble cog in the proverbial wheel. This gives rise to frustration, a weak sense of worth resulting in anger. This anger can lead to the *inexcusable* – violence against his wife or girlfriend whom they perceive to be weaker. No matter how many times the male may expiate, if he fails to obviate his anger, he will relapse repeatedly.

The above explanation does not, even in the smallest way, justify the male's reaction to how society has defined him; it does not absolve him from personal responsibility. On an individual level, he should refuse to embrace how society has defined him (this is approaching the issue from a psychological perspective) but on a macro level (which requires a sociological perspective), society can create or foster conditions that would mitigate these drivers of anger in its males. In other words, I believe how a society is structured is a more potent force with respect to how it creates its members. Thus, certain kinds of males fail to neutralize the anger-inducing aspects of this particular kind of society (whereas most males are more successful at mitigating them for one reason or another).

The second aspect of this matter is what I call *Locus of Identity*. For too many men, their identity is tethered to and centered around a reality of their own creation. *The underpinning of this reality, his identity, is the woman he dominates.* If she does not comply with his edicts, he beats her. If she leaves, she, in effect, takes his identity with her and for that, he will kill her and sometimes, himself. For all practical purposes, the locus of his identity is her – more exactly, she and what she does constitute the reality that he dominates, thereby feeding his need for power and, more importantly, his sense of identity.

To what extent is society culpable for this aspect of spousal abuse? Certainly the perpetrator is responsible individually. Society, however, is not guiltless. Its responsibility should extend beyond an un-yielding enforcement of aggressive laws against spousal abuse. Societal norms need to be re-calibrated to empower women to refuse to accept the burden of being the center of anyone's world except their own. Society should make all the tools and resources available to women so that the propensity to accept the role that these kinds of men need them for is diminished. True, there will always be a few women who will submit, but society should not facilitate this mindset.

Society also needs to aggressively fight to reduce, if not, eradicate discrimination based on sex (along with the other deleterious and denigrating forms of discriminations. How's that for wishful thinking?). As long as women are denied, overtly or tacitly, access to opportunities to express their humanity (their dreams, ambitions and hopes) the same as men do, men will continue to view the male-female difference as the basis for un-equal treatment.

Men, as a significant group, refuse to share society's limited resources. This treatment of women as third-class humans creates the stepping-stone between discrimination and violence against them; it perpetuates misogyny. Religion and other societal forces continue to mount a formidable stand against the kind of changes needed to nearly eradicate violence against women.

In summary, few men are born as misogynists; they are created and nurtured by a society defined by men. If indeed, "In the beginning, God created them, male and female; He created them" *then, in the end, society created them, the privileged and the female; it created them.* Thus, until society places the value and worth of women on par with men, 1 plus 1 will always be less than 2.

Their masculinity is counterfeit – their manhood is bogus

Males Who Impersonate Men

The weak are dangerous. The fearful are dangerous. To hide their weakness and their fear, they often attempt to exert their will – project power. Consequently, more often than not, they abuse it. Many humans often feel powerless because they see power as something to be exercised over another. They fail to understand that sublime power is power one exercises over oneself. This failure is often the basis for abuses; weakness and fear give life to this kind of baleful power. This is especially true of men who are homophobic and men who sexually harass women.

The homophobic male refuses to acknowledge his own weakness (consequently, by definition, his mind is small). He feels compelled to compensate for this condition by projecting an image of virility. One way to accomplish this is by attacking someone different from him – different in a way that makes he himself feel superior. This is the reasoning of a weak man. Because he is weak, he fools himself into feeling strong and achieves this feeling by preying on others that he perceives to be weak. He can only feel strong relative to someone outside himself; he does not understand that genuine strength is best measured by comparing oneself to oneself – over time.

The homophobic male, in addition to being weak, is also fearful. These men define manhood in terms of their heterosexuality. Homosexuality creates a kind of tension and uneasiness within these heterosexuals. They fear what is different. They fear the tension and uneasiness because of having defined manhood and masculinity in heterosexual terms. These fearful men fail to understand manhood and masculinity are no more than secondary or tertiary; humanhood is first and paramount. These homophobes commence with the wrong premise and thus, cannot ever free themselves of the fear. Humanhood should always prevail over manhood/masculinity and humanhood should not recognize any other category as being superior.

For those homophobes who claim to act in the name of religion, they may or may not be weak and fearful, but they are at best hypocritical and stupid. Hypocritical because their "righteous indignation" should prevail upon them to also attack or excoriate those who lie, steal, get drunk, commit adultery or fornication, deceive or mislead, and so forth. After all, most "holy" books proscribe all of the above *and more* and yet almost no one is attacking those who violate those commands. Stupid because how could a "God," the Creator condemn what all the current scientific evidence shows is a natural/genetic predisposition – as much as heterosexuality?

When I was a much younger man (with more hair and less belly), I was propositioned by a gay man. I politely declined his advance, and he moved on. Some time later, I shared the details of the incident with another heterosexual man who loudly declared that if he had been propositioned by a gay man, he would have "beat the hell out of him." He asked me why didn't I. He even asked me was I gay or bi-sexual.

Puzzled by the questions, I answered, "Neither one."

"So why didn't you kick his ass?"

"Because there was nothing to fight about."

Of course, having thought much more about the issue over the years, I could have given a better and more insightful answer to the question, but the point I wish to make is that something pathetically and blindly visceral is at work with respect to homophobia (but that visceral reaction is the product of acculturation and not instinct).

With regard to the other matter, for quite a while, I am flummoxed about why a man (men) would make un-wanted salacious and sometimes degrading remarks to women. These men are of the despicable ilk. They define their manhood in terms of a sexual framework. Again, these men are weak and fearful as are the homophobes – though not necessarily in the same way.

Imagine this: If women made genuine and aggressive advancements toward men, I venture to state that most of those men would not sexually harass them. As obvious as that may seem, it goes to the heart of the matter. Part of the reason why these men may harass women is based on the realization that a polite advance would likely be rejected and rather than suffer that rejection, they accost them in such a way that the rejection would be meaningless (at least on the surface). If they were not, they would be comfortable with possible rejection because they would not see themselves as powerless because their power would not be glued to being accepted by another or defined by domination over another. Fear of rejection is an underlying drive with respect to sexual harassment.

Secondly, these men, in their heart of hearts, are weak; their power is shallow, and to compensate for that, they seek to project power over women by sexually harassing them. They do not value the humanity of a woman and as a subsequence they do not value the sexual aspect of a woman's humanity. To these men a woman's sexuality is seen as a means for them to dominate; this domination is an attempt to exert power – power they lack within. Hence, they are weak. Their masculinity is counterfeit; their manhood is bogus because it lacks the primary ingredient -- respect – respect for the humanhood of women and respect for their own selves.

Homophobic men and men who sexually harass women are actually disgusting males who impersonate men. They are impersonators because an authentic man does not derive a sense of worth or power by harassing gay people or harassing women. An authentic man is human first and is coincidentally male second or even third.

The weak are dangerous. The fearful are dangerous. Males who impersonate men are dangerous.

racism ... both plagues this country as well as serves it

The United States Of White America

Researchers, historians, politicians, religious leaders and a host of others – some who were perspicacious (insightful) and some who were moronic – have all contributed to the vast number of tomes written about the often procellous relationship between Whites and Blacks in this America. The reality of racism in the United States of White America has proven to be an issue that both plagues this country as well as serves it.

The Future of Racism
Racism in the United States of White America will remain potent until a critical mass of Blacks unchain their minds by acting and thinking as a collective with respect to the advancement of our race. Education would be the fulcrum upon which unity and self-reliance would be balanced. Then and only then would we become a force to be reckoned with so that Whites would be forced to share power and resources. The nature of power is that it is never relinquished willingly or generously. It must be seized. In the case of racism, power must be seized, *not by violence*, but by occupying a space from which we can dictate mutually beneficial terms to the racists; we seize power by being powerful. We become powerful by saving enough of our today for our tomorrow. Otherwise, racism will thrive like a virulent parasite.

Power and Resources
At its source, racism is a framework of beliefs and subsequent behaviors designed to facilitate the projection of power over a specific group and/or the denial of access to or the possession of scarce resources by that specific group. The cleavage between the dominant group and the non-dominant group must of necessity be superficial but justifiable. What justifies discriminating on the basis of the superficial is a system of lies, misconceptions, half-truths and unadulterated ignorance (deliberate in most instances, not so, in others). To ensure that the structure of lies and half-truths appear to be completely true, the dominant group must do what it can to create a context in which the lies appear to be rigidly correct and immutable.

Legacy
Economics was a primary driver behind the enslavement of Africans. Ripping their families apart, systematically raping the girls and women, treating them like mules or cattle, proscribing

them from learning to read or write and establishing an entire host of laws to ensure their continued enslavement guaranteed that the African slaves and their descendants would remain subservient and utilitarian. In short, the only resources made available to the slaves were those that would perpetuate their station in life in the United States of White America.

Most Whites of that era stupidly believed that Blacks were intellectually and morally inferior; they were not seen as being equal to Whites. Therefore, why should inferior beings enjoy the same access to or possession of scarce resources as Whites? This belief was simply one component of the justification of slavery and its aftermath.

Slavery ended. Nonetheless, the freed slaves were disallowed equal access to scarce resources. Technically they were free. In reality, their freedom was more nominal than substantive with respect to access to resources. Therefore, the question screams: What would be the expected outcome if one group with complete control of society's resources (good-paying jobs, safe and clean housing, respectable education, *et cetera*) blocked access thereto for centuries and suddenly grant former slaves access *only* to inferior jobs, unsafe and inferior housing and inferior education? This question is key and fundamental. Very few Whites acknowledged the connection between breaking a person's legs and then accusing that person of not being able to run as fast as people whose legs were not broken.

The legacy of slavery was the creation of an entire underclass of freed men and women who were scorned, censured and objurgated to nearly the same extent they were when they were slaves. For all practical purposes, the status of the former slaves had changed little; but the attitudes of most Whites had changed from disdain to disdain and resentment in combination with fear – fear that they would have to share or compete for the same resources. Stated differently, I am reminded of something someone once said about how we are viewed: "Wanted! Singers, dancers, athletes, entertainers and the like ... all others considered dangerous."

Reinforcement
That mixture of disdain, resentment and fear all but ensured that Whites would do all they could to establish and institutionalize a system that would reinforce the execrable beliefs they held about Blacks. To that end, they limited access to the scarce resources as itemized above. Such actions facilitated the perpetuation of an

underclass about which the Whites could continually point to as unworthy of equal treatment and equal access to opportunity.

Thus, the likes of Martin Luther King, Jr. and others decided to seize power. Subsequent to their actions, the combination of legislation and the dying off of a violent racist generation weakened – but did not eliminate – institutionalized and societal racism. Racism had to adjust or morph from something egregiously and dastardly overt to something more subtle and pernicious – but equally as instrumental. In short, racism serves a very useful purpose the root of which is economic but the expression of which ramifies in a multitude of ways.

The Mind of a Slave
But Whites are not the only culprits in this drama. Many Blacks think and therefore behave as did the slaves that Harriet Tubman bemoaned. She claimed she could have freed many more slaves than she did if only more of them realized they were slaves. So it still is with too many Blacks today; they are slaves.

Many Blacks announce that Whites are not superior to them but they act as if Whites are. Many Blacks favor light-complexioned Blacks over dark-skinned Blacks. Many Blacks believe that straight or curly hair is better than kinky hair. These Blacks behave as if looking more European than African is better. Many Blacks believe the fiction that the White man's water is wetter and that his mind is better and that her beauty is more beautiful.

On the opposite end of this pitiful continuum, many Blacks choose ignorance over education as a repudiation of White culture and yet complain of being at the dirt end of the totem pole which is often a direct consequence of that choice of ignorance over education. Many Blacks also fail to see they are the type of Black person they are running from when they escape the "ghetto" in search of a better neighborhood. They are running from the likes of themselves.

The minds of these Blacks are locked in chains. They are victims in search of a perpetrator. They provide the excuse for many Whites to paint us all with the same broad brush. (It is easier for them to do so rather than to assess us on an individual basis.) These Blacks may correctly accuse Whites but they stupidly truckle and plead with "Massa" to open the door.

America has too many slaves and too many others who are intoxicated by their white-skin privilege that keeps racism virulent in its effects and sinister in its methods.

Having sex standing up is the only way to contract an STD

Penciled In Thoughts On Paper Minds

One of the most fascinating things about the human mind is that in an important respect it is like paper, especially in the beginning. Like paper, others can write on it (only in pencil), and like paper, the human can decide whether to believe what is written on it or whether to erase it. Most of the writing, however, is never erased.

Humans can be led to believe almost anything. This is especially true if the culture they are born into present certain ideas and notions as true or if they hear something often enough and if the stupidity/ignorance is presented in an organized fashion.

Humans used to believe that diseases were caused by the "gods" because someone wrote that on their minds. Many humans used to (some still do) believe that women were intellectually inferior to men because someone wrote that on their minds. Currently, there are also humans who believe that if the young boys in their village swallow the ejaculate of the older males, their passage into manhood is assured. They believe that because someone wrote that on their minds. Furthermore, some humans believe Blacks are intellectually inferior vis à vis Whites, and other humans believe that if a woman is raped, her family should kill her because shame is brought on the family. In short, humans will believe almost anything written on their minds and the list of examples (from the bizarre to the sublime) is endless.

Obviously, the more people who believe what is written on their minds, the easier it is to get younger people to accept what is written without fear of the beliefs being erased. Thus, the list of hypothetical beliefs noted below is no more shocking than what was once or is still believed:

- In order to avoid burning in hell after dying, the number 23 must be branded on a child's forehead if the child is younger than eight (unless the child is a twin, then she should be branded only if she is older than eight).

- Having sex standing up is protection against contracting an STD.

- Spanking a groom and bride on their bare buttocks with a paddle made of pine wood during the marriage ceremony will guarantee a long and happy marriage.

- Running around the outside of the place of worship three times while naked, in the dark, will ensure forgiveness of the sin of fornication.

- Eating snakes is a sin. Eating squirrels once a year is a requirement for redemption.

- Drinking horse urine reduces fevers. Adding a cup full of dog urine to your bath water brings good luck.

- If a woman gets pregnant after eating the root of a certain plant, she has been unfaithful.

- People with gray eyes are more intelligent that those whose eyes are blue or green, and there is no such thing as brown eyes.

- A long tongue portends a long but unhappy life.

The list of hypothetical beliefs as represented above can extend *ad infinitum*, and for each one, there is a comparably asinine one that was once believed or is still believed. Humans can believe almost anything because they seldom challenge or even question what is written on their minds by their families and the other parts of society. The idea of erasing a belief is as foreign to many as is the idea of cutting off one of their feet. No ideas or beliefs are written in stone; most people simply do not want to erase the penciled in thoughts of their paper minds. If only they lived and breathed the following advice then the stupid would not be so stupid and the wise would be wiser:

There is no idea or belief I so dearly cherish so as to shield it from rigorous scrutiny or thoughtful challenge. There is no idea or belief I esteem so highly that I will not alter it or abandon it – sacrifice it in favor of standing even closer to the truth.

... she would threaten to shoot them right there on the spot.

Shades Of Different Black

Being an African American Black in White America places one in a curious mix of conditions that give rise to the existence of at least four shades of being Black. Each African American Black has the noteworthy opportunity to select which shade (or shades) she wishes to be despite the actual amount of melanin in her skin. In other words, being born with a certain amount of skin pigmentation is one thing, but being a particular shade of Black as an African American Black is another.

To this day, however, there are African American Blacks who bear the scars of self-denigration and/or obsequious adulation of non-Blacks. Those African American Blacks disdain their physical "blackness" and so they resort to plastic surgery to alter their nose or lighten their skin color in order to appear less African and more European. Equally as egregious is that before a particular non-African American Black woman proudly flaunted her round derrière, many African American Blacks would use several fashion techniques to hide it – even allowing photographers to air brush this mark of beauty. (They even choose to "father" children who are White as opposed to Black.)

Of course, this is not say that surgery is never appropriate. Sometimes a nose can be disproportionately large or misshapen. One's skin can be blotched or acne scarred. One's buttocks can be very much too big. My criticism is directed at those who make such changes due to their desire to look more European than African because they have swallowed and digested the spurious notion that beauty is White and ugly is Black; these folks are "Uncle Jacksons."

The other shade of Black that some African American Blacks choose is less obvious but equally repulsive. They are modern-day Blacks in search of a plantation. These Blacks see themselves through the eyes of their "White masters," and hence, their decisions, attitudes and ideas mirror those of the men and women who discount African American Blacks. These self-disrespecting Black humans justify their eager pursuit of White companions or partners and their rejection of those who are Black by claiming that Blacks are gold-diggers, emasculating or otherwise deficient relative to Whites. These Blacks are so blinded by their profound self-disrespect that they refuse to acknowledge that Whites are just as gold-digging, emasculating and otherwise deficient with regard to positive traits. (The proof is as close as the nearest television, newspaper, radio or history book.)

It is one thing to side with a White person against a Black person because the Black person is wrong – that is an honorable thing, more so especially if the Black person would side against a White person if the White person were wrong. It is another matter, however, to side with a White person *because* he is White – the rightness or wrongness of the Black person notwithstanding. For Blacks of this shade, acceptance by Whites is the grand prize, even if it is attained at the expense of Black people. These kinds of Blacks are especially foul when they achieve status or power granted to them by White society; these folks are "Uncle Thomases."

The third shade of Blackness is identified by the kind of mirror used to explain reality. These Blacks look in the mirror and ask, "Mirror, mirror on the wall, who is the neediest victim of them all?"

"You are," their mirror replies.

To these Blacks, everything can be reduced to just two colors that stand in stark contrast: Black and White. Every wrong or slight they suffer is because they are Black. They can dribble a basketball but cannot multiply by 7, and so when they cannot get a job, it is because they are Black. They fail a drug test because the White system is stacked against them. They can explain and justify all their misery, pain and disadvantage in life with three words: "Because I'm Black."

There is enough truth in that statement to sufficiently drug them into believing everything in their life is a Black versus White issue. They fail to recognize where being a victim ends and where their self-inflicted wounds begin. They add their own garbage to the garbage that White society throws into their world; these folks are "Uncle Jay Jay" and his brother "Uncle Alfred."

The final shade of Black presented here are those who value their own humanity in such a way as to also value the humanity of others. They have no delusions about the United States of White America and none about the Disjointed States of Black America. This shade of Blacks seek to improve themselves and where possible help other Black Americans without enabling those who are other shades of Black. One such person earned a reputation for saving hundreds of enslaved African Americans via the Underground Railroad during the Civil War. When asked how she was able to save the hundreds she did, she is reported as having replied, with bitterness, that she could have freed thousands if only she had been able to convince them they were slaves. That woman was Harriet Tubman. (Even then, some Blacks did not see themselves as they really were. Thus, they had little incentive to change their plight.) Her modern day counterparts are "Auntie Tubmans."

Auntie Tubmans have a clear idea of who they are and who other African American Blacks are relative to White Americans. They respect White people but they do not shuffle before them, and they do not believe White people's water is wetter. They love their Black people but will not enable their self-hatred or decisions to wallow in ignorance.

They recognize Blacks are victims of White institutional racism, but to some extent, they are also victims of their own choosing; and where they are victims of White bigotry, they are not helpless victims. Auntie Tubmans understand that oppression by Whites does not have to lead to thinking like a victim. Auntie Tubmans understand that White people are not better; their blood is not redder and their brains are not better. They know Whites are as stupid as Blacks and Blacks are as intelligent as Whites. Auntie Tubmans also understand that Black people do not have to look like White people in order to be beautiful people.

It is said that once Harriet Tubman led a slave away, if that slave began to be timorous or to reveal a change of heart, she would threaten to shoot him right there on the spot.[1] She and others of her ilk were the best shade of Black. We Black people have enough damn Uncles; we desperately need more Aunts.

---

[1] I wonder, which of the "Uncles" would she have had to threaten to shoot?

Thus, I embrace the dark side

The Dark Side

When I was younger, as an African-American pre-teen and teen, it was considered an insult to be called "black." The word was often uttered with contempt and disdain – almost no one wanted to be called that five-letter word. Back then we referred to ourselves as "colored" or "Negro." For centuries, most African-Americans swallowed – some eagerly and avidly – the self-defacing, self-emasculating and self-deprecating *credo* that the darker the skin, the more inferior the person in all the ways that matter. Thus, African-Americans who were light-skinned and had so-called, "good hair" (i.e., curly or wavy as opposed to kinky), were deemed as superior to their darker-skinned counterparts.

Even to this day quite a few Whites and far too many Blacks are biased in favor of the lighter-skinned Blacks. In fact, I have heard some dark-skinned Blacks say they would not want to have children with an equally dark-skinned person because the children would be dark. That kind of slave mentality is evidence that they are ass-licking admirers of Whites. They do not simply respect the humanity of Whites; they worship them. Blacks who disdain their own color are a waste of beautiful skin. I find their attitude and self-disrespect to be repulsive and deeply disgusting.

I have always found dark-skinned African-American women equally as beautiful (okay, maybe slightly more so) as their light-skinned counterparts. In other words, I have never thought light-skinned women were more attractive than those with darker complexions. From my perspective, it has always been the full-lips, the round derrière and tinted (lightly or darkly) skin tone that arrested my attention.

So, to my point: As far as my own body is concerned, I, as perhaps most other humans, am not satisfied with my body. For one thing – or two – the hair on my head has been replaced by the pounds around my mid-section. Furthermore, genetically speaking, I was born with what I consider average looks. So if I came across a magic lantern, rubbed it and was subsequently confronted by a genie who would grant me only *one* wish and that wish had to be related to my physical appearance, what would I request? How would I alter my physical appearance?

On a scale of 1 to 10 (with 1 being very light or pale complexioned and 10 being very dark of skin), I am about a 7.5 to an 8. Given that I would be granted only one wish, I would not ask for a healthy head of hair or a strikingly handsome face or a sculptured physique. I would ask for a darker skin color – a 10. Darker skin, more than any other one thing, would improve my looks as far as I am concerned.

Thus, I embrace the dark side, for it is that side that I find myself, not with pride but respect – profound self-respect. I respect all sides but I *love* the dark side.

... especially when a discussion is shaped and contaminated with egos

Truth Lies In The Gray

I do not wish to detail the numerous wrongs many White people have perpetrated and continue to perpetrate against Black people (there are many documented instances of how White racism is relatively vibrant though somewhat less overt – Barack Obama's election to the U.S. presidency notwithstanding). I do not wish to describe how many Black people perpetuate the negative stereotypes and cripple themselves with their own self-destructive behaviors and attitudes.

What I wish to do is present why I believe substantive and productive discussions about race in America are painfully difficult and often futile. Certainly, it is understood how shifts in cultural norms, values and perceptions are glacially slow and in fact, as stated by Max Planck (a German physicist and one of the founder of quantum theory) regarding fellow scientists but applicable to cultural matters, "A new scientific truth does not triumph by convincing its opponents and making them see the light, but rather its opponents eventually die, and a new generation grows up that is familiar with it." Two events have done more to reduce racism in American than anything else: The enforcement of the Civil Rights Act of 1964 in concert with the deaths of many of the racists of that time.

In any event, it is reported that Voltaire, an 18th century French philosopher, was once challenged by another who wanted to engage him in debate. Voltaire refused and explained that a debate with him would consist of an argument involving six people. "How so?" the young man asked (since he and Voltaire were alone).

Voltaire elaborated: On one side there would be who you think I am, who I think I am and who I really am versus who I think you are, who you think you are and who you really are.

This is more true than not, especially when a discussion is shaped and contaminated with egos, the need to save face, the urge for one-upmanship, pre-conceived notions, superficial rationales, reinforced ignorance, resistance to admitting truths that are contrary to long-held beliefs, and so forth. All of these and more perfidious traits are present except when two people can be honest with themselves first and then with the other. This is why close friends and not strangers or casual acquaintances can discuss controversial issues without resorting to the follies commonly seen when most others debate the same issues.

Until White people and Black people – at least enough of them – can take an honest and less slanted look at themselves and then at each other (when the conversation will be between two people instead of six – so to speak) with the intent of honestly and sincerely grappling with the issue of race, we can only hope that as one generation dies, the next one will shed more of the flawed ideas and baleful notions of the previous.

... not even "God" ... can change the meaning of the word

The Word For Used Toilet Tissue

From time to time, there has been much debate and controversy about the use of the word, "N_ _ _ _ _" (written hereafter as the "N-word"), especially in the Black community in the US. By "N-word," I specifically refer to the word that rhymes with "bigger" and is most often pronounced by Black people as rhyming with the word, "bigga." Either pronunciation carries the same weight[1] and either pronunciation is used to refer to African American Blacks. The use of the word within the African American Black community has generated tremendous heat between the camp that believes the word to be colloquial and acceptable or demeaning depending on the context versus the camp that believes the word to be inflammatory, degrading and revolting no matter the context. Hence the question: Should Blacks embrace the word as having various shades of meaning or should we eschew it with disdain at all times?

To begin with, many words are essentially defined by their context, and that context also includes the one using the word and the associated inflection or tone. For instance, the word "dog" could be used to reference a scoundrel, ("He's a low-down dirty dog.") or a friend ("He's my dog."). Or, take the word, "shit." "She's full of shit" compared to "She bought some good shit." In these and other instances, the same word can take on diametrically opposite meanings depending on the context.

Accordingly, many Blacks feel at ease using the "N-word" as a disparaging term identifying a Black person or they use it as a term of endearment and respect for a Black person depending on the context. More specifically, many Blacks use the term to describe a gauche, uncouth, low-life, ignorant or criminal Black person. On the opposite end, many Blacks use the term to indicate friendship or adoration. (e.g., "He's my "N-word.") In almost all instances, however, no matter who utters the word, the reference is to a Black person, especially an African-American Black person.

---

[1] For those who think the pronunciation makes a difference, I present the words "floor" versus "flo," "more" versus "mo" or "it came loose" versus "it came a loose." In short, the second pronunciation is simply the "ghetto" or "ebonic" way of pronouncing the word. The meaning remains the same.

True, a few Blacks have said that White people can be the "N-word" too – usually meaning "Poor White Trash" (I view this as a feeble attempt to mitigate the connotations of the word) – but they almost never actually call them as such or if they do, they use the term, White "N-word"; however, they almost never say, Black "N-word," which goes to my point: The term is almost always understood to reference Blacks whether the context is favorable or unfavorable.

For most of my life, I, too, have used this word – both as a favorable or unfavorable term – until two events changed my mind – 180 degrees.

Event One
Sometime ago, I read a newspaper article about a White man who was being charged with a hate crime because as he was beating a Black man, he was also calling him the "N-word." The White man did not challenge the assault charge but did challenge the hate crime charge because he stated that Black people regularly refer to themselves as the "N-word," and so his use of the term while assaulting the Black man did not rise to the level of a hate crime. I do not know how the case was resolved, but the incident gave me cause for pause.

It became clear to me that the nuances associated with the use of the term by Black people completely escaped the assailant (admittedly it could also have simply been a legal ploy). In his mind, and probably in the mind of many Whites (racists or not), the use of the term by Blacks sanctions the use of the term by non-Blacks – context and gradations be damned. After all, the term was created by Whites as an excoriating term to define Blacks and even though Blacks may have, by its usage, expanded the definition, should Whites be forced to acknowledge the new expanded definition of the word?

Event Two
Few books have altered my view of reality as did a book entitled, *100 years of lynchings* by Ralph Ginzburg. As unforgivably and unbelievably naïve as this may sound, I had no idea how unfathomably deep and broad, how evilly wide and long the unmitigated hatred of and the utter contempt for Blacks was – especially in the South. White America and its institutions directly or tacitly sanctioned White terrorism against Black Americans during that 100-year period following the end of the Civil War.

Yes, I was aware of the atrocities that came with the enslavement of Africans and their descendants in the United States. The systematic ripping apart of families sold into slavery where they were subject to rapes, beatings, castrations and all manner of exploitation and utter subjugation. I was also aware of the establishment of Jim Crow laws designed to institutionalize and legitimize a caste system designed to relegate Blacks to less than secondary status as US citizens.

But I was not aware of the *details* of the post-Civil War wicked cruelties many Whites had perpetrated against Blacks. The above-referenced book cited newspaper articles – written by Whites – that described almost 5000 lynchings of Blacks in America. The newspaper articles (*sans* photos and the author's comments) read like accounts of the Spanish Inquisition. The unadulterated enmity Whites felt for Blacks was focused, virile and unequivocal.

The articles explain that many innocent (and some guilty) Blacks were tortured, mutilated (more particularly castrated), raped, dismembered, burned alive for offenses that included:

- *Looking* at a White woman
- Arguing with a White man
- Defending their families from attack by White people
- Owning valuable land that White people wanted
- Persuading other Blacks to consider moving back to Africa
- Being in the wrong place at the wrong time
- Looking like one who was accused of a crime
- Accidentally startling a White woman
- Begging for food (not stealing, but begging)
- Wearing a military uniform after returning from serving in the military (the uniform was the only clothes the man had)

- Being around White people

- Refusing to be humiliated by dancing at the demand of a jealous fellow farmer

- And so forth

There were also many instances in which Whites later acknowledged they had lynched the wrong man (or men) but felt no compunction. *NONE!!*

In cases where the Black person may have been guilty of a real crime, they were blatantly denied due process. There were also cases in which a Black person was found "not guilty" by a White jury but were lynched anyway.

Many of the lynchings were public events that drew hundreds – sometimes thousands – to witness the methodical, step-by-step torture of a Black man or woman. Afterwards, they would cut off a finger or ear or other body parts as a souvenir or as an item to be sold. Post cards containing photos of the lynching were sold and mailed all over the US.

To add injury to more injury, the United States Senate refused more than a dozen times to federalize the crime of lynching.

It became clear as I read the book that many Whites manifested a deep and visceral hatred of Blacks. Reading that book brought to life, in the most vivid way short of actually witnessing the events, the historical fact of how repulsive we as a race of human beings were to many Whites. All the while before, during and after the event, Blacks were casually but disdainfully referred to as the "N-word." Knowledge of this kind of terrorism and hatred gave the "N-word" a most profoundly accurate meaning to me. I came to realize the *only meaning of the word.*

Conclusions
That word conjures up an image of what White people judged to be foul, scornful, contemptible, revolting, despicable, loathsome and evil – or stated otherwise – what White people thought of Black people. Not Jews, not the First Nations, not Latinos, or other non-Whites. This term was designed to reflect White people's view of Blacks – all Blacks – not just unscrupulous, low-life

Blacks – all Blacks no matter if they were fathers, mothers, children, lawyers, business owners, physicians, teachers, President of the United States. As long as they were Black, they were considered the "N-word."

Yes, I understand words and their definitions can change because language is vibrant and dynamic, but that particular word has not (because it can not) morphed into a word so different in meaning that its original meaning is lost or its definition appropriately expanded. In short, no amount of using it in a different context could rid it of it foul-smelling, feculent stain despite the fact most Whites today do not view Black people in the same way those of previous generations did.

In other words, no matter how much we as Black people use the word in a different more benign or affectionate context, its original meaning looms large in ways that cannot be ignored or obfuscated. The word cannot be sanitized because its original meaning is stamped into stone. **Not *even "God" – so to speak – can change the meaning of that word*.**

Black people who use the word – whether referring to other Blacks or not – demean their own humanity and continue to give life to the original and only meaning of the word – one of contempt and scorn for all Black people. Not even the worst of the worst of Black people deserve to be called by such a word because in its origins it meant that **all** Blacks were less than their White counterparts or any other humans – including most animals. The word meant Blacks were less than the slimy droppings of a pigeon. It was irrelevant to the racists that Black people are no worse than White people and that White people are no better than Black people.

Consider this: History tells us that, for some Jews, the name of their "God" was considered too sacred for any one to even utter. On the opposite end of the continuum, I believe the "N-word" is too despicable *for any one*, especially Black people, to utter or write.

Continuing with a similar path of reasoning, it is currently a crime punishable by imprisonment, in more than a dozen European nations, to deny the holocaust. The holocaust was one of humanity's darkest displays of raw evil. Drawing a parallel (at least in my mind): To use the "N-word" constitutes not only a flagrant denial of the history of slavery in White America and the subsequent Jim Crow laws, but also an overt approval of all forms of White racism against Blacks. It is tantamount to joining the Ku

Klux Klan at best or eagerly helping them to find the rope to lynch you with, at worst.

If denying the holocaust can be deemed a serious crime, why can't we as Black people "outlaw" the use of the word that was designed to paint us as less than a piece of used toilet tissue that White bigots used to wipe their asses? Our use of the word, even within a different intent or context, does not in any manner render it acceptable, no more than a Jew wearing a swastika to a Halloween party changes what it stands for.

The "N-word" is forever contaminated and heinous; it is offensive to all the senses as well as to the moral sensibilities of anyone with even a half a sense of self-respect – its context notwithstanding.

Being stupid is among the top nine

Three Sounds Of Stupid

Stupid Comment #1

A man is thinking about seeking revenge for the murder of his brother. His sister says, "Killing the man who killed our brother won't bring him back." That is a stupid thing to say!

If that is the reason why the man should not seek revenge then it follows that he should do what it is that would bring his brother back. But given that nothing will bring his dead brother back, he should do nothing – not even testify in court about the murder or weep and mourn his brother's death or support the idea of locking up the killer. None of those things would bring the brother back either. That is why the comment is *stupid*: Bringing the victim back is not the issue, so why state something so inane. The man knows that avenging his brother's death will not bring his brother back. The sister's response is as stupid as saying, "Drinking Kool-Aid won't stop the rain."

Stupid Comment #2

Some African-American Blacks will tease or criticize other African-American Blacks who speak standard or proper English as "talking White." *Stupid!*

All African-American Blacks talk like White people. Some African-American Blacks talk like educated, well-spoken White people, and the others talk like un-educated, intellectually inert White people.

Stupid Comment #3

One of the most fascinating things I have read – not because of the words but because of where the words are printed: "In God We Trust." The motto is printed on US currency. Of all the places to attach those words, the government chose to place them on the one thing people trust as much if not more so than "God." Never mind what people say; money engenders the kind of trust that would make "God" jealous (assuming "God" gives a damn). Humans will steal money, lie to get money, kill to get money, slave to get money, demean themselves to get money because they trust it. They trust what it can do. Even religious leaders beg for it

– as much as they claim to beg "God" for whatever. Voltaire once quipped, "When it is a question of money, everybody is of the same religion" (Famous Quotes and Authors). "In God We Trust" are the words – the words that are not nearly as loud as the very actions surrounding money. That contrast between the words and the actions is not necessarily *stupid*; but inscribing the words on one of "God's" main competition is.

Conclusion:

To be sure, there are many more instances of how humans manage to utter stupid things. There are also several ugly things that humans can be. Being stupid is among the top nine.

A Sweetest Sound

When someone you love says, "I love you," or you hear the welcomed laughter of friends, or the comforting words during a dark moment – oh how sweet the sound. But, one of the sweetest sounds is simply – silence. Sometimes silence, well-placed and conscious silence, is as sweet a sound as it is powerful.

Much of what we speak is not in response to a question as much as that we often speak in response to comments or statements. Most humans love to pontificate or otherwise express their views or give advice on almost any matter presented especially in the presence of two or more people. It is in these and other instances when silence can be so sweet a sound.

Every statement or declaration is not necessarily deserving of a verbal response. Not every incorrect statement merits a correction. Not every lie has to be debunked. Not every assertion has to be challenged. Sometimes the best rebuttal, the best reply, the best answer is deliberate, thoughtful silence. Two noted scholars were debating the issue of quantum mechanics at a party. After the discussion abated, a third scholar – who was more of an expert than either of the two – was asked why he sat there without saying a word. "I had nothing better to say than what was being said" was his reply.

Deliberate, strategic silence (as opposed to being naturally reticent or being in an uncomfortable situation) requires discipline and being at ease with being quiet and allowing others to indulge. This is not to say one should embrace a kind of "vow of silence" for there are times when speaking is critical. It is part of the way we grow and learn or help and contribute. But there are many times when saying nothing does far more good than speaking even one word. The key is to know when to speak and when not to.

Someone once said, "Speak only if you can improve upon silence." Aside from being asked a question (and even on some of those occasions), is what you are saying better than saying nothing at all? This is not an easy question to answer and implementing such a principle is even more challenging, but the aphorism remains valid: "Speak only if you can improve upon silence."

During the Vietnam War, I, (as most other males my age), had to appear before the draft board. After reviewing my case, they classified me as being married and a father thereby effectively exempting me from being drafted. As a devout Jehovah's Witness at the time, instead of getting up and leaving, I began to argue that I wanted an exemption based on being a minister. One of the men on the board interrupted me and, in effect, told me that some people keep talking and end up losing what they gained. In a nice way he was telling me that it is hard to put your foot in your mouth if it's closed. That was one my first lessons about the sweet sound of silence.

They will go to arduous lengths to avoid saying them

Three Beautiful Words

When asked, "What are the three most beautiful words in the English language?" people often respond: "I love you." Though beautiful (and powerful), those words are frequently misspoken or misapplied – ofttimes said without really giving the matter the thought it deserves. At the other end, the notion of speaking those three words, for some, creates anxiety or discomfort resulting in those words not being uttered enough or spoken to the right persons.

There are, however, three other words that are equally as beautiful. What is most tragic is that many people will often fight not to speak these other words; they will go to arduous lengths to avoid saying them despite how obvious it is they should say them and despite the powerful effect those words have in promoting the well-being of all involved. I also submit these three words are spoken far less often than the words "I love you" though they should probably be spoken more so. Those other three words are, "I am wrong" or "I was wrong" and their sister statement, "You are right."

Stated with sincerity, those words are twice nice. They can avert wrath, ameliorate rage or otherwise ease a tense situation. Furthermore, they can foster respect more effectively than always being "right." At the other end, to utter those beautiful and euphonious words sincerely reflects both humility and self-respect. With regard to self-respect, when a person loves and respects himself, there is no puerile-type shame in admitting error; acknowledging error or a mistake is seen as acknowledging one's humanity or limitations and not as being of less value.

Resipiscence (a $59.13 word meaning recognizing one's own error; seeing reason once again) does not require one to truckle or grovel, but simply to intelligently accept that absolute truth and absolute right does not begin and end with who you are – an idea that is easy for most humans to declare but far more difficult to actually embrace.

It is true, however, that admitting error or wrong can bring with it, dire or inimical consequences. It may subject one to being flayed or excoriated because some people would interpret such an admission just as a ravenous lion would view a wounded calf.

Nonetheless, for the most part, admitting being wrong has more of an upside than not.

As humans, we thrive where there is love but I think, admitting error is as potent an ingredient for our tranquility and growth as any. Saying, "I love you," has more force if, when appropriate, one can also say, "I was wrong."

Beliefs often defy the rational, bolster the superstitious and foster the ignorant.

Beware What You Believe

It has been said, "Facts are stubborn things." Perhaps, but not as stubborn as beliefs and not nearly as dangerous. Time and time again, whenever facts and beliefs are at odds with each other, nescient beliefs win – often decisively. True, there are times when facts and beliefs are congruent – joined at the hip – but far more often the two are locked in battle for the prominent position of acceptance. Facts and beliefs will often intersect, but more than they should, they move in opposite directions.

Much of the suffering on this planet can be traced to people whose minds are cemented with unchallenged, blindly accepted beliefs of what is right, wrong, good, bad, true and untrue. Much of what humans suffer on this planet is due to cherishing what they believe is true – whether the facts are supportive or not.

More often than not, humans sheepishly believe what they are told with respect to "God," religion, women, men, children, politics, government, history, sports, business, marriage, sex, how to behave, how not to behave, and almost anything else. From the cradle to the grave, most humans rarely challenge prevailing beliefs, and when those beliefs are challenged, they tend to resist any notion that they might be wrong with all the vigor of a drowning man fighting to stay afloat. They will often dig in and hold their position (i.e., belief) in the face of overwhelming facts to the contrary. Such humans will ignore or even despise facts rather than subject their beliefs to rigorous scrutiny or change them. Too often facts get in the way of their beliefs.

One reason for this tenacity is that beliefs (based on facts or not) determine most of what a person is and how she interfaces with her world. To know what a person believes is to explain the person. Thus, something attached so closely to one's identity makes it risky to challenge – even if the challenger is the person herself. Connected with this notion is the concept of cognitive dissonance which is that state of mind and heart that arises when a person realizes that what she believes does not fit the facts. The resulting emotional tension and angst is called cognitive dissonance. To avoid cognitive dissonance, most humans cling to their deleterious beliefs. The state of cognitive dissonance is too painful, and changing one's beliefs to match the facts is often a distasteful option.

To that end, humans are adept at accepting facts supportive of their beliefs, rejecting those that contradict them as well as drafting and then contorting those that are ambiguous or neutral. This explains why most arguments or debates end with the opposing parties even more convinced of the correctness of their beliefs. Few people, after even a dispassionate debate, end up declaring they were wrong and are now convinced of the correctness of the formerly opposite view. People do not like changing their beliefs: facts to the contrary be damned! They are comfortable with beliefs that impersonate facts. Beliefs can produce comfort; facts can be the bug in the soup.

One story illustrates how many humans respond when facts and beliefs clash.

A seven-year-old math whiz bragged to anyone who would listen about how smart her father was. She believed her father to be the smartest person alive. Weary of her bragging, one of her classmates decided to see for himself whether the girl's father was as smart as she claimed. He approached his schoolmate's father and posed a question.

"How much is eleven times eleven?"

The father chuckled and replied, "One hundred and twenty-two"

The little boy looked at his seven-year-old classmate and smirked and retorted, "No, eleven times eleven is one hundred twenty-one."

The father snapped back, "Eleven plus eleven is twenty-two so eleven times eleven is one hundred twenty-two."[1]

The little girl turned to the boy and exclaimed, "Wow, I didn't know eleven times eleven was one hundred and twenty-two, I thought it was one hundred and twenty-one! Told you my dad was the smartest man in the world."

This example presents a profile of humanity when beliefs clash with facts. Humans will redefine, ignore, and otherwise trample over facts if they stand in the way of cherished beliefs. Thus, there

---

[1] My mother's husband actually believed that 11 x11 was 122 for that very reason. (Proving that some people are both sincerely and possibly certifiably stupid.)

should be no surprise that beliefs – those that are benighted or baneful – are what fuel human's inhumanity to humans. It is more because of beliefs, rather than facts, that history abounds with wars, pogroms, racism, inquisitions, classism, sexism, injustices and a host of other foul things that humans do because of what they believe.

It is what many men believe about women that fosters sexual harassment. It is what heterosexuals believe about homosexuals that breeds homophobia. It is what Muslims, Hindus or Christians believe about each other that drives naked bigotry. It is what White people, Black African-Americans and Latinos believe about each other that feeds racism and suspicion. It is what the rich and the non-rich believe about each other that creates classism. Facts matter little; beliefs matter most.

To be fair, facts are often elusive and difficult to secure and sometimes even more difficult to understand. Some are even unknowable. But beliefs often defy the rational, bolster the superstitious and foster the ignorant. They often parade as facts or as being based on facts. Yes, there are beliefs that have led to advancements in society and brought enlightenment and justice, but I assert many of those particular beliefs were rooted in facts or at least, were not contrary to facts.

One should also beware of the "logic" one uses to believe one thing over another. There is the story of a young boy at school. He was taking a class in simple logic. The teacher provided an example of logic by saying that if it takes four people 12 days to build an addition to a house, then it would take eight people just six days to build that addition.

To show the teacher that he understood, he said, if it takes four boats 12 days to cross the ocean, it would take eight boats just six days to cross the ocean.

As cute (and illogical) as the little boy's response, that kind of reasoning infects what many people believe and accept as truth. True, sometimes the illogic nature of one's beliefs may not be as obvious as the little boy's. That fact requires an even more rigorous examination of some commonly held beliefs. Something may make sense on the surface but not after careful review.

To that end, I believe people should hate being wrong. Hate being wrong so very much that they want to know when they are so they can alter or modify their nocent and/or paralogistic belief accordingly. They should abhor walking around being wrong. "Hear the other side," is a cogent Roman principle. Even more insightful was Napoleon Bonaparte's declaration, "I am never angry when contradicted. I seek to be enlightened" (Bonaparte, N Guide). Related to that, there was once a business executive whose staff came to know that whenever they presented an idea, they also had to present the merits of an opposing idea. His position was that beliefs are not sacred; facts are. And when the facts are few and nebulous then beliefs must still be challenged.

To be certain, I do not advocate challenging every single idea or belief (for instance, there is no reason for me to challenge the idea that the speed of light in a vacuum is 186,282.397051221 miles per second unless I were a scientist or teacher or someone for whom such an idea was relevant). I do advocate, however, to at least question any idea or belief that impacts how you decide to live life or what you decide to believe as relevant to yourself and others.

Therefore, to me, the altar upon which all I believe rests is in the following summation: *There is no idea or belief I so dearly cherish so as to shield it from rigorous scrutiny or thoughtful challenge. There is no idea or belief I esteem so highly that I will not alter it or abandon it – sacrifice it in favor of standing even closer to the truth.*

The ability to believe is one of the things that separates humans from other animals, and it is the very thing that makes humans so dangerous. Thus it is the duty of each human to shine the truth on his beliefs to minimize the dangers associated with fallacious beliefs. To beware what you believe, you must prove what you believe, believe what you can prove and *always be ready to believe otherwise* if the proof leads you elsewhere.

I posit each person has a quasi-genetic/cultural set point(s)

The Reason And The Obligations

The French call it, *raison d'être* or "reason for being." I have often pondered what is my raison d'être or as others before me have framed the issue: "What is the meaning of life?" "Why do humans exist; for what purpose are we – am I?"

Theologians and philosophers have cogitated on those same questions many times before I was born and will continue, no doubt, to ponder it long after I die. Most theologians point to the Bible as the source of the answer whereas others have observed the human drama and come to conclusions based on those observations. As far as I am concerned, theologians and philosophers can only speculate and present their opinions or interpretations.

Suffice it to say that I do not embrace any book as the "Word of God" for reasons stated elsewhere in this book. With respect to philosophers who reach conclusions based on their own perspectives, I submit their speculations are no more valid than that of most other humans who indulge in self-reflection and contemplation, including mine.

Carlespie Mary Alice believes that only the Ultimate Being, the Prime Source, knows what is the purpose of humans. Only that Person knows why He, She, It or They created humans. I will not conjure a guess, for it would hardly be more valid than anyone else's. It is a legitimate question beyond the scope of humans to answer (holy books and prophets, notwithstanding). It is correct to say that I do believe there is a reason why the Ultimate Being created humans, but I do not believe there is sufficient information provided from which to know or even infer that purpose.

Nonetheless, not knowing that purpose(s) does not preclude me from asserting that humans have two pivotal obligations – no matter the real purpose of their existence. Achieving the secondary one facilitates the primary obligation. In fact, the first obligation is best attained by successfully fulfilling the second.

That second obligation for each individual is to surpass or exceed herself and thereby actually transcend herself. The obligation is to be a synergistic being so that after adding up all that constitutes herself, the result is something greater than the sum of the component elements. I will elaborate.

One of the initial steps toward becoming a synergistic being is to be *profoundly self-knowing and self-perceptive* as a result of being intensely and constantly idiotropic (introspective). Profound and meaningful self-knowledge and self-understanding require significant time and an array of diverse experiences including observations of the human drama and interactions with others. This self-knowledge and self-understanding can be succinctly explained by stating that you should not be able to surprise yourself with respect to why you do, say or feel what you do. You truly know and understand who you are because there are no un-explored corners in your psyche; you are fully exposed to yourself.

This is not to say that you can know and understand every infinite particle of your personality, but it does mean that anything you do not know is either minimally relevant or so very similar to what you already know. Self-knowledge and self-understanding would naturally require that you could articulate and explain yourself with considerable precision and blatant honesty.

To not have this deep self-knowledge and self-understanding, means you are less than who you could be. To not know and understand who you are means you are simply you; you are not greater than yourself, you have not exceeded yourself, you are not a synergistic being. To know and profoundly understand who you are and then to *take command of that person* and *master* that person, means you are more than who you are; you are synergistic – you have transcended yourself or more specifically, your set-point.

(*Be certain that I am not spouting some mystical or spiritual homily. I am saying study and subsequently know who you are – your strengths, your weaknesses, your proclivities, your secrets and your beliefs – and then take possession.*)

I posit each person has a quasi-genetic/cultural set-point(s) with respect to how well she understands and masters herself – a point beyond which to evolve requires concerted, focused and persistent efforts. A point that represents the minimal and the fundamental level at which one comfortably settles naturally and without much incentive. In other words, the "you" that you would be with little or no effort to be otherwise.

One of the most effective ways (though not the only one) to evolve (or sometimes, burst) beyond one's comfortable set-point is to question ones motives by asking, "Why" much like the 4-year-old who seems to take pleasure in responding to each answer to a question with the question, "Why?" The questioning of your motives, feelings and behavior by asking, "Why?" until you cannot sensibly continue (along with other questions, too).

You can achieve this knowledge with brutally truthful answers that forces one to dig deep for the core answers to who you really are. By refusing to settle for your first, second, third or fourth, *et cetera* answers can you then transcend or evolve beyond your set-point to become a better person – a person best able to fulfill humans primary obligation.

With that special knowledge and understanding of self, you would now be able to master and take command of yourself. To take and maintain command of yourself is a function of self-validation and channeling your energies toward dominating yourself as opposed to dominating other persons.

This state of being makes it far easier to meet our primary obligation:

Whatever our purpose is, as humans, our primary obligation, as far as I am concerned, is to honor and respect (not necessarily love) the humanity of others. As simple or Pollyannish as this may seem, it cuts to the core of why humanity stands in the condition it has and does and probably will. There can be no greater purpose than to esteem the humanity of another and this is best achieved through becoming a synergistic being.

WATER AND OIL

LIKE

GOD AND RELIGION

Of all the institutions in society, religion is the primary one which claims to derive its authority and legitimacy from a supra-human source. Such a claim merits rigorous scrutiny given the power and impact of religion. Thus, the following …

I do not claim to be absolutely correct

What I Believe About "God"

Part I

I have read The Bible, the Quran, the Talmud, the Book of Mormon and newspapers, magazines, textbooks and comic books.

I have studied the teachings of theologians and scientists, creationists and evolutionists. I have pondered the philosophical thoughts of paupers and moguls, gangsters and aristocrats. I have queried whores, drug addicts, virgins and clowns.

Having read or heard the answers, I studied and compared them to the things that humans do. I saw the human condition played out in the drama.

I have contemplated butterflies and teardrops, shark attacks and the moon light. I have pondered tornadoes and sidewalks, dark energy and spiders. I also stripped my mind as naked as I could get it to question and challenge what I believed and even what I knew (or thought I knew).

All this and more I did because I wanted to know what does this reality, this life, this drama mean? Said differently – albeit implicitly, "God" or no "God" – which is it? Is "God" a notion, a fanciful creation of the human mind born out of a need (innate or learned) to believe in something greater than ... or is "God" real – an actual being? In my mind, this question is the starting point from which answers to my other questions can begin.

Having examined the views of atheists, agnostics and theists, it is precisely clear that all three play a part in the human drama. Having examined the views and ideas of atheists, agnostics and theists, I concluded that a Prime Source or "God" (I use the term "God" as a matter of convenience) exists.

It is what I believe about this "God," however, that separates me from most other "believers" and "non-believers." My contemplations and observations of the human drama and other aspects of this reality compel me to believe that "God" is significantly different from the conventional depictions.

I am a deist. That is what I believe about "God" – the Prime Source and the Uncaused Mind.

More importantly, I do not claim to be absolutely correct. I only claim that each time I spat on, beat on and stomped on what I believe about "God" – as a way of testing – my belief stood back up and was ready for more.

What I Believe About "God"

Part II

I *believe* that a Prime Source, an Uncaused Mind/Intelligence who transcends time, space and other elements of reality created the universe and its fundamental components – both living and non-living. (It is quite possible that this Ultimate Being is a plurality as opposed to a singularity.) Most humans call this Being, "God." Though with reluctance and reservation, I will use this same nomenclature.[1] In any event, I believe "God" receives undeserved credit and unwarranted blame for what happens in the human drama.

As a deist, I assert that "God" has abandoned us to our own devices. (Perhaps in deference to our "free will" or perhaps for some enigmatic reason that resists our understanding or sense of morality). To misquote a Bible passage, "In the beginning, God created them ... male and female, God created them. *After that – we were on our own."* "God" stopped creating and so "God" stopped being involved.

Thus, the road we travel and *all* that happens on it are determined by the maleficent trinity: *Whimsical Chance, the Workings or Agenda of other Humans and alas, Our Own Doings.* Hence, "God" should not be blamed for "miracles," the "holy" books, a person surviving a massacre, a person finding a job, a person winning an Oscar, or whatever else people do not want to take full credit for. Conversely, "God" should not be praised for the wars, rapes, robberies or other things humans seem to have a proclivity to perpetrate against their own kind.

As an important aside (to elaborate on one particular matter), I reject any book as being inspired by or produced by "God." If "God" is almighty and is the creator of the human mind/brain, then such a "God" should be able to produce a document that is not subject to differing interpretations. The words of such a profound Intelligence would resonate at the same frequency and

---

[1] My hesitation is due to the religious connotations that spring from the word, "God." But given that I reject religion as being of "God," using the universal term "God" serves to elucidate my stance against religion. Thus, I use the term – with qualifications.

tone for each and every human – those words would defy any explanation/interpretation other than what "God" meant. To date, there is no such book. From any one "holy" book, differing and often conflicting interpretations abound. Thus, I reject each and every so-called "holy" book that purports to reveal the actions and thoughts of "God." We are on our own – without "God."

Therefore, prayer is a form of wishful thinking or a non-psychotic form of talking to oneself. Worship (formal and informal) is emotional masturbation whereas any positive effect credited to religion or the "hand of God", is nothing more than a placebo effect. Religion, and all its trappings, is a purely human construct as are all other institutions of society. *"God" and religion are two sides of two different coins – and one of the coins is counterfeit.* Connecting the two constitutes a fatal flaw in thinking.

To give "God" any more of a part in the equation of human affairs would be to paint "God" as manipulative, sadistic, and a devil in angel's clothing with nothing better to do than to "play God" with the human species.

These concerns reveal the limitations of language when referring to "God."

"God" In Quotation Marks

As you will (or have) observe while reading this book, I enclose the word "God" in quotation marks. I do so for simply one reason. Given that the term "God" is so universal and despite its connotations, it can serve as a convenient surrogate term for that which is responsible for the existence of universe.

The word that is meant to refer to a Supreme Being, a First Cause, The Prime Source is dripping wet with religious connotations – connotations which tarnish what I believe (based on what I can infer from observations of this reality and by abstract reasonings) to be a Being or Beings who have nothing to do with the flawed human construct called religion, but have been inserted into religion to give it credibility and authority and by extension and convenience, its leaders the power to interpret or explain.[1]

You will also note, however, that with respect to pronouns, I occasionally use the expression, *"He, She, It or They"* because I cannot infer the nature of "God" in that regard. Besides, referring to "God" as "He" implies a justification in the eyes of males to claim a divine right of dominance over females. I actually suspect "God" is neither male nor female, and I cannot dismiss the possibility that "God" is a plurality as opposed to a singularity. In short, "God" is probably an "It" or a "They" – a gender-neutral term. These concerns reveal the limitations of language when referring to "God."

I suppose the more accurate term(s) could be Supreme Entity, Ultimate Being, the Uncaused Mind, *et cetera* but for expediency's sake as well as to emphasize my point about the actual relationship between the First Personage and religion, the term "God" (in quotation marks) will suffice.

---

[1] Read essays 77 and 79, What Religion Does and A Glass Of Power For The Thirsty.

If it can survive the ordeal of critical thinking and logic

My Road To Deism

Most humans navigate through this reality without subjecting what they believe about "God," religion, morality, and other major aspects of life, to the rigors of critical and logical thought. At best, some may silently question certain matters but not in any significant way – not in any way that would reflect conclusions which are the product of careful deliberation of the various sides of the issues.

As a young child, I was exposed to the teachings of Jehovah's Witnesses; my mother studied with them intermittently but was never baptized. After her death, I lived with her mother and sister. They would send my cousins and me to the Kingdom Hall of Jehovah's Witnesses, but they themselves never went. One of the teachings of Jehovah's Witnesses is that the doctrine of the Trinity was a false doctrine based on pagan beliefs. I accepted their teaching on this and other matters without much thought. I got baptized at age 14.

One summer, while working a temporary job, I would catch a ride with a man who studied the Bible and who believed in the Trinity. He and I would debate, and he would prevail – decisively. I told my fellow believers about those discussions. Subsequently, I met a man, a devout Jehovah's Witness, named Harold Lloyd Flemings. This man had a deeply profound effect on me. He showed me scriptures I could use to refute the doctrine of the Trinity. Harold's approach was that of a critical thinker. Logic and reason supplanted blind belief and faith was to be based on logic and critical thinking as supported by Bible scripture.

From that moment on, I studied the Bible from cover to cover. I immersed myself in scripture and the teachings of Jehovah's Witnesses. I successfully challenged Catholic priests, Baptist ministers, people of the Baha'i faith, Black Muslims and a host of all kinds of religions and philosophies. I believed the Bible to be the inspired Word of God and that Jehovah's Witnesses was the one true religion. I preached from door to door, gave sermons on Sunday, performed weddings and funerals. I prayed each day and tried to live by the "Word" of "God."

For 20 years I embraced that religion because to me it made more sense than any other religion I encountered. It appealed to my intellect. I did not accept it on faith alone. Keen and accurate knowledge of the scriptures was my mission. When confronted with a new notion, I would immediately assess how it compared to the scriptures. This methodology was not without its cost; several times I was even at odds with the local leadership of Jehovah's Witnesses. But that was a cost I was willing to bear because I believed my position was rooted in scripture.

Nonetheless, over the years there were several questions that pricked my mind because certain teachings and practices among Jehovah's Witnesses raised some concerns; they did not appear to fit snugly with the scriptures as did many of their other beliefs. I was comfortable with my dismissal of other religions because I could point to scriptures that decisively refuted their belief system. I must confess, however, that I did not ruthlessly apply my critical thinking methods to Jehovah's Witnesses' teachings as I did other religious teachings.

Finally, however, things boiled over. I could no longer ignore the nagging questions that pricked my mind. In short, by using the same logic and critical thinking I used to dismiss other religions, I used with respect to Jehovah's Witnesses. Subsequently, my belief in them collapsed under the weight of critical thinking and logic. In December 1985, I formally rejected Jehovah's Witnesses and their belief system by submitting a letter to that effect.

Thereafter I searched for "truth." I attended several churches of different religions – believing that my zeal for Jehovah's Witnesses may have blinded me and that perhaps another religion would actually make sense. I also explored New Age and mysticism as well as a branch of African paganism. I consulted astrologists and psychics as part of my search for truth and "God's" purpose. None – not one – synchronized with my intellectual processes. In short, they did not make sense. They failed to satisfy my intellectual appetite – my thirst to know.[1]

I also plunged into reading or re-reading the works of philosophers such as Spinoza, Hume, Kant, Locke, Descartes and so forth. I read other works of atheists, theists and agnostics as

---

[1] As might be starkly obvious, I have no emotional need for religion. Something as important as how to live life and what to believe as a citizen of the world should make sense – it should appeal to the mind. Furthermore, I, by no means, wish to present a profile of myself as an intellectual. I do, however, wish to present a profile of myself as one who values proof – proof that can stand up to intellectual challenges.

part of my search. I even re-visited the doctrine of evolution. Having done all these things, only one idea connected with my need for things to make sense (or at least not require that I suspend reason and critical thinking): I became a deist (by definition first and by designation later). I became a deist after an 8 year search for some semblance of "truth."

By definition, a deist is one who believes that a Being(s) who transcends infinity is responsible for the existence of the universe and its component parts including life. Furthermore, the only means to know anything about this Being is by pure reasoning based on the critical and logical observation of nature or reality (given that this Being stopped participating in the human equation after their creation).

Thus, as a deist, I believe that this Being **does not and has never** intervened in human affairs. To that end, there are no divinely inspired books, no men or women who have been commissioned by "God." There were/are no miracles (i.e., interventions into human affairs by the Being). Stated otherwise: In the beginning "God" created male and female; after that, we were on our own.

It can be stated that this Being or "God" has left us to our own devices. Therefore, holy books, religions, and all their accoutrements – all of them -- are purely human products. Prayer and faith are types of wishful thinking; they are forms of mental masturbation. In short, if "God" does listen to prayers, those prayers remain ignored – not answered with a "yes" or a "no"; they are ignored if heard at all. Also questions about life after death cannot be answered except to say: I do not know. No one knows (that is to say, no one can prove it). Religion is an elaborate human construct from beginning to end and from in to out.

Deism makes sense to me.[2] Atheism does not. Agnosticism does not. Theism does not. Evolution does not. And yet, I am not glued to deism; I am glued to whatever makes sense, and if it means I must alter what I believe or reject it, I will – if it makes sense to do so. If it can survive the ordeal of critical thinking and logic, I will embrace it. I feel obligated to frequently ruminate on the ab-

---

[2] In response to some who say, "There are no atheists (and by extension, no deists) in the foxhole," I say that I have survived my "foxhole" experiences as a certified deist. I did not pray when, for many, it would have been the thing to do.

truse matters of "God" always ready to confirm or reject with equal ease what I believe.

I understand that there may be matters beyond the reach of logic and critical thinking but religion or the service to or worship of or the belief in "God" should not be one of them. If religion is supposed to be the guiding force in how we should live life and interact with others then what could possibly demand more logic and critical reasonings? If religion were excused from being subjected to those things then we would have precisely what we have today – hundreds of different and conflicting religious beliefs which serve to add to the chaos and confusion of life on this planet. To say that religion does a great deal of good is a different point; all human institutions do some good.

The fundamental issue I have with religion is that it purports to be of "God." If religion presented itself as simply another human institution such as government or family, that would be fine; it would be fine if it left "God" out of the picture. Claiming divine support and authority feeds blind bigotry and counterproductive behavior and ideas. It excuses or justifies the otherwise insane.

If logic and reason are unnecessary (or secondary) but "faith" is, then who is to say belief in a "God" named Koa Boo Boo is right or wrong? And who is to say that this Koa Boo Boo will not one day arrive on earth riding a bull moose to save humans from themselves by requiring that they sacrifice whales? Furthermore, this religion requires that men wear blue pajamas, shave their heads and that women must wear two pair of panties and shoes that are at least a size too large (the reasons for which could be any number of things – use your imagination).

Additionally, the leaders of this religion are ordained by submitting to 99 lashes on their buttocks *sans* pajamas or the two pair of panties – after passing a rigorous exam based on the Koa Boo Boo's written word. Lastly, the founder of this religion claims that Koa Boo Boo appeared to him while taking out the garbage one night and subsequently inspired him to write a book filled with aphorisms and stories of miracles and divine guidance.

My intent is not to ridicule but to illustrate that accepting the religion of Koa Boo Boo (as a matter of faith) is hardly different from accepting any religion on faith. No doubt the worshippers of Koa Boo Boo could cite examples of how their prayers were answered much like the ancient worshippers of Zeus, Baal, Osiris, Coyolxauhqui or Molech did.

If such a religion existed, the burden of proof of a divine origin should be on the adherents, not the critics, and faith would be insufficient as the basis for acceptance. The teachings and creeds of the religion should not be exempt from reason and critical thinking – otherwise the religion of the "God" Koa Boo Boo would be as valid as any religion today.

In any event, I am comfortable embracing the evidence of the existence of some ultimate Being (by inference based on reason and the observation of what humans refer to as nature and the universe), and I am comfortable proving that such a creator does not intervene in human affairs at all (again, by observations of reality on this planet).

Could I be wrong on either count? Most certainly because:

There is no idea or belief I so dearly cherish so as to shield it from rigorous scrutiny or thoughtful challenge. There is no idea or belief I esteem so highly that I will not alter it or abandon it – sacrifice it in favor of standing even closer to the truth.

But based on what is available to my mind at this time, I am satisfied with being 99% deist and 1% wrong.

Both orthodoxies are faith-based

Ye With Too Much Faith

After having studied the religionists-creationists' explanation of how life appeared and having studied the evolutionists' explanation of how life originated and evolved, I can only conclude that both teachings require a heavy dose of faith – the kind of faith defined as the belief in something (or someone) without empirical evidence or the kind of faith that dismisses contrary empirical evidence.

Both orthodoxies are faith-based, and the only difference between the faith expressed by a religious zealot and that of a devout evolutionist is the subject of that faith. True, both groups have erected an elaborate and well-organized framework of dogma, doctrines, theories and tests designed as the underpinnings of the faith for their respective positions.

As a deist, I do believe that a superior Being(s), who transcends all external infinities, is responsible for the existence of the universe and its component parts including life – but my view of that Being is not congruent with the theists or religionists; I also reject the Bible and all other "holy" books as being divinely inspired.

My deistic beliefs are not rooted in religious notions or personal biases framed in science. I have no vested interest in believing that an intelligent Being created or, on the other hand, that evolution occurred instead. Neither belief impacts me; neither belief changes, improves nor diminishes my life. I simply chose to believe what makes sense to me with no regard to an agenda or motive. And, according to my own *credo* about whatever belief I accept, I am ready to reject what I once believed and to embrace heartily something different provided it makes sense. For now, I believe in a Prime Originator.

There are a few reasons why I reject evolution as a viable alternative to non-religious creation by an Ultimate Being just as there are several reasons why I reject the theory of creation as presented by religionists. One of my primary objections to the belief in evolution is based on the concept of probability and its cousin, randomness.

Together, those two elements make it necessary for faith to be an integral part of the belief in evolution. What is immensely fascinating is how, in our legal system, probability is recognized and is often used to determine the guilt of an accused. This phenomenon is called circumstantial evidence.

Many a person has been found guilty of heinous crimes based solely on circumstantial evidence. Most jurors are not deliberately aware of how they actually utilize the concept of probability. When deciding guilt or innocence based on circumstantial evidence, what is implicit in the decision-making process is the question, "How probable or likely are the series of events or circumstances to have occurred by chance?" One or two coincidences may be possible (happen by chance) but several or major ones ... not likely. Our experiences as participants in the human drama provide us with sufficient guidance as to how likely an event or series or events are due to chance.

That said, the impressive order, the mind-boggling complexity and precision operation of the entire universe – from the macro to the micro – from the sub-atomic to the galactic – are too much for me to accept as a function of chance or coincidental happenstance. The probability of just one part is immense; the probability of the whole is incomprehensible.

To make my point a different way, I will present the following information. Proponents of evolution posit that over a period of billions of years that matter evolved *(never mind how the matter got here in the first place)* from simple chemicals to living cells, to primitive fish, land animals such as reptiles, mammals, to primates to humans. In short, evolutionists believe that given enough time, even the most improbable can happen not just once but thousands if not millions of times. *Time is the most important ingredient in this concoction.*

In his book, *Struck by lightning ... The curious world of probabilities,* Jeffrey S. Rosenthal (2005) presents a few fascinating points about probability (p. 176-194). *Keep in mind, he accepts the theory of evolution as true.*

He states evolution requires the mutation and recombination of genes. This must occur *randomly* since evolution precludes the guidance of a superior Being or Intellect. The operative word is, "randomly." The randomness must be sufficient to create a wide variety from which some will flourish and some will die (survival of the fittest, aka: natural selection). If the randomization is not sufficient, then stagnation occurs and evolution ceases. Therefore, the randomization of mutation and recombination must be *just right*.

Mr. Rosenthal goes on to state that to be human requires the right combination of DNA strands. Given that the total number of possible DNA strands is 1 followed by almost 2 billion zeroes, a large portion of those strands must be exact in order for a life form to be human. Keep in mind, evolution is a function of the *randomness* of mutations and recombinations. What are the odds (the probability) of the right combination of DNA strands to arise out of random mutations and recombinations?

To answer that question, I point to another section of Mr. Rosenthal's book wherein he addresses the issue of how long it would take a *million* monkeys to type a particular sentence. "It would take those monkeys over a trillion, trillion, trillion, trillion years to have an even 1% chance of typing the sequence 'It was the best of times, it was the worst of times.'" He goes on to state that the million monkeys could do so if they had an *infinite* amount of time available to them.

My question is, which is more likely to occur, a million monkeys successfully typing the above sentence or a mindless chemical reaction (at least the monkeys have a mind) occurring which converts the non-living to the living and thereafter evolving based on the random mutation and recombination of DNA strands to form thousands of varieties of life forms? *Whichever one you choose it would take more time than scientists say has been.*

Mr. Rosenthal provides another example in his book about randomness. He records a random sequence of numbers obtained from rolling a single six-sided die 50 times. He goes on to say that that particular sequence of numbers has never been created before and the "CIA couldn't reproduce in a million years!"

Furthermore, he states, "In all of human history, there have been about 100 billion people. Even if each of them created similar 50-digit sequences, once per minute, for 100 years each, the odds would still be less than one chance in a 1 followed by 20 zeroes that any of them ... had ever created my special sequence above."

To make a final point, he declares, "Suppose the CIA has a million computers, and they can each produce a billion sequences a second. It would take them 25 trillion years, working around the clock, to have even a 1% chance of hitting on my special sequence. In other words, it will never happen."

Placing these facts within the context of the sequence of molecules necessary for a bird, a worm, a dinosaur or a human to exist and given the nature of random chance and adding all the time you wish *(which would have to be more time than has passed)*, I reject evolution as even being plausible.

Statisticians present the idea that 1 chance in 1 followed by 50 zeroes is considered an impossibility. Evolution requires infinitely greater odds. I say infinite, because one has to consider not only the existence of lower life forms but all varieties of life and then the existence of the entire unfathomable universe. *One has to apply these odds over and over again because each step along the evolution continuum requires the randomization of mutations and recombinations.* Thus, maybe with regard to a single event, the near impossible occurred (not really, but I will indulge the evolutionist for the sake of argument) but not many, many, many, many, many times as would be required for evolution to be effected so that we have what we have today.

Lastly, scientist also tell us that a small strand of protein molecules is necessary for some larger strands of molecules to function but that same smaller strand of protein molecules could not function in the absence of the larger strand of protein molecules. They both must exist and function in order for either to exist and function. Furthermore, both strands must be complete (in form and function) or no processes can occur. Thus, evolution (along with natural selection and random chance) could not explain the reality of this phenomenon.[1] A superior Intellect appears to be the only explanation.

No doubt, any evolutionist reading this piece would probably discount the basis upon which I reject the theory of evolution. Just as a religionist would reject the ideas I present in other part of this book wherein I reject religion. Nonetheless, neither orthodoxy makes sense to me.

As an aside, I believe some scientists refuse to see the frailties of the theory of evolution because they cannot accept the notion of "God" as Creator because of what religion has done. Religion has given "God" a very foul name. These scientist fail to disconnect

---

[1] Stephen C. Meyer in his book, *Signature in the cell: DNA and the evidence for intelligent design*, presents cogent and compelling scientific evidence that guts the theory of evolution and elevates the theory of Intelligent Design as the only logical alternative. Though Dr. Meyer is religious, he does not taint his presentation by invoking "God" or religion.

"God" from religion but instead they erect an elaborately specious argument baked with speculations and suppositions. It is tantamount to proverbially throwing the baby out with the bath water. Belief in evolution requires faith – faith in the power of time and chance to initiate vastly complex (living and non-living) micro and macro universes and their component-occupants.

As stated before, I could be wrong and if so, I would accept evolution as easily as I currently reject it. But as hard as I try, it does not make sense to me just like religion makes no sense to me. As a juror of sorts, I reject the case made for evolution. My verdict: Evolution is guilty by reason of being **Not logical.**

This work presents only one of the issues I have with the concept of evolution – a concept that is borne out of the confluence of sciolism and sophistry. A concept based on the same thing heaven, hell, salvation and damnation are based on – **faith.** [2]

Given that I reject religion (along with its notion of a "God" who participates in the human drama) and given that I reject evolution as a viable and logical possibility, I am left with a deistic perspective. That is to say, I can infer from the available scientific evidence that a prodigious Intelligence is responsible for the existence of the universe and its component parts, including life. I can also infer from my observations of the human condition and my experiences in the human that this Intelligence does not and most likely, never has, interacted with the human element post creation (despite what religion claims). In any event, faith is not included in either of my equations.

---

[2] Famed evolutionist, Richard Dawkins' book, The greatest show on earth: The evidence for evolution, lacks the scholarly tone and convincing evidence that supposedly characterizes evolution. In short, his arguments have the form and structure of truth and logic, but not the substance. Faith remains a critical, albeit un-named, component of evolution – his book, notwithstanding.

... those beliefs engender division, antipathy and misery

Explaining Imagine

The world is replete with varying beliefs about "God" and religion. These varying beliefs have been the source of much of the pain humans have suffered over the millennia. Even to this day, those beliefs engender division, antipathy and misery. Having either read or listened to many of these varying and often contradictory beliefs, I ask you to imagine the following:

Imagine a "God" who had nothing to do with the Bible, the Koran, the Talmud, The Book of Mormon or any other "holy" book.

Laws proscribing theft, rape, murder and so forth would still exist and would still be violated as they have been even with these "holy" books in circulation. Besides commenting on morality, these books purport to present doctrines such as details about such subjects as, the essence of "God", baptism, prophets and prophecies, gender roles, *et cetera* – all of which provide fodder for debate, division, persecution and even pogroms.

Most importantly, however, someone once said that the author of a "holy" book is not as powerful as the person who has been deemed authorized to interpret it. God" may **speak**, but the mullah, the minister, the monk, the prophet, the priest, the preacher, the pope, the whoever, **explains**. (No wonder there is this phenomenon: same book, different interpretations.)

Imagine a "God" who is something other than a "He" or a "She."

How "God" is referenced has subtle implications and ramifications with respect to how humans define their gender roles. Referencing "God" in terms of one of the sexes, and not the other, buoys a sense of entitlement to govern or dominate the gender not chosen to reference "God."

Imagine a "God" who banned/forbade the practice of religion with all its accoutrements.

There would be no churches, temples, kingdom halls, synagogues, or mosques. No need for prophets, popes, cardinals, elders, nuns, ministers, deacons, mullahs, priests, preachers.

Additionally, there would be no need for religious rituals, baptisms, holy water, robes, or collection plates.

Also, no place or time would be considered "holy." Thus, one less reason to argue or kill (albeit true that humans will always find plenty of other reasons to do so) and one less reason to feel superior (or to feel "saved" or "righteous").

Imagine a "God" who had nothing to do with our successes or our failures.

There would be no reason to "thank God" for winning the ball game, or receiving an award, or finding a job or escaping death. After all, why would "God" help you do any of those things and yet let millions suffer hunger, disease, genocide, rape and torture? That kind of "God" would have misplaced priorities.

Imagine a "God" who did not need a Satan against which to stand in contrast.

Sufficient is the "evil" within humans without the need for a being who personifies "evil." Is it that humans are more comfortable pointing to something outside themselves to assign blame for much of the horrors we experience? Assuming that "God" is "good," Prison Earth is filled with enough evil humans who stand at the opposite end of that continuum.

Imagine a "God" who did not need a hell with which to punish or a heaven with which to bribe.

How righteous or honorable is the person who lives a certain way because he wants to receive an award or avoid punishment. How would worshippers live if there were no prospect or living in eternal bliss or eternal torment? If heaven is a reward for "righteous" behavior and hell for "wicked" behavior, by which standard is one judged? Is it Christianity, Islam, Shintoism, Hinduism? Which branch or sect of those religions?

What happens to infants who die? What happens to those who convert from one religion to the other? Why punish/torture even the most vile human being for an eternity? How does eighty years of being "wicked" justify billions and billions and billions and billions and billions of years (i.e., forever) of excruciating torment?

Imagine a "God" whose ego did not require adulation, sacrifice or worship from humans.

"God" – the creator of a universe of unimaginable size, power, and complexity versus human beings. Why would such a Being require, demand puny humans to worship, praise and heap adulations on it? (Read essay 78.) Is it not possible for humans to respect and love each other in the absence of worshipping "God"? Of course! I present atheists and deists who are law abiding and exhibit behavior characterized as loving, and decent.

Imagine a "God" who placed emphasis on love rather than doctrine.

Is "God" part of a Trinity, or is "God" a distinct separate being from the other two members of the Triune? Is hell the grave or a place of torment? Is the cow a sacred animal or a delectable source of protein? Is pork unholy or best served fried? Or are love and respect for each human more important? How much sense does it make to observe the Sabbath but lie, or steal or even kill during the other six days of the week? How much sense does it make to condemn homosexuality but pray to "God" to bless your country as it engages in activities of which not even the prophets of your religion would approve?

People declare that all religions teach love and respect for human beings, but they insist on overlaying that notion with all sorts of doctrines and ideologies that turn the simple and sublime into complicated and convoluted.

Imagine a "God" who did not need humans to kill or punish in his/her/its/their name.

Put succinctly, why does an all-powerful "God" need humans to kill each other in defense of "Him" or "His" system of worship? "God" is in the best position to kill because "God" would know all the relevant facts and motives; humans cannot. "God" would, presumably not kill the innocent while killing the "guilty"; humans often claim that "collateral" damage is unavoidable.

I ask you to please do the following:

Imagine a "God" not made in the image of "HuMan."

... like a woman masturbating

Religion 101
(Introduction To Religion)

Religion is the wrong solution to the right problem.

Religion and "God" are like oil and water. Together you have oil that is not useful or water you cannot drink.

Based on what religion has done, if "God" didn't know any better, "God" would be an atheist.

Does the sun rise to hear the rooster crow or does the rooster crow so the sun will rise? Stated otherwise, is there religion because of "God" or is there "God" because of religion?

Religion is like a woman masturbating; it may make her feel good but it doesn't produce life.

Religion and "God" are like the unicorn and the horse. It is the fool who thinks one is correctly related to the other.

Religion is adroit at neutralizing the mental dexterity of its believers. It forces some to bend over so it can have its way with them – a lubricant may or may not be used. Or at other times, it seduces some to bend over so it can have its way with them – kissing and cuddling may or may not be a part of the trick. Either way, it is perfidious or pernicious – whichever it has to be.

A person without religion is like an eye without a stick in it.

All the above have massacred the other and others as well.

What Religion Does Well

One of the most powerful and long-lasting institutions in human society has been and remains, religion. Almost every society, no matter its place on the continuum of technological achievement, has been influenced by, if not actually founded on, religion. Each religion has established its system of beliefs from which appropriate behavior and thinking are defined. The consequences for violating the precepts of the religion can range from ridicule or scorn to ostracism or execution including – for those who believe – burning in "hell" in an after-life.

Many believe that without religion there would be chaos and anarchy along with moral depravity; religion has been considered vital to the existence of a viable society. Of course, anyone even mildly familiar with the history of human beings will also note that much of human misery and travails can be traced directly to religion. Wars, massacres, resistance to new scientific discoveries or new ideas and so forth, have all been an integral function of religion.

That is not to say that in the absence of religion there would be no wars, massacres, resistance to new scientific discoveries or new ideas, and so forth; all of these activities have more to do with being human than anything else. Religion, however, has more often than not, encouraged, blessed, required or facilitated these human activities as much as governments and other institutions of society. What sets religion apart as more guilty is that it claims to be expressing the "will of God" – something supra-human.

For believers or participants, religion has been supremely effective at achieving two things:

- Dividing

- Controlling

Obviously, the extent and intensity of its ability to control and divide rises and falls in step with the vagaries of life on this planet. Nonetheless, religion remains a viable force to reckon with even in so-called atheistic societies.

A fundamental development or shift in what would normally be logical thinking must occur to effect this division and control. A person must suspend or dismiss certain functions that occur naturally, for the most part, in the mind. This suspension of those faculties is often explained as "faith."

This phenomenon, or faith, allows the person to believe two critical things. First, the person *believes* "God" favors a specific religion, and then (more importantly) the person *believes* the leader(s) of that religion know, understand and can interpret the "Will of God." Once he or she embraces both beliefs, the shift from otherwise logical thinking is complete.

If this suspension of certain faculties does not occur, then a clash between "faith" and reason arises. This can lead to the emotional/mental phenomenon called, "cognitive dissonance." Cognitive dissonance is that uncomfortable anguish that occurs when one realizes that one's beliefs are obviously contrary to facts. Our mental and emotional construct is so designed that we feel the need to resolve cognitive dissonance by either denying, ignoring, minimizing or (as rarely happens) changing our belief.

Division

Religion divides people by virtue of the fact that there are different religions, and that followers of one religion do not want to be considered a member or worshipper of any other. "I'm Catholic." "I'm Hindu." "I'm Muslim." "I'm Southern Baptist." "I'm Buddhist." "I'm this or that and, therefore, not that or this." These divisions are real. Just ask a Jew if he wants to become an Episcopalian or ask a Jehovah's Witness does she want to become a Hindu or anything else other than what they are.

Given that religion is a prominent element in society and constitutes part of most people's identity, it becomes another way people distinguish themselves from others. These divisions, like divisions in other aspects of life, may form the basis for conflict, discrimination, hatred and so forth. It feeds a sense of superiority or piety – at worst. At best it is **another** way for one to be different from another based on a human construct. It becomes another needless way to divide – supposedly with "divine" approval.

Control

Control is the most malevolent aspect of what religion does: Control with respect to what to believe/not believe or to do/not to do or to say/not to say.

- Some Muslim taxi drivers refuse to transport people who are carrying alcohol or dogs (except seeing-eye dogs)

- Some pharmacists refuse to fill prescriptions for birth control or the so-called "morning-after pill."

- Hindus will not eat beef – the cow is sacred

- Jews and Muslims refuse to eat pork –- pigs are unclean

- Jehovah's Witnesses refuse to accept blood transfusions – blood is sacred

- Some religions forbid the drinking of alcohol or even caffeine; others say it's fine to drink if it is done in moderation

- Other religions forbid having photos of themselves taken – it is idolatrous

- And so forth and so on, *et cetera*

Then there is the violence that pours out of this control.

- Shia Muslims and Sunni Muslims have killed each other

- Hindus and Muslims have butchered each other

- Catholics and Protestants have slaughtered each other

- All the above have massacred the other and others as well.

History, both recent and distant, tells us that religion – its control of its believers – is one of the most virulent ingredients for much of the suffering humans impose on themselves and each other.

There are those, however, who declare that religion has saved and/or improved the lives of those who believe. Those who believe claim that the "good" counterbalances the dark section of what religion does by a significant margin. Drug addicts and alcoholics, criminals and other miscreants have all pointed to religion as having altered their lives for the better. They give credit to "Jesus" or "The Lord" or "Allah" or "God" or "Buddha" or so forth. My response is that these transformations, real or not, are due to the "placebo effect" as opposed to some intervention or assistance from a deity.

In medical research, experimental drugs are often tested against a harmless and chemically ineffective "drug" called a placebo (usually an ordinary sugar pill). Scientists understand the power of the mind – the power of belief, and its effect on the physical body. More specifically, there are occasions where simply the belief that a pill/medicine – issued by an authority figure such as a physician – is an actual treatment for a particular illness can result in an improvement – at least temporarily. In some instances, as much as 30% of those taking the placebo rather than the actual pill have reported improvement in their health. Thus, the placebo works because the one taking it (not knowing it is a placebo) *believes* it works – whether it actually does or not. The difference in the outcome between those on the placebo and those on the actual medication must be significant enough to rule out the psychological effects that may present during the trial: Mind over matter versus medicine over matter. *I assert any positive effect in a person's life that he or she attributes to "God" (via religion or not) is a placebo effect.*

Religion is a human facility that passes for a divine one just like a placebo passes for the real thing. Thus, if a drug addict believes "God" or "Allah" or some other supreme entity is the force behind her change, then, like a placebo in a medical drug trial, there can be a successful outcome. (But the same effect can be achieved by believing in oneself or other people.) That also explains, however, why religion fails to work for many religious observers with regard to their behaviors and attitudes.

At this point, let it be noted that I reject the notion that "God" has anything to do with religion. Religion is a human creation into which "God" has been inserted. For religion, "God" is a necessary convenience or a tool to justify religions' activities, their precepts and framework; invoking "God" bestows power and credibility onto the leaders, prophets or others who claim divine guidance or power. Nonetheless, "God" has less to do with human affairs than

Abell 1835 IR1916[1] has to do with planet Earth. Stated another way, if "God," then not religion; if religion then not "God." Combined, however, becomes a venomous toxin that effectively divides and controls.

---

[1] The most distant galaxy observed to date.

... the laws of timing and consequences would provide boundaries ...

If I Were "God"

As a deist, I believe "God" created humans and subsequently left them to their own devices without interference or intervention of any sort. Subsequently, we suffer domination, abuse and hatred at the hands of those of our species – humans' inhumanity to humans. That is how "God" has been "God."

But if I were "God," what would I do that would be different from what "God" has done with respect to life on Prison Earth?

My first choice would be to empty Prison Earth of all humanity and eradicate every single piece of evidence that humans ever existed. (Plants and non-human animals would remain.) There simply is too much senseless grief, pain, hatred and exploitation with no prospect that humans will ever change – not collectively or in sufficient numbers to create a critical mass to effect universal change.

The stupidity of humans is perpetual, ingrained and insurmountable. The existence of a few who are noble in deeds and willing to think independently and critically is not enough to create the bulwark necessary to negate the anguish that characterizes the human drama. In short, humans are frail, flawed and foul, as history and current events would verify.

But, if I chose to spare humanity its deserving fate, I would do several things differently (too many to list here). The very first thing I would do would be to eliminate religion; forbid it. There would be no religious buildings, no so-called inspired holy books or religious holidays. Prayer would be considered unnecessary; the thought of it would be nearly laughable. There would be no religious leaders; they would have to find another framework within which to exercise power and authority. Religious dogma and doctrine would be replaced with nurturing that part of the human psyche that fosters selflessness and respect for other humans.

Another thing I would change would be the timing of consequences (see essay 30). For example, smoking or chewing tobacco would cause nearly instant and grievous pain. Drinking alcohol would be fine except when one has drank an amount – as determined by one's physiology – that approaches inebriation or some other harmful state. At that point one would commence to experience severe physical trauma. So much so that one would stop drinking long before reaching that threshold. Eating would be pleasurable; eating more than the body needs at that time would be exceedingly painful. Like drinking alcohol, the body would indicate when one is approaching the point of eating more than one should. The same principle would apply to any drug. In short, addiction would not be possible because at a certain point (depending on the drug and its purpose) there would be no pleasure or positive effect – only profound *debilitating pain*.

Rudeness, disrespect, and similar behavior would serve to shorten one's life span. Kindness, courtesy and respect and the like would serve to lengthen one's life span. For instance, one who is characteristically and consistently rude, greedy or selfish would probably not live past the age of 23. A kind and respectful person could live to be 101. A boorish 17-year-old could change and possibly live to be 79 – depending on how much damage her rudeness and anti-social behavior has done. A kind person could change and become vitriolic and thus shorten his life. In summary, one's behavior would have a direct and *significant* impact on the quality and length of one's life – immediately.

Of course, I would take into account the frailty of the human condition but ruthless, selfish or deceitful conduct would be life shortening; though that type of behavior and attitude would impact others, it would have a direct physiological impact on the perpetrator. Each act or word (good or bad) would add to or chip away at one's life span – depending on the extent or intensity of the act.

With respect to criminal behavior, timing and consequences would be more exacting and, in some instances, instantaneous. To illustrate my point, the more money a person embezzled (and the more distress such an act caused others), the more years his life would be shortened. (To emphasize this point, Bernard Madoff, the man who bilked investors out of billions of dollars, would have died decades ago – long before his greed would have reached the point it finally did.)

A would-be robber, at the very moment he *commenced* the robbery would immediately begin to vomit and buckle over in crippling agony until his arrest. The same thing would happen to a would-be burglar or murderer. A would-be rapist would experience excruciating and tortuous pain in his genitals for several days once he *attempted* the rape. Hitting a person illegally or un-ethically would cause the perpetrator far more pain than the pain inflicted on the victim.

The other thing I would do if I were "God," would be to clearly and unambiguously defined for humanity, what is good or bad, nice or evil. (And if there were ever any doubt or dispute about my definitions, the consequences – positive or negative – would resolve any doubt.) My definitions would supplement that part of humanity that intuitively (perhaps instinctively) knows when kindness has been supplanted by unkindness, and so forth.

Under my Godship, I would honor the "free will" that I instilled in humans but the laws of *timing and consequences* would provide boundaries for the phenomenon of "free will." In other words, a human would be free to do as he wished; he would, however, bear the consequences more so than his would-be victim. In fact, by definition, a victim is someone who bears the negative consequences of someone else's bad behavior. If I were "God," I would alter or reverse that process. That fact alone would diminish much of the misery on this planet.

To be sure, there are other things I would do if I were "God"; nonetheless, these are the primary things. Much to my grief, however, I am not "God," and so humanity and I suffer on Prison Earth.

Viola! Seize power by explaining "God."

A Glass Of Power For The Thirsty

Over the course of several thousand years, many groups of men have convened to codify "divine" or "holy" arrangements so that future generations would continue to observe the terms of those accords. This would also preserve the power these men and their subsequent designees/heirs would exert over the masses. The most potent and insidious method to create and maintain this power was through their self-bestowed authority to interpret. After all, *"The power of the prophet lies not in his bringing the word of God to mankind but in his interpretation as to what the purported word of God means. Truth, it seems, does not determine what the prophet says; instead, what the prophet says determines what truth is"* (Siu, 1979, p. 181). In short, if power is the wine then interpretation is the glass.

People flock to religious buildings each week or so to listen to someone else explain what "God" meant by one or more passages in whatever book they deem divine. Worshippers may read the same book at home but decide to trust the explanation of what he/she may or may not have read to another human. Imagine the power given to the one who interprets.

Given the nature of humans, it is no wonder that different men issue different interpretations of the same "words" of "God." "God" apparently does not take the time to interpret or explain. Instead, self-appointed men do, and hence they wield profound power. Imagine the grief, pain, suffering and injustices that would have been avoided and the clarity achieved if "God" did all the interpreting (*and rigorously enforced that interpretation in unequivocal ways*) of everything "God" was purported to have said or meant.

Imagine that of all things.

But, given that "God" has done no interpreting or explaining of the various "holy" writing, humans took it upon themselves to do so and bestowed upon themselves supreme power. The result – a confusing hodgepodge of differing and opposing religious ideas and the justification for the horrific, the dastardly and a vast array of other ugly human deeds: All because "God" failed to interpret what humans believe to be "God's" own words.

Some may claim that their "Holy Book" interprets itself. Such a claim is specious given that different religious sects exist because their leaders still interpret the "interpretation" differently. Shame on "God" *(if "God" is actually responsible for the written work)* for leaving such an important task undone thereby leaving a vacuum that humans rushed to fill – much to the detriment of the entire human race.

But then again, no shame should be on "God" if "God" did not have anything to do with any of the so-called divine books anyway.

The world has a motley array of factious religions. There are different types of Christians, different sects of Jews, different kinds of Muslims. Then there are Hindus and an assortment of sects, cults and other religions (not to speak of the several which have come and gone). Each religion avers it knows the will of its "God(s)." (In the case of Buddhists, however, there is no focus on a supreme being, but rather, a state or condition to be attained. Nevertheless, they postulate that their *ethos* is 'the way'). Each of these religions has its prophets or teachers, mullahs, elders, bishops, priests, preachers, reverends, ayatollahs, popes, monks or other bosses; "God" spoke (or speaks) but they interpret. Their interpretations formulate the basis for their religion being different from the others – hodgepodge of factious entities.

The power of these people pivots on the necessity, perceived or real, to interpret a revered book or tome. Different people, after reading the same books, decided on different understandings or interpretations. What greater source of power is there when one claims to speak for or explain what "God" Almighty meant? They opined that "God" spoke, words which were subsequently recorded, and whatever "God" said needed to be interpreted.

Viola! Seize power by explaining "God."

Some grabbed this nocent and addictive power by claiming that "God" actually spoke to them and appointed them. Others cite their special education and training regarding the sacred yet arcane book(s) the understanding of which requires someone who is cabalistic (well versed in obscure or esoteric matters). Still, others are elected or deified by other humans to be the interpreter of "God's" words. In any event, these humans drape themselves in the "divine" mantle of power, and the masses follow with alacrity and near-complete credulity. No wonder these intoxicated feudal lords are always thirsty with glass in hand.

Consequently, the world has seen massacres, invasions, discrimination, domination and conversion by conquest all because "what the prophet says determines what truth is," and far too often, those "truths" require or justify the feculent, the truculent, the hypocritical, the arbitrary, the obscenely contradictory and the intellectually arid. History, from ancient to modern, is replete with instances of these nefarious outcomes.

What is most bemusing and disconcerting to me: If "God" is almighty, omniscient, supremely loving and divinely moral, why has He/She/It/They allowed human interpreters to facilitate or enact some of the most egregious horrors ever known? Why would "God" allow conflicting notions of who and what is correct, moral and true to be perpetrated by these moguls? Why cannot "God" merely communicate directly and clearly, precisely what we should know and do? If humans can quickly declare and disseminate to the masses a pronouncement then an almighty being should be able to do the same far more effectively and efficiently. In other words, why does "God" not cut out the middleman and simply tell us what should be? And, if the need for interpretation does arise, then why cannot "God" do the interpreting?

When asked these questions, the prophets or teachers, mullahs, elders, bishops, priests, preachers, reverends, ayatollahs, popes or other bosses reply with their sciolism, their doxology, their dogma and/or their parisology. Stated another way, these interpreters want to keep their powerful jobs and thus, answer those questions accordingly. Even more sadly, their followers have, for the most part, elected not to exercise their human right to *think* for themselves.

So I ask: Does "God" enjoy the pain, confusion, and evils wreaked on humanity because of these interpreters, or does "God" lack the power and knowledge to author a book(s) that disallows conflicting interpretations? Or, since nature abhors a vacuum, maybe the interpreters stepped in with their misology because "God" is too busy being "God" somewhere else in the universe.

Perhaps the basic premise is fallacious. Maybe there is no book or writings of divine origin. Maybe all these "holy" books are the mere figment of human inspiration. Maybe "God" had nothing to do with those books that are evidently much of the source of the power religious leaders exert. These books, because they are not of "God's" making, provide the need for someone to interpret – a need that leads to power.

religion provides one additional reason to...

Religion: Reductio Ad Absurdum

On 15 March 2002,

> A school fire in the holy city of Mecca killed 15 girls, apparently victims of bureaucratic incompetence and rigid religious customs that dominate this strict Muslim society. The school doors had been locked from the outside and the windows barred to protect the girls from unrelated men.
>
> And despite official denials, witnesses say religious police initially blocked male firefighters from entering the school and forced some girls who had managed to escape to go back inside to retrieve their obligatory black cloaks and scarves. (Slavin, 2002, p. 8A.)

The article goes on to say that many in Saudi Arabia are questioning their "extremism."

On 14 June 2002, a jury convicted 29-year-old Jacques Robidoux of the first-degree murder of his infant son, Samuel. In 1999, Jacques stated that his sister had received a vision from God telling him and his wife to stop feeding their infant son solid food. For 51 days, Samuel was fed only his mother's breast milk; he died three days before his first birthday.

The Robidouxs belonged to a sect called the Body. This sect rejects modern medicine and government. Jacques said he believed the sight of Samuel's misery was a test from Satan of the family's will and that a miracle would save the baby (Lavoie, 2002).

History and the present are stuffed with examples similar to the above (to varying degrees) from every sector of the world. Most certainly, most humans (including Muslims and Christians) would not condone the behavior of those cited above. Most religions, however, to some degree or another, condone some form of behavior as being the will of "God." It is this fact that frightens me and gives me cause for deep concern.

First, there is no agreement on what "God" wants – no agreement among Jews, Christians, Muslims, Hindus, *et cetera*. Secondly, there is no agreement on who "God" is. These two phenomena feed confusion at best and promote all that is foul and evil about humanity at worst. Without religion, humans would kill, rob, rape and otherwise wreak mayhem. Religion, however, provides one additional reason to kill, rob, rape and otherwise wreak mayhem and do so in the name of the "Highest Authority in the Universe." How frightening is that?

Of course, I have made a significant assumption

Distinctions Without A Difference

Christians are distinct from Buddhists who are distinct from Muslims who are distinct from Hindus. Catholics are distinct from Mormons who are distinct from Jehovah's Witnesses who are distinct from Baptists who are distinct from whichever group you may wish to consider, and each of the above is distinct from the others. But in what regard are they all the same?

History, current events and my personal observations indicate that among all the above, there are liars, thieves, rapists, murderers, the disingenuous or imperious as well as other varieties of miscreants or the frail. But also among them are persons who are kind, self-sacrificing, generous, loving, and otherwise magnanimous. In short, with regard to human behavior, the distinctions cited earlier are without salient differences with respect to fundamental human behaviors.

If religion is supposed to improve our relations with others and provide guidance with regard to navigating the human drama, it has no more or less effect than not having a religion at all. Religion has proven to be feckless or nugatory in making a pertinent difference despite the threat of hell-fire or the bribery of heavenly bliss.

Of course, I have made a significant assumption: Religion does (or rather, should) make a difference in the lives of its adherents – a positive difference that flows from the distinction between it and the non-religious. Given that the distinctions may be without practical (or even relevant) differences, what purpose does religion serve? How is it meaningful?

Several years ago, my best friend, his lady friend and I sat down at a restaurant. He had to use the rest room before our server came to the table. As he rose to leave, he asked us to order a particular brand of beer for him (because he fancied himself as a connoisseur of beer, and he only drank that particular brand). After he left, I suggested to his lady friend that we order a different brand and not let him know; we did just that. When he returned, he began drinking the beer – thinking it was what he had asked us to order. He drank it without comment until we told him about the ruse. We all had a good laugh. Religion tastes the same way. If you believe the distinctions constitute meaningful differences, they do – but only in the mind and not in any useful or significant way.

Christians are not different from Buddhists who are not different from Muslims who are not different from Hindus. Catholics are not different from Mormons who are not different from Jehovah's Witnesses who are not different from Baptists who are not different from whichever group you may wish to consider, and each of the above are not different from the others. Distinct but not different, and as proof I present history, current events and other facts of life in Prison Earth.

These same questions and issues apply to the non-Christian religions also.

Revelation Versus Evolution

Most religions claim to trace their origins to "God," either directly or via a prophet(s). That would mean the religion[1] was "revealed." In fact, one would expect a religion that "God" gave to humanity would be complete and intact – with no need for evolution in the form of revisions or adjustments. Yet almost all religions have *evolved* from the primitive to where they are today.

In more direct terms, if "God" reveals a religion (along with its teachings, practices and so forth) then it should *not* need to evolve; it would be complete. Or if there is a need for revision "God" would inform the believers in no uncertain terms?

For example, with respect to teachings, the early Jewish religions believed that witches should be killed or at least ostracized. Now, they do not support that idea. Early Christians believed sex between a man and woman should be performed in the "missionary position," only. Centuries later, they relaxed such requirements. Also, Catholic priests were once allowed to marry but later they were proscribed from doing so. Church garments or raiment evolved from simple everyday wear to what we see today (e.g., the clerical collar, robes, maniples, biretta, and so forth). In short, the original profile of the early Church (Catholic or Protestant) compared to the profile today clearly indicates an evolution, which would belie any claim of revelation from "God."

So, did "God" tell Christians to start celebrating the birth of Jesus? The early Christians did not. Did "God" tell the Jews to start wearing yarmulkes? The early Jews did not. In short, pick almost any religion and compare its beliefs and practices today with those that were present, or not, at its inception. Evolution, more often than not, will be evident. Revelation would be of "God"; evolution is a human phenomenon.

Either religion is one that is revealed by "God" and hence complete and in no need of any adjustments, or it is not revealed by "God" but rather is a human concept which is naturally given

---

[1]Simply stated, my working definition of religion is a formal system of worship and beliefs about "God" that includes doctrines, dogma and edicts.

to evolving. If there is an evolution of beliefs, ideas and practices, shouldn't "God" induce the evolution by revelation? Yet, there is no record of "God" revealing additional details or beliefs.

Some would explain that "God" simply provided the framework but left the details subject to evolution. That is difficult to accept given that the early Church morphed into the Catholic Church out of which Protestantism was spawned only to splinter into an array of conflicting religions. If that is "God" providing a framework but leaving the details subject to evolution, what does religion reveal about "God"?

P.S. These same questions and issues apply to the non-Christians religions also such as the Hindus and Muslim religions.

Four More *Said* That Need To Be *Things*
(or vice versa)

I. ### Who's Playing Tricks?

Religionists have often said that the greatest trick the "Devil" ever played on mankind was to convince people he does not exist. Two of the greatest "tricks," as far as I am concerned, however, are that religion has convinced the masses that "God" endorses religion and that "God" gives a damn what happens to us in this life. (If you want to argue that "God" cares, I present the thousands of years of wars, rapes, murders and deceit that have victimized the innocents – as revealed by a cursory study of history and watching the television news today.)

II. ### Big Business

Religion has more to do with money than "God" has to do with religion. It is a tax exempt enterprise that looks like a business, wobbles like a business and quacks like a business; it is a business. And as a business it runs on money. From the mega-churches to the story-front holes in the wall churches, they are the same as major corporations to Mom and Pop operations. Their products range from hope to piety in exchange for your credulity and your money (and not necessarily in that order).

III. ### The Question Of Heaven

The 19 men who hijacked four US planes on 11 September 2001 believed that upon dying they would be ushered into heaven and rewarded with a bliss that would include being serviced by dozens of virgins. Many, if not all, of the families and friends of those they killed believed their loved ones were also blessed with a heavenly existence. Which belief is correct? Did the hijackers go to heaven or did the people they murdered go to heaven? Is there more than one heaven? If the people the hijackers killed were, in fact, "infidels" they would not be blessed with a heavenly existence; if the hijackers were evil – according to others – they would not go to heaven. Where is the truth of the matter about "Heaven?"

IV.   The Question Of Hell

Jews, Muslims, Hindus and most other humans do not accept Jesus as their "personal savior" and thus, according to many Christians, not qualified to enter heaven. If not heaven, are they assigned to "Hell"? What of the victims of the Spanish Inquisition or the victims burned at the stake for being "witches"? Did they go to hell or did those who murdered them in the name of "God"/Jesus go to hell?

Furthermore, if Satan is ruler of Hell and is an avowed enemy of "God" then who really is the sadist? If people suffer immeasurable agony for an infinity (compared to being "evil" or a "non-believer" for less than 100 years) as a result of "God" sending them to Hell as punishment, is not "God" guilty of complicity by feeding into Satan's sadism? How is "God" holy and the "Devil" not, given that both are complicit in the endless torture of those who are not considered worthy of "Heaven?"

They had their priests, temples, rituals and ceremonies.

Why "God" Never Says, "You're Welcome"

It is not uncommon for a winner of an award to stand before an audience and begin his acceptance speech with the words, "First of all, I want to thank God ...." Such a comment raises questions about the one uttering the words.

With respect to the one speaking such words, is he speaking out of humility or arrogance? Humility in that he is giving credit to "God" as opposed to taking the credit himself or arrogance in that he actually believes that "God Almighty" paid special attention to him relative to the others who did not receive the award? Or that "God" paid attention to him rather than to the millions of others on this planet who suffer hellish horrors each day?

I claim that it may be neither arrogance nor humility but convenient ignorance borne out of the refusal, reluctance or simple failure to raise the questions I just have. Of course, the common response to this issue is that it is about faith. By all measures, however, the kind of faith believers often talk about is the kind which requires the suspension of reason, logic and even common sense. Believers often counter that faith in "God" defies reason, logic or common sense.

What is interesting is that if one lived in ancient Rome or Greece and questioned the relevance or intervention of Zeus, Jupiter, and so forth, the answer the believers would have given would sound eerily familiar to the one's today who believe that "God" (Yahweh, Allah, Jehovah, Vishnu, Jesus, *et cetera*) deserve thanks for the good and no blame for the bad.

They would cite "faith" as the primary ingredient in accepting or minimizing the illogic of their belief. Keep in mind those ancient worshippers believed in their deities with the same vigor and zeal as those who believe today (in whatever "God" they have chosen to believe in). Yet, by all accounts, almost everyone today has dismissed those ancient "Gods" as false or not real! So, did their "thanks" rise no farther than their voices could carry?

To that end, how was belief in Baal, Molech, Dagon, Amen-Ra, Osiris or other deities of the ancient world different from the beliefs in the "Gods" of today? They had their priests, temples, rituals and ceremonies – all designed as part of their worship and the *giving of thanks*. What proof is there that the ancient "Gods" were false and the ones today are not? Imagine this, if you will, a thousand years from now (if humanity survives), humans look back on this time and regard the religions of today much like we regard the religions of the ancient past. In any event, giving thanks to the "God(s)" of today is just as effective as giving thanks to the "God(s)" of yesterday.

In short, "God" (feel free to pick anyone of them you prefer) never says, "You're welcome" because the reasoned evidence reveals that "God" does not indulge the religious sensibilities of humans; how else could one explain the issues I just presented?

... God likes to hear them.

Out Of The Mouths Of Babes
"Let Us Pray"

On 16 April 2003, a popular singer was hospitalized; he had suffered a severe stroke. Shortly thereafter, a prominent minister and an influential radio disc jockey asked listeners and other radio disc jockeys and their audiences to place their hands on the radio at a certain hour and recite a prayer for the hospitalized singer. Later, the singer's mother and others thanked all who did so; she and others believed that prayer has power and that "God" would hear their supplications and answer accordingly.

The following is a conversation between a father and his young daughter about the situation.

Baby Girl: "Daddy, why are all those people praying for _____?"

Father: "Well, baby girl, prayer has power."

Baby Girl: "What kind of power?"

Father: "The power to change things, or in this case, the power to heal."

Baby Girl: "Is prayer more powerful if a whole bunch of people pray to God?"

Father: "I don't know if it is more powerful, but... I guess so."

Baby Girl: "So God will really listen to a prayer if a lot of people pray, but if only one person prays, He won't?"

Father: "No baby, God also listens to prayers from one person."

Baby Girl: "Then why would the reverend ask everybody else to pray? Wasn't God listening to _____ mother's prayers?"

Father:	"Yes, but other people felt the need to pray for God's help."
Baby Girl:	"What would happen if nobody prayed for him? Would he die?"
Father:	"Well, not necessarily."
Baby Girl:	"Does praying make sure he won't?"
Father:	"No ... not necessarily."
Baby Girl:	"Is God more likely to answer prayers because a lot of people are praying and would that be fair to the person who only has one person praying for him?"
Father:	"That is up to God. A person could still die even if a lot of people are praying for him."
Baby Girl:	"Then why pray?"
Father:	"Well, people also pray for God's will to be done. If it is God's will for him to live, he will or if it is not, he won't."
Baby Girl:	"If something is God's will, then how will praying affect it? If something is God's will, won't it happen anyway, prayer or no prayer?"
Father:	"Prayer is also an expression of love for the person."
Baby Girl:	"Can you show love without praying for him?"
Father:	"Of course."
Baby Girl:	"Then why pray since God's will will be done any way, and there are other ways to show love for _____?"
Father:	"Well, maybe in a certain way, God is moved by prayers, especially if a lot of people pray. God is loving and prayers could have an effect."
Baby Girl:	"Oh, just like when a lot of people sent a whole bunch of letters to the mayor to make him change

	his mind? So, a lot of people praying can make God do what they want."
Father:	"You can't make God do what you want, but God still likes to hear a lot of prayers. A lot of people praying ... prayer has power."
Baby Girl:	"Oh, OK. God is like granddaddy. He loves to hear us beg before he gives us anything... then he still might not give it to us."
Father:	"No, baby girl. Prayer also shows you have faith in God, faith that God hears you and will answer ..."
Baby Girl:	" I get it. Prayer shows you have faith that God will do what's He's going to do whether a million people pray, or one person prays or no one prays. So prayers really don't do anything, except that God likes to hear them, and we should do what God likes."
Father:	"Well ... Baby Girl, it's hard to explain but when you get older you'll understand so in the meantime, just remember to say your prayers."

Is God good to the kids in Africa who are starving and being killed?

Blessed

An 11-year-old girl heard her grandfather respond to the question, "How are you?" with the words, "I'm blessed."

"Grand daddy, what does blessed mean?"

"Baby girl, it means God is good to me. It means that grand daddy is alive and feels good."

The little girl thought for a moment. "If a person doesn't feel good does that mean he's not blessed?"

"Well, that depends. The main thing, sweetie, is that God is good to the person. That's what really makes the person blessed."

"Is God good to the kids in Africa who are starving and being killed?"

"Hmm, that's a good question, baby girl."

"Maybe they're not blessed. They don't feel good, and God is not being good to them because they are starving and being killed," she replied.

"I wouldn't go so far as to say that … being blessed … is something God just does."

The little girl sat silently for several minutes. Then she said, "It seems to me God doesn't bless some people, but He blesses other people."

The grandfather replied, "God doesn't bless bad people."

"Does that mean that the kids who are starving are bad since they are not being blessed?"

He sat silently for several long minutes. "Grand daddy has faith that God has blessed me … I just believe, and you will, too, once you grow older."

The little girl hunched her shoulders, smiled and hugged her grandfather. Later, as she grew older, she came to believe that "God" neither blesses nor curses. Humans are left to their own devices without the hand of "God" interfering either to bring good or to stop evil.

Eventually, she felt "blessed" that she became a deist.

... what merit is there in a site being "holy"

Holy Is As Holy Does

On 28 September 2000, right-wing Israeli politician, Ariel Sharon visited a Jerusalem shrine holy to Jews and Muslims, igniting clashes that mark the start of the second Palestinian uprising.

In November of 2008, Armenian and Greek Orthodox monks brawled – physically – with each other at the Church of the Holy Sepulcher – a site declared holy by both sects (Novinite).

Each of the major segments of religion have a host of sites their tenets have declared to be "holy." The Buddhists, Hindus, Christians, Muslims and Jews all have sites they have declared to have holy status. Designating a site to be holy is usually based on some pivotal event believed to have occurred at the site.

To be sure, a site is declared sacrosanct because some human(s) decreed it to be so or a site is declared sacrosanct because some human(s) claimed some deity decreed it to be so. If a deity – not some human – wanted a site to be treated as holy, it would seem logical or appropriate, if not imperative, that there be some sort of indisputable or miraculous indication that a place is sacred. There is no such proof; there is only the word of another human. Nonetheless, even if a miraculous event actually occurred at a particular place, it would be no more sacred a place than the behavior of those who believe it to be so.

To push this point further, what merit is there in a site being "holy" when the believers behave ruthlessly, bigotedly, and otherwise inhumanely? Which is more relevant and important, a holy site or a holy people – and by "holy" I do not refer to a person's status or position, but I refer to respecting other people's humanity and being kind, loving and otherwise honorable in how you treat and interact with others.

As I stated earlier, a place is "holy" if the people on it are; a place is a no better than a garbage dump or landfill if those who believe it to be "holy" behave as humans have typically done, especially when religion is involved.

Insulting or demeaning the Supreme Being would be an entirely different matter

Coming To "God's" Defense

Most religions that center on the worship of a Supreme Being(s) declare that their "God" is powerful or even almighty. Additionally, they proclaim their deity to be wise, fair and omniscient. That combination of qualities begs the question, "Why do worshippers feel compelled or duty-bound to leap to 'God's' defense or act in 'God's' behalf?"

It is understandable that a woman would defend her child if someone slandered his name. It would not be unusual for a son to defend his parents if someone libels their names. A man or woman would normally take offense if someone demeaned or insulted his or her spouse. In each of those instances, and in many more, love and respect for the person being derided would invoke protests, anger and the like. Such reactions are understandable especially given that the one(s) being derided and the one(s) doing the deriding are *both humans.*

Being human results in there being imbalances or an uneven distribution of power and other resources. The strong and advantaged often prey on the weak causing others to defend the weak. The strong, however, seldom need the weak to defend them. Extending that issue, insulting or demeaning the Supreme Being (Vishnu, Jehovah, Jesus, Allah, Yahweh, "God," and so on) should lead one to think similarly. If the Supreme Being is as described in the first paragraph of this work, why does this "God" need worshippers to come to the rescue? *Would not "God" be the best person to address any personal insult or sacrilegious behavior?*

If the Supreme Being were omniscient and fair then if someone hurled insults at His/Her/Its or Their divine character, then this "God" would know the motives and who the culprits really are. No innocent victims would be swept up in the vindictive rage of a zealous mob, and no innocent persons would suffer unjustly because of the disrespect shown by the guilty. Also, the punishment would fit the offense. In short, "God" would be the best one to defend "God."

To say that defending "God's" honor is the duty of the worshippers is to say that "God" has dumped a huge responsibility onto beings whose knowledge and perspectives are limited, biased and otherwise, comparatively frail. Is that a fair thing for a fair "God" to impose on human beings?

One of the most interesting passages in the Bible – one that stands in utter contrast to the rest of that book – is the account of Gideon in the Book of Judges. According to that account, Gideon was instructed by the "God" of the Hebrews to tear down the altar of the "god", Baal, along with its sacred pole. (Of course, to me, I ask the question, Why didn't "God" just strike down the altar and pole and make it obvious who did it and then dare them to rebuild the altar or pole?) In any event, Gideon did during the night.

The next morning, citizens/worshippers of Baal were outraged and wanted to kill Gideon. Joash, Gideon's father, said: *"Are you going to plead Baal's cause? Are you trying to save him? If Baal is really a God, he can defend himself when someone breaks down his altar. Let Baal contend with him"*(Judges 6:31, 32).

No matter whether Joash was sincere or simply trying to save his son, what a profoundly sagacious point. One can pose the same question with respect to responding to what anyone says or does about "God." If a person believes his "God" to be supreme and all-knowing then "God" is in the best position to respond to any perceived disrespect.

Instead, people kill, persecute or scorn those who disrespect or speak disparagingly of their "God." This is not say one should not be upset or even angry if someone else disdains the particular "God" one may worship. (I also suspect that some worshippers have taken action to persecute or prosecute those who speak ill of a particular "God" because they needed to justify some personal, political or economic motives) In any event, to take actions against such a person(s) implies that "God" Almighty wants humans to do what only "God" could do best.

Does a real "God" need puny humans to defend Him/Her/It or Them? If someone chooses to ridicule, scorn or curse "God," at best one should ignore the offender and at worst be angry. In either case, let "God" do what only "God" should do instead of frail humans.

Maybe "God" deserves no credit and no blame

Maintaining "God's" Image

Millions believe humans were created in "God's" image. Yet, it appears that humans spare no effort to maintain "God's" image with an array of explanations, the impact of which any public relations firm would kill for.

Since life on this planet is rife with grief, travails and angst, these realities must be explained in such a way so that "God" is always, at best, good, loving and irreprehensible, and at worst, mysterious and inscrutable. Hence, the need for the representatives to interpret reality! More specifically, to safeguard this image of "God" so that "God" could never look bad or culpable, the representatives have promulgated many interpretations of reality, including some of the following:

If a woman escapes being murdered by an enraged co-worker because she arrives to work late, she has "God" to thank and not luck. The other six people murdered at her job were allowed to die so that their families and friends could appreciate the life "God" has given them, the survivors.

If a man is laid-off from his job and loses his house, it is said that "God" would not allow him to suffer more than he could bear and so if he breaks, he cannot blame "God." This adversity should make him stronger. The other man, who was not laid-off from his job (at the same plant), has "God" to thank for the blessing.

"God" answered the prayers of many: the child's cancer went into remission. But then the child finally died of cancer anyway. "God" called the child to heaven. Furthermore, the child's display of courage and faith in the face of death was a lesson for his family and the hospital staff. Either way, "God" is blameless.

A tornado decimates a town killing dozens and yet a toddler is found safe thirty feet up in a tree. "God" saved her. Regarding those that died: "It was their time."

A talented singer struggles for years and finally wins several prestigious awards. In his acceptance speech, he thanks "God." Another equally talented singer struggles and yet never succeeds. "'God' has other plans for him."

If you pray to "God" for success and you have success, "God" answered your prayer. If you experience failure then "God" said, "No."

Two persons drive commercial planes into office buildings, killing thousands. The thousands go to heaven. The pilots also go to heaven (I do not know if it is the same heaven) to be serviced by a bevy of virgins.

One Bible: Yet many different religions are based on it – religions that contradict each other and sometimes the book itself.

One Koran: Yet different sects are based on it – sects that contradict each other and sometimes the book itself.

One Torah: Yet different sects are based on it – sects that contradict each other and sometimes the book itself.

One Book of Mormon: Yet different sects are based on it – religions that contradict each other and sometimes the book itself.

Is "God" the source of the Bible from which differing religions sprang forth? Is "God-Allah" the source of the Koran from which differing sects sprang forth? The same question applies to each of the so-called holy books. Yet, if you pose the question you are told to have faith and not to question "God" – so "God" can still look good rather than confused or inconsistent.

And the examples go on, and on, and on, and on, and on, *ad nauseam*.

The point is, "God" must always be cast in a favorable and positive light. Therefore, "God's" representatives" and their harem of followers always make sure that no matter how convoluted, strained or bizarre the explanation/interpretation, "God" must look blameless and deserving of credit thereby ensuring the continuation of their power over their flocks. Hence, cute, little maxims are chanted as a mantra:

"Everything happens for a reason." (You're supposed to think the reason has something to do with "God" or some guiding force in the universe.) See essay 48.

"There is no such thing as a coincidence." (... not even the fact that a former childhood neighbor that you barely knew was the one flipping the burgers that you bought at a fast food restaurant.)

"That which doesn't kill you makes you stronger." (Does that saying apply to a child who is abused for years and grows up to become a drug addict and prostitute only to die penniless and broken at age thirty?)

"What goes around comes around." (AKA: You reap what you sow. Can't we all think of people who were cruel and mean whose lives were no better or worse than those who were sweet and nice. For every example, one can cite where someone reaped what he or she sowed, there are examples of where that did not happen. Lastly, some believe that if you don't reap it in this life then you will in the next. That's convenient because no one can prove it.) See essay 49.

"God" is never late. Whenever it happens it will be right on time." (Another way of saying don't hold "God" to your time table, even though without knowing "God's" time table one can never say "God" was early, late or on time. How convenient.)

"Blah, blah, blah and yadda, yadda, yadda."

There is a visceral compulsion for most people to give "God" credit for the positive and where there is horror, chaos and agony, they *interpret* (notice that operative word) it as something constructive so that "God" looks good or blameless, no matter what.

These acts of interpretation ensure the power of the chosen few because their followers do not question the efforts to maintain "God's" image. Protecting "God's" image protects the power of the leaders. The other side of the coin is the followers who masturbate their own minds and then tell themselves that they really connected with truth, with "God."

Embracing these interpretations so that "God" is blameless makes them feel good without having to really connect and actually have an intercourse with their critical, analytical but ignored self. Thus, the power of the prophets, ministers, mullahs, priests, nuns, reverends or monks is preserved and perpetuated. (See essay 79.)

I propose the following: Maybe "God" deserves no credit and no blame for any of the events in the human drama. Maybe "God" is a passive or inert component in the human equation. Thus, there is no more a need for the prophets, ministers, mullahs, priests, nuns, reverends, monks, and so forth than there is a need for applying a band-aid to treat dementia. "God's" image does not need to be protected; if "God" is concerned with image, He, She, It or They can handle it without any human assistance. Actually, it appears that "God" does not give a damn about image given that (speaking as a deist) life on Prison Earth is replete with image-demeaning realities and has been since humankind's beginning, and it appears will remain so until humankind's end.

Such a "God" cannot be blamed for the evils...

Playing "God" Or Being "God"

On 10 October 2006, a local news station in Detroit featured a segment in which the news organization collaborated with a local franchise to provide school supplies and back packs for needy students at a K-8 school in Detroit, Michigan. The students were elated and expressed their gratitude. The segment ended with the school principal being asked about her reaction to this act of kindness. Among other things, she stated this was "a gift from God."

In February 2008, I attended a meeting of real estate investors chaired by a woman who, among other things, stated that "God" had determined her mission was to help others learn how to invest wisely and profitably in real estate.

Throughout my adulthood, I have heard the rich, the poor, the elite, and the plebeian credit "God" with everything from selecting the proper color shoes to saving them from a rapist – and everything in between.

This raises the issue of priorities. Priorities identify not only what one considers important, but they also reflect one's character.

If "God" gave those students the gift of school supplies and backpacks, why not deliver the child who is being abused by his or her parent(s) – in the same neighborhood as the students who received the gifts? Why not give the gift of life by saving an Iraqi child or a Hindu girl or a Mexican boy from being raped and killed or otherwise abused? How can "God" give the gift of school supplies and not give the gift of safety and protection to the many children in the world – or at least in Detroit, Michigan? If those indeed were "a gift from God" then what does that say about "God" and "God's" priorities?

I could present the same question using a myriad of different issues and instances. The "believer," however, will assert that "God" works in mysterious ways and that "God's" ways are higher than humans; thus, the rhyme and reason for "God" intervening in one instance but not in another is abstruse and recondite. Such an explanation is convenient (to say the least) and requires one to suspend the use of the same faculties we normally would use if you were propositioned by a homeless man who wanted to sell you the house at 1600 Pennsylvania Avenue in Washington, D.C. for only $19.63.

The idea that "God" does not and has not, in any way or in any instance, intervened in the affairs of humanity is too frightful an idea for most humans to contemplate. But I ask: Which is the better "God"? The one whose priorities allow Him (or Her, It or Them) to help you find that job to support your family while another family is killed by a stray missile? Or a "God" who does not intervene in human affairs, at all, thereby allowing time, chance and the human element to determine the realities (the good, the bad and the neither) of all life on this planet?

If you choose the former as the better of the two then you must accept the notion (based the realities of this life) that a "God" who picks and chooses who lives or who dies, who thrives or who barely survives, who enjoys life or who suffers the agonies of injustice, wars, lynchings, and so forth, and who does not – that Being is playing "God."

Whereas, a "God" who is detached and non-intervening is being "God." Such a "God" cannot be blamed for the evils and cannot be credited for the good. Such a "God" is an equal opportunity abandoner or ignorer. Such a "God" does not play "God" but is "God."

I, as a deist, can only loathe "God" if "God" is playing "God," but I can at least respect "God" if "God" is being "God."

What did You do today?

Questions I Have For "God"

Whereas, I have examined and studied, several of the world's major "holy" books, and;

Whereas, as a consequence of such examinations and critical thinking, I do not accept those "holy" books as communications from "God" or any other "divine" being, and;

Whereas, after having studied those books and having observed the application of the teachings of those books, I do not accept those books as the moral compass for humanity, and;

Whereas, I have listened to, spoken to, or queried, ministers, priests, preachers, pastors, elders, deacons, bishops, parishioners, and a host of other religious leaders regarding matters relevant to the above-cited tomes, and;

Whereas, I have examined, studied, reviewed, read, the beliefs, ideas, theories, dogmas of evolutionists, creationists, atheists, agnostics, theists, philosophers and theologians, *et cetera* and;

Whereas, I have observed and participated in the human drama and;

Whereas, given the above matters, I elect to believe that an incomprehensibly powerful and intelligent Being/Personality does exists and did create the universe and its fundamental components (both living and non-living),

I present these questions for that Being(s) whom I reluctantly agree to call "God":

What are You? Who or what do You define yourself to be other than Creator?

What did You do today?

Is there anything You do that takes longer than an hour, or a century?

Are there other Beings like You? Are You a plurality or a singularity? Do You have formidable enemies?

Why is there anything? (Why isn't there nothing?)

Why did You create the universe?

Do You have needs? If so, what are they? If not, why not?

Why did You create humans? What is the plan ... what is the point?

Are we the best humans You could have made?

Why is death part of the human experience and the natural order of things?

Were the first humans morally different (in an inherent and intrinsic sense) from humans today or have humans always been morally frail, flawed, fragile and otherwise foul?

What happens to humans after they die?

Why did You create the orangutan and the butterfly, the platypus and the hummingbird, the aesthetically pleasing and the otherwise?

Why do animals die (if they are not killed)?

Why must some animals serve as food for others – and do so in a violent way?

Are there other "intelligent" life forms other than humans and Yourself? If so, where are they? Why did You create them and what are they?

Are there other life forms You did not create?

What matters to You? Is there anything that is important to You?

Why haven't You left us with a moral guide that cannot be challenged as truth and cannot be interpreted in so many differing and opposite ways? If You are the all-powerful Creator, shouldn't You be able to present such a guide given that You must know how the human mind is wired so all humans would know what is truth, what is "right" and what is "wrong"? Couldn't an almighty "God" favor us with information that simply is not subject to various interpretations no mater where, when or how a person is raised?

Does it really matter how we live our lives, given that we all die and are all subject to calamities no matter what? Does it really matter how we live our lives since, often enough, we don't always reap what we sow, and sometimes we sow what we did not reap?

Is there another reality or life after death? If not, then isn't it sadistic of You to allow humans to be born into squalor and suffering, to live in pain and grief and to die in the same predicament? If there is a life after this reality, what is it? Does how we live now impact the kind of life we will live afterwards? If how we live now is important, then why don't you instruct us how to live now? (The Bible and other books in that genre, notwithstanding).

Do You love humanity? If not then why don't You put us out of our misery? If You love humanity then why don't You end our misery? Why do You allow us to treat each other the way we do (wars, crime, lying, hatred, selfishness, prejudice, and so forth)?

Is human life sacred? If so, then why do You allow it to be treated with contempt and disdain?

Why do You allow religion to exist since so very much of human misery, confusion and pain are attributable to religion?

Why do You allow religion to exist since so very much of human misery, confusion and pain are attributable to religion?

Is this all there is?

Est Is Totus Illic Est?

One night I dreamed about an inamorata of mine who was murdered more than 30 years ago by a man who tried to rob and rape her. Thoughts of her led me down a familiar path of questions about this reality we call life on planet earth.

The title of this piece, translated from Latin, is an age-old question that philosophers and other thinkers have pondered: "Is this all there is?" After ruminating on this profound question (even after considering what theologians and other religionists have preached and confidently declared), I always reach the same answer: I do not know.

And that grieves me deeply.

At this point, let it be noted that I am a deist. Translated, it means I believe "God's" involvement with humanity and this planet began and ended with their creation. I reject any and all beliefs that "God" spoke to "prophets" or inspired any books to be written. "God" does not and has not intervened in the affairs of humanity. To believe otherwise, one would have to accept that this reality is an indictment against "God" for the crimes of unconscionable discrimination based on religion, sadism of the worst sort and willful obfuscation of the facts relative to our safety and well being. As a deist, I subscribe to a different Gospel: "In the beginning, "God" created the heavens and the earth ... After that, we were left on our own.

But that leaves the question presented in the title still unanswered: **Is this all there is?**

We live, then we die. Whether it be for two seconds, two minutes, two days, two hours, two weeks, two months, two years, two decades, two centuries – we all die. If, in the end, this is all there is then the one who died two centuries after birth did not fare any better than the one who lived for two seconds. In short, what difference did living longer make? Of course one can argue that while living, one can contribute to the lives of others, make a positive impact on society. Perhaps, but to what avail when all is said and done, when all are dead especially since everyone dies whether they benefited from the goodness of others or not.

Now if there are a heaven and a hell then there are a set of disturbing questions and issues. For instance, the matter of there being a hell would paint "God" as a maniacal sadist in league with "Satan." Imagine the person who does not believe and hence does not behave as "God" supposedly requires. As a punishment for being a sinner or non-believer (being a gambler, or a liar or a mass murderer, for instance) for even two hundred years, the person would suffer unimaginable torture for *eternity!!!*

How does that punishment fit the crime(s)? Even among humans, life imprisonment ends at death. But for living a life contrary to what "God" has prescribed, one must suffer unimaginably excruciating agony for hundreds and hundreds and millions and millions and billions and billions and trillions and trillions of years – and more? What kind of all-powerful Being would do such a thing to an inferior life form, especially if he or she happened to have been born into a religion of which "God" does not approve. Which begs more questions about heaven.

Which heaven? The heaven of the Hindus or the heaven of the Muslims (with 70 virgins for men, and I have no idea what the women who go there would get) or the heaven of the Protestants, or the heaven of the Catholics, *et cetera*? Which group is correct given that they do not agree on many of the fundamental matters? Which one is the real Heaven? They all cannot be correct. So why would someone who happens to be born into the so-called "correct" religion (or converts to it) get to be so lucky while others who sincerely believe, but are wrong, would fail to gain admission to the bliss of Heaven?

Thus, I reject the notion of heaven and hell (as well as Nirvana or re-incarnation, albeit for different reasons) as presented by religions and their associated writings.

So again, *Is this all there is?* Where are my mother and my friend who were murdered as well as everyone else who has died? Is there a reality after death other than what religion has preached, or is this current reality all there is?

I do not **know**. No one **knows**, but many believe.

I know that what religion teaches about this does not convince my mind or heart – it fails to make sense on any level. I weep with grief not knowing the what and the why. No doubt I will go to my grave never really knowing as have my mother and my friend. I can only conclude the following: Either "God" is irrational, sadistic and virtually psychotic or there is something very different from what we have been told that occurs after death. Either the curtain drops and the lights go out and it's just over or something else that makes sense but at this time, is elusive and evasive with respect to my efforts and desire to know.

So, still I ask: *Est is totus illic est?*

THIS SON AND HIS MOTHER

Dear Mama,

Though my eyes have long dried, my heart still bleeds tears for thee.

Your forever-grieving son

... being my mother's husband and the ruler of our hell

Helpless

Awakened by the tugging on and the shutting of rickety dresser drawers, I stared in grief at a woman whose eyes, lips and nose were puffed with pain. She moaned that it was time for me to get ready for school as she set out my clothes, but I continued to stare. She did not look or sound like my mama, but she was.

I then realized that my prayers were hollow words and that I had another nightmare while wide-awake. The sounds of fists and feet bludgeoning her while she screamed and pleaded for him to stop were quite real. The sounds of her gasping to stay alive while being strangled were not a product of my imagination. And, I really did catch a glimpse of what I had prayed would turn out to be merely a horrible dream.

Mama had survived another episode of being crumpled, broken and mangled, and he was once again being my mama's husband and ruler of our hell.

I could never save her.

**NOT
EVEN
ONCE.**

Neither then, nor any of the many times thereafter.

And I did not save her when he used me as unwitting bait and took me to watch him murder her.

Too late, I grew a pair

4,654 Days

From 19 September 1950 to 17 June 1963: The number of days from my birth to the death of my mother. 12 years and 9 months of childhood memories seared into my mind.

During those days, I heard and saw him choke my mother to near unconsciousness then beat her then choke her again to near unconsciousness then beat her again – repeating that pattern until he was tired. I would tremble as if I were convulsing.

During those days, I saw him chase my mother into the street – in broad daylight – beating her with the buckled end of a belt – stripping her red dress off, revealing her slip and bra. I would tremble as if I were convulsing.

During those days, I saw him come home as she was peeling potatoes. He beat her because that is what he did on Friday or Saturday nights. I would hear her scream and plead for him to stop. I would tremble as if I were convulsing.

During those days, I would follow her onto the street, in the middle of the night as he kicked us both out the house – she, tugging on her short slip and I in my underwear running down the street. I would tremble as if I were convulsing.

During those days, I would hear him rant and then tell my mother to wake me up. She would come to my door and call me. I would never answer on the first call ... I would stand before him, listening or answering the questions of a drunken fool as my mother stood by, helplessly until he decided to go to bed. I would tremble as if I were convulsing.

Near the end, she wished I were older so that he would not beat her anymore. She knew I was not ready ... too young, too frightened.

Near the end she became brave; she left him – and her seven children – only she stayed nearby. She would meet me on my way to school and walk with me the rest of the way – everyday. No more beatings and humiliations. No more broken ribs or face broken beyond recognition. No more screaming and begging. I would no longer tremble as if I were convulsing.

On day number 4,654, he took me with him to go looking for her. (He retrieved $40 from his pocket and gave it to me. "I won't need it where I'm going." His intentions did not even dawn on me.)

We found her, with her mother, visiting with neighbors – a family. He and I stood on the front porch. She came to the screen door. In the softest and sweetest of voices he asked her to step out on the porch with us. She shook her head. He pleaded ever so kindly, in a whisper, like a lover who wanted to make amends. He pleaded.

Finally, she stepped out onto the porch. Folded her arms and asked, so matter-of-factly, "Now what do you want, Odis?" He reached into the breast pocket of his jacket. She held out her hands and in a terrified voice, "Don't stick me, Odis." There, as we stood inches apart, he produced a gun and began firing. I panicked. I fled as he continued firing. (Later, I learned, he reloaded and continued shooting – shooting her a total of at least 11 times).[1]

After running less than a block, I shut down. I stopped the horror from rushing in. I began walking as if nothing had just happened. I stopped my mind as I wandered aimlessly. I ended up at a store and bought an apple and corn chips. I wandered back to the house. I asked to see my mama. The police would not let me see her. I saw the pool of her blood on the living room floor (She had stumbled back into the house – pleading for her life as he continued shooting. Reloading again ... then sat on the porch steps waiting for the police.)

The next 30 years, I did not cry. I would remember her death day but shed no tears. Then, 17 June 1993, I had a brutal and life-altering epiphany. For the first time, I wept like a broken child. Thirty years of pain and grief and shame crushed me.

I did not save my mother. The terror of living with him snuffed out any courage I might have had. (Even in my marriage, I was disgustingly weak. Yielding, compromising, and acquiescing just to avoid conflict – trying anything and anyway not to be even remotely like him.)

---

[1] The newspapers inaccurately stated my mama and he were arguing. There was no arguing. He calmly and gently begged her to come out. She kept saying no – in the most gentle of ways. Nothing was said, in words or tone to telegraph any anger, hostility or murderous intentions.

Too late, I grew a pair. And also,

Too late, I grew into a man who, if it were possible, would avenge my mother in ways that would even make the "Devil"[2] glad he wasn't my mother's husband. (*Would I rather that than to see my mama again if I had to choose between the two?*)

In this life, my regrets are plenty but none compares with the regret of failing to save my mama. My heart still bleeds tears for her. My heart still beats with her love for me and mine for her. Her last 4,654 days and my first 4,654 days ... too soon she departed, and too late I arrived.

Epilogue

Yes, I am drenched with a kind of guilt for being used as unwitting bait in my mother's death and for being worthless as her protector. I also have a sustained disdain for a man who has been dead for more than 30 years. Amazingly, (as far as many social scientist are concerned) I never resorted to anti-social behavior such as drug use, poor performance in school, committing crimes and so forth. I have been able to segregate my guilt and hatred so that they do not interfere with my functions as a productive human being in society. With regard to my marriage, I started out as a weak and always yielding person. I was conflict averse. Later, I began to respect my needs and wishes. In either case, however, I did not resort to violence; nothing could make me emulate the man my mother married. I also, without effort, was the very opposite of the kind of father he was.

In any event, I am accepting of (having reached a kind of resolve) the feelings of guilt and loathing that spring from failing to protect my mama; and I cannot forgive the man who snuffed out her light. To me, to feel guilt-free would besmirch my mother's memory, and to forgive him would be to dishonor it.

Oh, to be able to return to day 4,653 of my life and know what I know now.

---

[2] I use the term "Devil" metaphorically to illustrate the kind of unbridled savagery I would unleash against him if it were possible ... the extent of my abiding hatred for him.

Mama was begging and pleading with Almighty God

The Power Of Prayer

It was a Saturday night. I was awakened by my mother's loud sobbing and pleading. It was similar to the kind of sobbing and pleading she would do whenever her husband would beat and break her body. Only this time, her husband was not even there. She was actually praying. Mama was begging and pleading with Almighty "God" that when her husband did come home, he would not ...

He came home.

If it had not been for that living room wall, she would have landed in the front yard. At least the wall had heard her prayer.

What is the rhyme and reason of it all?

> **THE BEYOND**
>
> It seemeth such a little way to me
> Across to that strange country,
>   The Beyond;
> And yet, not strange, for it has
>   grown to be
> The home of those of whom I am so fond.
>
> And so for me there is no Death;
> It is but crossing, with abated breath,
>   A little strip of sea,
> To find one's loved ones waiting
>   on the shore,
> More beautiful, more precious
>   than before.
>
>   ELLA WHEELER WILCOX

> MEMORIAL SERVICE
> FOR
> MARY ALICE McKINNEY
>
> NATIVE OF
> ALABAMA
>
> PASSED AWAY
> JUNE 17, 1963
>
> SERVICE HELD
> UTTER-McKINLEY'S
> SOUTHWEST CHAPEL
> JULY 24 AT 1:30 P.M.
>
> OFFICIANT
> REV. GEORGE E. HILL
>
> MUSIC BY
> UTTER-McKINLEY ARTISTS
>
> INTERMENT
> PARADISE CEMETERY

Pieces Of A Heart

Above is a copy of my mother's original obituary. I was given the original one after my mother had been dead 43 years. This "post card" was an insult that I felt I had to correct. Oddly enough, I had written an obituary of my own many years before because I was not able to attend her funeral. I was told that her husband had shown contemptuous temerity by attending her funeral (under police guard), but I did not know her memory suffered additional insult with an obituary will less information than most greeting cards.

Excerpts Of My Eulogy For Mama

On June 17, 1963, my mother's husband used me to be an audience so she could see her own death right before my very eyes. I could not save her. I could not protect my mother.

I stand in this time and space knowing that not an iota of reality will be altered except that which occurs within my own being; this eulogy is for my comfort alone. I will not insult the memory of my mother, Mary Alice McKinney, by deifying or apotheosizing her; I will not taint her humanity by casting her in "sacred light." (For after all, to be a fine human being often requires more than to be a "god.") Painting her as someone more than she was would be to assail her memory. I will, however, honor and esteem her, for in my mind, none before, during or after her time, is worthy of more.

I accept that each person's reality is the fusion of choices she makes often under circumstances larger than herself. Circumstances determine available choices, and each choice made creates new circumstances. This process constitutes the details of life as life leads us to death. Thus, my mother made choices; she suffered then died – my siblings and I survived.

From moment one to moment last, for 4,654 days my mother and I were together. There is so much I did not know about my mother; she was too busy surviving each of the "hells" her husband inflicted:

Now my mother lies in a mass grave (because the cemetery where she was interred was managed by people who dug up un-marked graves and dumped the bodies to make room for new ones). I stand here and now to pay tribute and honor. Most of my memories of her, however, are dominated by the savagery of her husband and so I say:

Butterflies, hummingbirds – beauty, fragility – but sadly, too short they live, too soon they die.

In this life, I have come to regret several things, the worst of which are two:

- I regret I did not kill him before he murdered my mama
- I regret I did not kill him after he was released from prison

With respect to the first regret, I was utterly terrified of him. With regard to the second regret, I was prisoner of some religious notion that it was a matter for "God" to handle – and that "God" would. In short, how lucky for him and how tragic for my mother – on both counts: how painful for me.

Therefore, I stand here in this stream of time – the time that has come and gone and the time yet to come and go – and declare that I am only one in the countless billions and I understand I am minutia and that my mama was the same, except to me (and my brother, O'Dell and my sister, Venecia). Soon enough I, too, will die; I will stop, but time will flow over me and I will fade into a speck of a memory. Nevertheless, my life stands as a teardrop in a rainstorm and as words on her "headstone." When I die, she will die again.

Does she or will she stand elsewhere? Or will she forever remain in some unmarked mass grave? What is the rhyme and reason of it all? I have read/heard from the pastors, priests, elders, reverends, bishops, gurus, ayatollahs, monks, rabbis, *et cetera* but for naught. Their answers? Nugatory speculation, supposition, superstition, or stupidity. They really do not know

… I do not know – only "God" knows.

So I, **_Carlespie Mary Alice McKinney_**, my mother's first child, do say this about "God": Having pondered "God" and contemplated the human drama and its condition, I conclude "God" is either demented and sadistic *or* supremely sublime in a convoluted or perhaps abstruse and arcane way (the assumption, albeit debatable, is that these two possibilities are mutually exclusive and collectively exhaustive).

If "God" be the latter then it can be *inferred* that the agony and insanity of this life actually works for our best well-being (in another reality perhaps?). Thus, if a person like me, a *deist*, could come to know precisely what "God" knows and could then do things differently, he would not. He would not alter a single event in all of human history – not the raping of a child, not the slaughter of millions, not even the torture of Mary Alice McKinney, my own mother.

If, however, "God" be the former (the agony and insanity of this life does not work for our best well-being) then "God" is horrifically cruel and severely demented. "God" is the Devil guilty of unforgivably "playing God" with humanity – and eternal shame on "God" for doing so.

Whichever one "God" is (not ever knowing is what plagues my soul and tears at my heart), my grief lives as time moves forward. I miss my mama.

Mama, though my eyes have long dried, my heart still bleeds tears for thee.

Your forever-grieving son

too short the time ... too long the pain ...
****

"all the gods ... and a young boy"

in bed many nights
trembling to
the screams
the pleadings
the wailings

in the next room

in bed many nights
trembling to sounds of
the pounding
the smashing
the breaking
of her body

in the next room

never was there a savior
to burst
into the next room

to rescue my ***mary alice***

not jesus the christ
not allah the great one
not jehovah the yahweh
not god the almighty
    and
    not i

(were they trembling too?)

no savior for ***mama***

not once – not ever
not even when he
used me ... bait
hunted her down (to where
she hid)

and as he stood
shooting ... re-loading ...
shooting again ...
her face ... down in a
pool ... her own blood

    i fled

... 'cause the gods didn't
show up to save her

not jesus the christ
not allah the great one
not jehovah the yahweh
not god the almighty

Mama,
   Your time was stopped ...
   broken too soon

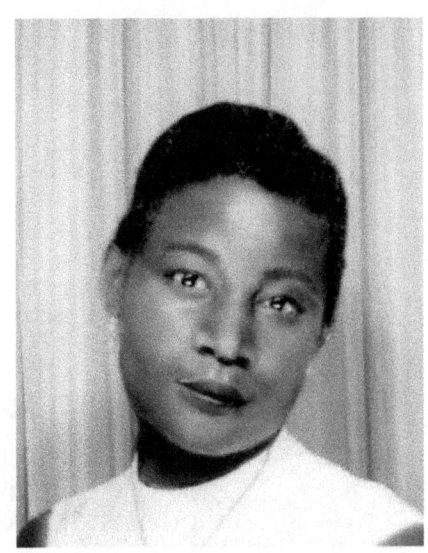

never heard her laugh out loud

a boy knowing his mother

together
twelve years

never saw her dance

but saw him
slam her, mangle her
break her and re-break her
often

never heard her laugh out loud

but heard him
choke her
as she pleaded
gasped and wailed
out loud

never knew her favorite color

but knew her life was
the black shade of tragic that he painted

a boy knowing his mother – always there

washing
cooking
cleaning

loving us
loving me
together
twelve years

I knew my mama
I did not know my mama

too busy
burning in a hell

too busy
praying
she'd make it through the next fire.

not the only woman

"nothing new under the sun"

<u>mary alice,</u>
not the only woman to
wash ... iron
the clothes of the man
who broke her ribs ...
cracked her face

<u>mary alice,</u>
not the only woman to flee
near-naked and bloodied
into the daylight streets
out of her hell

<u>mary alice,</u>
not the only woman to be expelled
into the midnight streets
but return to hell
in time to
prepare the devil his breakfast

<u>mary alice,</u>
not the only woman to
to suffer torture – for a decade ...
or be butchered
within reach of her boy child

<u>mary alice,</u>
not the only woman to
be hunted down
for escaping.

not the only woman to die
lying
in pool of her own blood ...
he standing in it

but
MARY ALICE,
the only woman

i call
"**mama**"

no wonder life is as it is on this planet

A Tale Of Two Siblings
(An Apple And An Orange From The Same Tree)

One of the most inexplicable matters relative to being "cut from the same cloth" is how diametrically opposite the pieces can be. Being pulled from the same womb is no guarantee that the facts of a situation/event will be painted the same. My mother's second child was a girl two years younger than I. She witnessed much of the brutality our mother suffered; she saw first hand much of the cruelty her father heaped upon our mother. My sister never knew a time in her life when her father was not the monster – except perhaps after he was released from prison for murdering our mother.

Two events that occurred in our youth bear mentioning. One night, when my sister was about 10, her father went on a rampage. This one was different from what he would normally do. He did not beat our mother. Instead, he kicked our mother and his own mother out the house in the middle of the night. Before he kicked his six children and me out, he asked the four oldest of us one question. He started with me.

He asked, "Who do you love more, me or your mother?" I trembled and said, "Mama." He then asked my sister the same question. She replied, "I love you more, daddy." At that moment, he turned her around, bent her over and literally kicked in the butt and shouted, "You're supposed to love your mother more! Get out!"

He then asked the next two younger ones (O'Dell and Venecia) the same question and they declared their love for our mother. He then ordered everyone out. After we left, he knocked out all the windows of the house and threw out all the furniture onto the street. The police arrived and arrested him. The next day, the newspaper referred to him as the "Human Hurricane." The poignant point of this event was that the sister I am referring to was a "daddy's girl" to a fault. Even in the face of his years of beating our mother and in the face of our mother loving her as she did all her children, this particular sister loved this ogre-beast of a father.

Less than two years later, her father used me as unwitting bait to shoot our mother at least 11 times (reloading his weapon while she lay in a pool of blood). Fast forward more than 15 years: I was sitting in a car with this same sister. We were having a calm conversation about our childhood and I stated to her, "If I were not a Jehovah's Witness, I would kill your father." Without hesitation, she retorted, "Yeah, and I'd kill you." From that moment on and for the next 13 years, I disowned her. I told people I had three sisters, not four. I did not mention her name when talking to my siblings and they knew not to mention her name to me. To me, she did not exist anymore.

In my mind, how could she not hate her father? She witnessed much of the cruelty and even experienced, firsthand, some of it on more than one occasion. Why would you say you would kill your own brother (I never thought she could actually kill me if I had killed her father) for avenging the death of your own mother – our mother? Even after her father served 9 years in prison (he was sentenced five years to life) for murdering our mother, she embraced him, welcomed him as her father. I rejected him in full but it was my belief in "vengeance being the Lord's" that allowed him to live and eventually die from complications of diabetes.

Same mother, different fathers – but the same mother who loved us all and endured years of violence to be murdered because she finally left. During my efforts to revisit the notion of "God" and religion (including forgiveness), I finally initiated contact with my sister. She admitted that what her father did was wrong but that she clung to him because "he was all I had left." She said she loved our mother, but she loved her father also – and his abuse and ultimate crime did not alter that. She also said our mother should have left her father earlier. Furthermore, she had recollections of more pleasant childhood memories; my childhood memories, however, are dominated by memories of her father's viciousness.

If murdering our mother could not alter her misguided affection for and devotion to her father, then what could? If she could not hate her father or at least disown him then no wonder life is as it is on this planet. A tale of two siblings (Carlespie and Theresa) is a tale of humanity and its own madness.

Where you are on that continuum depends on what happens when life drops you.

Humpty Dumpty Or A Cracked Rubber Ball

Social scientists tell us that a horrific event can traumatize some but leave others relatively whole. The question stands: What is there about those who are traumatized by a particular event that is different about others who can experience the same event yet prove to be resilient – not traumatized. (Traumatized, as some scientists would define it, is that one's ability to function positively in society is compromised as evidenced by drug addiction, alcoholism, violence, anti-social behavior, depression or post-traumatic-stress syndrome and so forth – as a way of coping with the trauma and its aftermath). Scientists describe those who are not thusly traumatized by a horrific event as resilient.

I suspect that both factors – being traumatized or being resilient – lie on a continuum, and that continuum is not necessarily linear. Furthermore, some may be traumatized but only for a period of time (days, months, years, decades – or not). Is the same true of resilience? Can a human display resilience for years but then later behave in a traumatized fashion? I ask for the following reason:

From about the age of one year until I was almost thirteen, my mother was physically and emotionally abused and broken by her lover-husband. Most of my childhood memories are those of her surviving such hellish torment. That treatment culminated in his using me as unwitting bait so he could murder her before my eyes.

From that night in 1963 to decades later, I did not cry over the loss of my mother whom I loved deeply. I excelled in school and even won an academic scholarship to one of the country's most prestigious high schools. I never used drugs – got drunk twice in my early twenties but never got drunk or buzzed or high since then; in short, I led a somewhat typical life emotionally and psychologically. I did not abuse (physically or verbally) my wife or children. I did not suffer sleepless nights or nightmares. I was, as most social scientists would describe, resilient; my mother's suffering and murder did not traumatize me.

But, in 1976, a dear friend of mine was literally butchered by a would-be robber. Then, in 1988 a lover betrayed me, and later, in 1991 she inflicted even more pain. All three times, I was overcome with pain and a sense of hopelessness. I was in agony – deep and potent. It took me a year to bounce back from the first incident and much longer with regard to the second and third incidents as I was depressed and in constant grief. Then, in 1993, I had a painful epiphany about my reaction to my mother's murder causing me to weep and grieve in a profound way. I cried and sobbed for the first time over Mama. Thirty years later! It was if she had just died. For the first time, my heart bled tears. Was I resilient or numb or in shock from 1963 to 1993?

What about the events of 1976, 1988 and 1991? Was I traumatized or was I something else such as grieving in a common way? Given how I reacted to the loss of the two other persons when I was older, would I have been traumatized by my mother's murder if it occurred when I was fifteen, or eighteen or twenty? Is being traumatized a function of many variables including age?

Whatever the answers may be, I suspect there are other elements on this resilient/traumatized continuum. Where you are on that continuum depends on what happens and who and what you are when life drops you.

She had no delusions about me

The Innocence Of Guilt
(When I Was Put On Trial)

THE INTERNATIONAL COURT OF HUMAN AFFAIRS HEREBY AGREES TO HEAR AND ADJUDICATE THE CASE OF:

The Conscience of Carlespie Mary Alice McKinney – **Plaintiff**
v.
Carlespie McKinney – **Defendant**

The Honorable Justices of the International Court of Human Affairs - Family Relations Division: **PRESIDING**

FORMAL CHARGE:
On this 17th day of June, the Defendant, Carlespie McKinney is hereby charged with the following offenses:

Cowardice: 30+ Counts.
Dereliction of Duty as a Son: 30+ Counts.

Opening Comments by the Prosecution:
It is hereby alleged that on numerous occasions commencing circa 1951 to 17 June 1963, the defendant failed to protect his mother from physical assaults perpetrated by her husband. It is further alleged that on 17 June 1963, the defendant did act as bait to lure his mother outside and then fled the scene as his mother's husband proceeded to shoot her more than eleven times – killing her.

Opening Comments by the Defense:
The defendant counters that he was three months shy of 13 on the day of his mother's murder and was also unarmed on 17 June 1963 and that he was **unwitting** bait as he was completely unaware that her husband was going to harm his mother. He further states that during the previous years, he lived in utter terror of his mother's husband.

The Prosecution:

We have taken the age of the defendant into serious and deliberate consideration which is why the number of counts is only 30+ as opposed to far more than that. It is estimated that at least by age 8 the defendant could have intervened to protect his mother. There are several incidents which led us to believe the defendant was unforgivably impuissant and cowardly – his age and the circumstance notwithstanding. The prosecution would like to enter the following as evidence:

In August of 1990, an 8-year-old boy in Pennsylvania found his father beating his mother. The boy repeatedly stabbed his father, William Jones, 59, in the back with an 8-inch knife. A coroner's jury declared the homicide to be justifiable (Goldman, 2008).

According to the Associated Press, in April of 2008, a 12-year-old boy fatally stabbed a 64-year old man in the throat who was attacking his mother in their home in Maryland.

The boy ran into the kitchen after hearing his mother scream and found his mother on the floor with a fellow resident astride her – choking her. After shouting at the man to stop, the boy finally grabbed a knife and slashed the man's throat (Boy, 12, kills man who attacked his mom, 2008).

In December of 2007, in Detroit, Michigan, a 7-year-old girl jumped in front of "an enraged ex-boyfriend, who pumped six bullets into the child as she used her body as a shield to save her mother's life" (Girl 7, shot 6 times saving mom, 2007). The child survived after 6 hours of surgery but lost an eye. Her mother was physically unharmed (Fund set up for 7-year-old 'hero' who saved mom, 2007).

These three incidents stand in stark contrast to the behavior of the defendant during the more than 10 years of abuse his mother suffered at the hands of her husband. Not once did the defendant ever intervene on his mother's behalf. He asserts he was terrified which in fact goes to our point: He was a coward and a disgrace.

At issue is not what his mother did or failed to do to protect her own self. (She in fact, did leave her husband and had initiated divorce proceedings shortly before her murder.) The issue before the court is the conduct of her son, the defendant.

The Defense:

On 25 November 2007, a 41-year-old Michigan man shot his estranged wife six times as she sat in her automobile with her nine-year-old son in the back seat. The boy was wounded (accidentally) as he watched in horror. The community responded with sympathy for the boy and even established a trust fund for him (Hunt, 2007).

With respect to the 12-year old boy who killed the man who was attacking his mother, the same article states, "Rarely is a 12-year-old implicated in a homicide *and even less often does a child that age kill someone to protect his mother*" (Boy, 12, kills man who attacked his mom, 2008 – Author's emphasis).

Imagine that your earliest recollections are your mother's husband beating her regularly in your presence or within earshot. **Imagine** being thrown out of the house in the middle of the night in your underwear with your mother dressed only in her slip. Imagine seeing your mother being beaten with a belt-buckle end of a belt in the middle of the street – no neighbors coming to her rescue. **Imagine** trembling at nightfall on the weekend knowing full well that another episode of beating of your mother was close at hand. **Imagine** the police treating the situation as a private matter and that there were no shelters to run to. **Imagine** hearing your mother gasping for breath as he choked her, let her catch her breath and then choke her again. **Imagine** being verbally abused by that same man and then **imagine** the worst: being used as unwitting bait to lure your mother to her death. All during the course of nearly the first 13 years of your life.

The other children noted earlier had not been terrorized from the time they were one-year-old to the time they were almost 13. That difference is significant. In fact, the examples the prosecution cited were the exception – certainly not the rule.

As a final point, I would like to cite the actual words of the victim, the defendant's own mother and have them entered into the records.

The Words of Mary Alice McKinney, the Defendant's Mother:

When Carlespie was about eight or nine, his family lived in a poor and rough neighborhood in Detroit, Michigan. One of the neighborhood families had children a couple of years older than Carlespie. Some of those children and Carlespie got into an argument; in effect, they were picking on him.

Carlespie told his mother about the incident and she remarked that if his two cousins were here, those kids would not "mess with" him. His cousins would "beat them up."

Secondly: Years later, shortly before she left her husband, she and her son, Carlespie McKinney (who was 12 by this time), were walking across the street in downtown Pasadena, California. She said, almost matter-of-factly,

"I'll be glad when you get bigger so your father won't beat me anymore."

Those two incidents clearly indicate his own mother knew he was not emotionally capable of protecting her (or even his own self for that matter). She knew that in time, he would not only be "bigger" but emotionally prepared to defend her. (If anything, the words she spoke to her son served as an indictment against her own four older brothers would did not protect her.) She had faith in her son – *for the future.* In fact, however, she did not wait for him to be "bigger" because she left her torturer shortly thereafter; she finally gathered the nerves and fortitude to leave him and all her children.

If his own mother, the victim, was aware of but respected his limitations and yet stilled loved him dearly, then the court should find him not guilty of cowardice. If he is guilty, it is of being what almost anyone would be if they had known the kind of terror he knew for almost the first 12 years of his life.

The Verdict:

The court understands the gravity of the abuse and terror the defendant suffered. There is no question but that to live under such severe and horrific conditions would tax any person's courage and fortitude. Nonetheless, the prosecution has presented a compelling and formidable case – thus the burden facing the court. After arduous deliberation, and sometimes vigorous debate, it was the words of the victim herself that tilted the scales. From her own words one can infer that she understood her son lacked the wherewithal to provide sufficient protection and security. The court cannot, in good conscience, supplant the victim's assessment of her son's capacity or lack thereof. It is hereby the decision of this body (six votes to five) to find in favor of the defendant.

Not guilty on all counts.

The After-Math

Reporter: "Ms. Prosecutor, what is your reaction to the judges' verdict?"

Ms. Prosecution: "We believe the court erred by giving too much weight to the words of the defendant's mother. The justices minimized the weight of the other evidence. We plan to appeal."

Reporter: "Mr. Defense Attorney, what is your reaction to the judges' verdict?"

Defense Attorney: "They made the only fair and right decision, the actions of the other young people notwithstanding."

Reporter: "Mr. McKinney, how do you feel now that the court has found you not guilty on all counts?"

McKinney: "I sat in court listening to all the damning evidence. Children younger than I were killing to protect their mother or at least willing to stand between her and death. My mother loved me and I, her. She knew my limitations. Nonetheless, I wish I had been a braver son. *That said, in my mind: Not guilty of cowardice. In my heart: Not guilty of cowardice by reason of it.*"

I will eat strawberry ice cream ...

To "Celemourn" My Mother

There are two days out of the year I set aside to both celebrate and mourn the birth and death of my mother. It is on those days, I disconnect myself, as best I can, from the rest of humanity to pay homage to the memory of Mary Alice.

On those days, I engage in her vices; I savor strawberry ice cream then crème-filled vanilla cookies along with a bottle of Pepsi Cola. I listen to songs by Jackie Wilson and "Green Onions" by Booker T and The M.G.'s as well as other songs that remind me of her. I reflect on her life as it overlapped mine. I ponder my earliest memories of her – I re-live the last day of her life and the seventh day thereafter as I saw her in a morgue.

I weep. I smile. I appreciate. I regret. I blame myself. I forgive myself.

That is how I celemourn her birthday and her deathday.

I wish she had seen me graduate. I wish she had been here to be a mother-in-law and a grandmother. I wish she were here to hug my grandchildren. I also wish she had been here to see the Afro hairstyle, bell-bottom pants, cable TV, CDs computers, cell phones, the internet, Oprah, President Obama and all the beauty and insanity of life on Prison Earth after 1963 June.

I wish she had been here to be my mama longer than she was. If so, she would have seen a terrified boy grow into a man capable of protecting "sheep" but terrifying the "wolves." A man who would have been a "Torquemada" and a "Marquis de Sade" on her husband; her husband would have sobbed and begged "God, Allah, Vishnu, Zeus, Baal (and anything else considered divine,) to die. "Hell" would have been a relief by comparison.

But, such was not the case.

Nonetheless, I refuse to let her memory fade into a distant or cluttered corner of my mind. As long as I breathe, she will not be forgotten, and my heart will beat love for her. Too soon she was gone, and I will leave soon enough ... then she will finally die in all the ways that death can come. Until then, she lives at the forefront of my mind's heart, and on two days out of the year, I celemourn her.

... his name is forever fetid, ignominious and foul.

A Name Too Foul To Speak

In the 1930's and 40's, a slimy slut bitch[1] gave birth to and raised a completely useless and contemptible male who grew up and married my mother and adopted me. This foul person was brutal and sadistic in how he treated my mother. Marrying this piece of feculent material and enduring his savage and vile treatment until she finally left him says many things (negative and positive) about my mother. Lest one thinks this person's opprobrious behavior was identified only with his cruelty to my mother, the following are examples of his parenting skills:

When I was almost 11 he thought it was time for me to learn how to masturbate. He took out his penis and told me to do the same. I did. He stopped. Put his penis back into his pants and left the bathroom. He then proceeded to tell his mother and his sister, who were visiting, about the size of my penis compared to his. (On a later occasion, he took me to some of his lady friends so I could give up my virginity. It appeared, however, the women drew the line at having sex with a 12 year old.)

Then there was the time he told me that out of all the women he had been with, "your mother has the best pussy." On an earlier instance he made a batch of "home brew" in the bathtub. He got me drunk (along with two of my siblings). I was about nine. About a year later, he stated that I was going to be smoking anyway so I might as well start now. He lit a Pall Mall cigarette and told me to take a puff. I did. I choked. (I, however, decided to follow my mother's example; I never touched a cigarette thereafter.)

Thus, I neither speak nor write[2] the name of that rodent. He is relevant only in that his truculent and murderous brutality dominates most of my childhood memories. It is for those and other reasons that his name is forever fetid, ignominious and foul.

---

[1] That woman physically and brutally abused my siblings while her son was in prison for murdering our mother. The state of California finally took them from her and placed them in foster homes or institutions. That is just one reason why I describe his mother as I do.

[2] The exception I have made is when I quote one of the last things my mother said when he drew his gun to kill her.

Father In The Legal Sense ...
Son In The Illegitimate Sense

Shortly before my mother's husband murdered her, his mother and sister told me he was not my biological father (though he was the biological father of my six siblings). For almost thirteen years the man I thought was my natural father was only my father in the legal sense of the word. I felt a sense of relief that such a despicable human did not father me.

A year or so later after my mother died, I asked my aunt (my mother's sister) who was my natural father. She said he was a man who denied being my father; he wanted nothing to do with us. She told me his name. That is the extent to which I have ever been interested. I have never asked anything else about him. Thus, I know his name and that he denied being my father.

To that end, I find it difficult to empathize or sympathize with children who long to know about the parent(s) they never knew (except perhaps for medical reasons). The oft-cited apothegm about having to know your past so you can understand who you are or to plot your future is non-sense presented as logic and something aphoristic.

In short, I do not care if I am the descendant of royalty or scum. I do not care if I am the descendant of geniuses or buffoons – or any combination thereof. I knew my mother – the only "ancestor" who matters; any other details about my heritage come close to being superfluous.

I was stunned

How My Mother Came To Name Me Carlespie

Family and longtime friends have always called me Carl. As an adult, most often, whenever I introduced myself – as Carlespie – the other person would remark how unusual my name was and that he or she had never heard of it. Admittedly, I took a tincture of pride in having a name practically no one else had.

I remember, after my mother died, asking her younger sister how did my mother come to name me "Carlespie." She stated that when my mother was pregnant with me, she (my aunt) had a girlfriend (whose name was Goldie) who had a boyfriend named Carlespie. (They all attended Northwestern High School in Detroit.) My aunt liked the name and suggested that my mother name me Carlespie. So, my mother did just that.

When I was 35, I introduced myself to a lady who immediately stated she knew someone with that same name – in fact, she knew his son very well. I remarked that such a thing was impossible; it just could not be. She offered to prove it. Later, she gave me an obituary for a Mr. Carlespie Johnson who also had a son whom he named Carlespie Johnson, Jr. I was stunned.

Later, while with the same lady, we called Carlespie Johnson's widow. She confirmed that her husband had a girlfriend named Goldie while attending Northwestern High School in Detroit. What a discovery! This Carlespie Johnson was the man whose name was the name my mother gave to me. What a startling string of events.

For the record, Carlespie Johnson was not my father. According to my aunt and grandmother, when my mother became pregnant with me, the man who was my natural father (whose name was, Raymond Gillespie West) denied his paternity. I suppose the similarity between Gillespie and Carlespie caught my mother's and her sister's attention. My aunt also stated my father had a sister who later became a local politician – information she volunteered. All I asked was how did mama come to name me.

... the confluence of stunning shock in concert with overwhelming relief

Why I Changed My Name

I was born to Mary Alice Richmond on 19 September 1950. Accepting the suggestion of her sister, Rosetta, she gave me the first name, Carlespie. Since my biological father denied paternity and forever left us, and since he and my mother were not married, my last name became Richmond. Hence, Carlespie Richmond was my full name until 28 November 1955 when my mother's husband of two years, legally adopted me. Thereafter, my legal name became Carlespie McKinney until 02 September 1993 when I changed my legal name to include my mother's first and middle names as my middle names. My legal name became Carlespie Mary Alice McKinney.

The reason I changed my name from Carlespie McKinney to Carlespie Mary Alice McKinney is attributable to an incomplete but insightful understanding of my reaction to my mother's death. When my understanding became complete, the rightness of my decision to change my name was enhanced even more so.

For the ten years my mother was married to the father of my six younger siblings, he was shamelessly unfaithful to her, and he brutally beat her often. His long-winded diatribes and vicious physical assaults constitute my earliest and most enduring childhood memories. Often times, he would wake me in the middle of the night and rant and rave stupidities and cruelties to my mother and me (as his children lay sleeping).

I also personally witnessed many of the merciless beatings and chokings, and that which I did not see, I could hear in the next room. Mama and I had also survived the midnight expulsions from the house into the streets dressed in our sleepwear. She endured a "hell" that never stopped burning, and we lived in utter terror of her husband, our personal ogre-demon. I was craven; I could not protect her.

On the other hand, I was my mother's first son. She would confide in me about her pains and how she looked forward to the day I would be bigger so he would stop beating her. I remember vanilla cookies, Pepsi Cola and music playing while cleaning house – my mother's only pleasure/vice. My primary and basic recollections of her, however, are primarily in the context of her surviving from one attack to the other. But my mother was my mama. I think of her, and I feel either pity or warmth, grief or love – without exception – even to this day.

On 17 June 1963, Monday at about 8:00 p.m., my mother's husband used me as unwitting bait[1] and took me to watch him murder her because she had finally left him. He pulled a handgun from his jacket and began firing at point blank. My mother stumbled; I ran (he ended up reloading the weapon and shooting her a total of eleven times as she crawled away). *I did not cry when my mother died.*

Every year, however, on 17 June, I would place my mind and heart to the awful events of that day in 1963; I would hurt, sometimes wallow in pain. Also, I would often ask myself, why did I not cry when she died, especially since I personally witnessed her murder. Later in life, this question would become more pressing whenever I would recount my behavior regarding other tragedies I suffered. Such tragedies as when I wept profusely – prayed to die – for months when an inamorata of mine was murdered in 1976 or when I grieved and lost almost forty pounds, when a relationship with a lover ended in 1991. Both events broke my soul, and I drowned in stark pain and agony. Yet, my reactions, in 1963 to mama's death were nearly phlegmatic and placid.

I remember loving my mother – as much as a young boy could. As a person, I feel deeply and cry too easily as far as I am concerned. I remember when my oldest son, LeGé, was struck by an automobile and suffered a broken leg when he was six years old. I locked myself in the bathroom and cried, not because he was injured but because he could have died had the car struck him differently. So, why did I not cry after seeing my mother murdered?

Finally, on 17 June 1993, thirty years later, I, as usual, contemplated my life and my mother. Suddenly, I collapsed into weeping. I sobbed as if she had just died. My heart tore open and I could not stop crying for days. I had experienced a painful epiphany.

---

[1] This is something for which I will forever loathe and despise him. There have been times when I would rather he come back to life so I could torture and kill him, than for my mama to return to life so I could be her son.

Into The Light

Her husband was imprisoned for nine years for what was unjustly agreed to be second-degree murder as opposed to what it actually was, first-degree murder. After mama died, I moved in with my older maternal aunt, Ruth and my grandmother, "Big Mama." Life was incredibly so much better. It was void of the pain and anguish I had lived with for ten of my 12 years. I missed and longed for my mama, but I also reveled in the *joie de vie*, the joy of life (albeit for only two years; thereafter, the burdens of being alive have been with me since).

In short, 30 years later, I finally realized that immediately following mama's death, I was so relieved not to be living with her tormentor that I essentially reacted to her death, (without conscious thought), as the means of my escape. I felt so free of the misery, the beatings, the pleadings for mercy, and all the other cruelties he wreaked on my mother and, to a lesser extent, me. This insight was characterized by utter clarity, and I did not mislead myself: I felt relief that *I* was not suffering- suffering through her sufferings. I shamefully admit, I did not think of *her* as no longer suffering, but of *myself* as no longer suffering. This relief from suffering overwhelmed and suppressed the anguish and suffering of losing my mama.

This sudden realization, 30 years later, caused me deep and acute embarrassment and grievous shame. To imagine that I felt more relief than sorrow, more joy than pain following my mama's murder (Mama, I am so very much sorry.) So, I pondered: How could I most respectfully mourn my mama? How could I honor her and at the same time resist the urge to overcompensate and subsequently deify her? (I strongly believe that glorifying my mama would actually denigrate her memory.) It was then that I decided to legally change my name to include her names. Thereafter, each time I signed my name, I would be honoring and properly memorializing my mama; renaming myself with her names would be giving her honor in a way that my tears could not. It was a superior way, this son could be his mother's son.

The Brighter Light

Nevertheless, my insight was incomplete until 02 January 1998 when I spoke with my cousin. I told her that I remembered something that I had almost forgotten. After the first few shots were fired and mama stumbled, I ran. When I had run less than a block, I stopped and began walking down a main street as if *nothing had just happened*. I meandered into a store and bought a bag of Fritos corn chips and an apple. I spoke to no one, and I did not think about what had just occurred; I simply traipsed around and casually wandered about until finally returning to where Mama died. Seeing all that blood on the floor,

I did not even react.

I had nearly forgotten this immediate aftermath.

My cousin said, as she had often opined why I did not weep when mama died, that I was in shock. She asserted I knew of no other way to process what I had seen. I had to shield my twelve-year-old psyche from the horror as best I knew how; I behaved as if nothing had happened. My behavior subsequent to witnessing my mother's death clearly confirmed to her that I had been traumatized. I finally agreed that she was more correct than not. I wept again – as if mama had just died.

So, I believe my reaction to my mama's murder was the confluence of stunning shock in concert with overwhelming relief resulting in a delayed onset of aching grief. These insights and the urge to best mourn and memorialize my mama, as others and I had not done in 1963, are why I proudly bear her names as part of mine.

P.S. If my mama could only know that my heart beats pain and love for her.

I stepped on my own face

Stepping On My Own Face

Some years ago I presented my driver's license and a check to a bank cashier. She looked at my driver's license and read aloud, "Carlespie Mary Alice McKinney." Her tone was one of muted curiosity and a hint of sarcasm. I have encountered this reaction only a few times over the last nine years since I changed my name to include my mother's first and middle names.

"Yes, indeed," I replied in a matter-of-fact voice. I did not want to inject any negative emotions into the situation.

"Interesting, different," she mumbled as she smirked ever so slightly. I looked at her nameplate.

"So is the name, P****," I responded in my same matter-of-factly voice and a poker face.

She continued processing my transaction without comment. Then, at that moment, I violated my own self. I stepped on my own face.

"Mary Alice is my mother's name," I explained.

She simply hunched her shoulders a bit and handed me my money without further word. I walked away hating that I yielded to the pathetic impulse to explain to a stranger, whose interest at best was marginal, an issue so dear and precious to me.

Most people, (including traffic cops) upon reading my name, say nothing. A small number, however, do inquire politely. To that small number, I simply state, "I changed my name to honor my mother." I do not go into detail about the manner of her death and my subsequent reactions. To tell them anymore would be a waste of breath.

At best, they could offer their polite and perfunctory sympathies but would remain untouched because they did not know my mother and do not really know me; they really cannot fathom my situation. So I do not waste my breath with anything more than a canned response – even if they inquire further.[1]

There is an even smaller group that reacts with rude or thoughtless questions/comments or reactions such as …

"Why would your parents do that to you?"

"Aren't you worried people might think you're gay?"

"I bet you had a lot of fights growing up with that name."

"Are you gay?"

"Did you mother wish for a girl?"

"Are you serious?"

I reply:

"They didn't."

"No."

"No."

"No."

"No."

"Yes."

Or I simply look at them with a poker face and give no reply.

I had concluded that most of those humans are not worthy of even the most terse explanation – only a terse answer, if anything. Nevertheless, in the situation at the bank, I abandoned my integrity by not focusing on the fact that I changed my name to honor my mother – a fact of which I am most proud; damn what others may think.

---

[1] This book, however, contains the full story for all to read. Part of my thinking is that anyone who purchases and/or reads this book would have more than a mere passing or cursory interest. Writing the full story is also an additional way to honor the memory of my mother.

I spent the better part of the day trying to understand why I gave her more than she deserved. I concluded this: Sometimes, I just want to be understood (which is why I write). I wanted to be understood even if but for a moment or by a stranger. *I allowed that desire to lower my guard and waste my breath.* In effect, I wanted that teller to do what she could not possibly do – understand and appreciate within the constraints of that moment.

I learned a little more about Carlespie Mary Alice McKinney that day. Now, I spend my words more appropriately.

I stood in my own way

As The Crow Soars

During the summer of 1965, 51 students from two middle (junior high) schools in the city of Detroit and I were selected to attend Cranbrook High School in Bloomfield Hills, Michigan. We were the first participants in a program called the Horizons Program. Inner city (urban) youths who displayed academic potential spent eight weeks on the Cranbrook campus. Cranbrook ranks among the most elite private secondary schools in the US. By summer's end, two of the fifty-two students were awarded full academic scholarships to attend Cranbrook as full-time boarding students. I was one of the two out of 52.

At that time, I was one of about four Black African-American students out of about 300 Cranbrook students (all boys). Nonetheless, I can accurately state I did not experience any racism – at least none that I could detect even after looking back on the three years I spent there. I graduated with a "B" average[1]; successfully competing with some of the most intelligent (and richest) students in the US.

My primary regret is that I wish I were not lost during those three years. I wish I had been more engaged. I was in it but not of it. I had not come to terms with the murder of my mother – hence I stood in my own way – unbeknownst to myself and to others. I performed well academically and to some extent socially. I soared with the other Cranes (Cranbrook's mascot) but I could have soared higher.

I felt alone, except for my best friend at the time (Edward K. Lee) and my favorite teacher/coach (Delvin Walden) – so alone that I went through the motions as I suffered through the cultural shock of coming from poverty to living at the opposite end of the continuum and coming from coed schools to an all-boys school. All this within the context of unconsciously struggling to keep the lid on the pain of losing my mother.

---

[1] I have always been at or near the top of any class I took (except Wood shop and Metal shop) from elementary school to graduate school. I only mention this lest any reader think that the Cranbrook teachers took it easy on me. They did not – a fact for which I am deeply grateful because it has served me well.

I soared with Cranes, not as a Crane but as a Crow; I just did not fit in. I soared high enough to pass but I did not excel – I did not reach the edge of my potential. But the best I could be at that time was less than my unencumbered best. If only this Crow had not been in such pain, he would soared even higher as a Crow among Cranes. Nonetheless, I am so deeply happy that I was given the privilege to attend Cranbrook because its impact and influence proved to be essential for my development in ways that extended beyond the academics – my personal baggage notwithstanding.

...more years behind me than in front of me

"Yestermorrow"

On 06, 07 and 08 June 2008 I attended my 40 year high school reunion and I enjoyed it more than I thought I ever would. I was especially elated to see my favorite high school teacher (math teacher, football coach and dorm master, Delvin Walden). I also enjoyed seeing the one classmate who helped me maintain some semblance of sanity (Ed Lee and I would listen to Motown music on his reel-to-reel portable tape player.) Despite the fact I had visited and re-visited the campus many times during the 40-year time span, things seemed different this time no doubt because most of those in my class came to celebrate also.

As expected, most of us had bodies and faces touched by time (some gently, some not so gently). We ate and talked of the times gone by. I was even given photos of my younger self I had never seen. I learned that out of a graduating class of 72 students about, six had died. Otherwise, we all had gone on to become physicians, attorneys, business owners, professors, husbands, fathers and so forth.

On the last day of the three-day reunion, after the last meal, while exchanging good-byes and promises to remain in touch, one of my classmates (Patrick) said he would see me at the next reunion in five years. Suddenly, almost without hesitation, I said I would not attend that reunion. My response muted the joy I had been feeling until that moment. He asked, "Why?" I explained why (the short version: "Once is enough") but not as precisely as I will now.

I must first state I am a person who regularly contemplates his mortality. I am grievously aware I have more years behind me than in front of me; I am running out of time to do what I aspire. I have attended funerals of several of my contemporaries or have seen their bodies challenge them to stay alive. Nonetheless, there was something unsettling about what my high school classmate said.

I realized that returning to my 45 year high school reunion would only serve to make me look at my own mortality in an especially vivid way – with **all** my senses. Joining my classmates to celebrate our common bond would constitute a formal acknowledgement of the passage of years; it would be a way of wishing yesterday could be tomorrow. Such an experience would be lachrymose and distressing. Another reunion would be too heavy a dose of contemplation because looking back should be done with sips not gulps. Even when I listen to the music of my youth or otherwise reflect on my past – it is not as strong a dose as reuniting with dozens of others for the purpose of paying homage to a time gone by.

Oddly enough and inexplicably, I would consider (the operative word is, "consider") attending a 60 year reunion if I should be so fortunate as to be alive and healthy; anytime sooner than that would be too much too soon. As strong as I think I am, "yestermorrow" is more than I want to manage.

I had a flash of insight

The Resurrection Of Mary Alice's First Child

In my early forties, I suffered a crisis of identity, validation and power. My heart was decimated by the collapse of a relationship in which I was weak and essentially pathetic. The demise of that relationship dropped me to a bottom from which I could only rise if I altered much of who I was. I could not, however, have accomplished that without the help of my best friend – someone who loved me enough to show me who I was and encouraged me to grow beyond. After six months of him not allowing me to look any where other than in the mirror, I had a flash of insight. From that moment on, I began to develop into a person I could honor. Subsequently, at the end of that six-month period, I wrote the following:

Identity

Where I have the choice to decide, I am who *I* have decided to be. Thus, I am self-defined.

My being male, Black African-American, or anything else is relevant only *after* I define myself in terms of my singularity. I am a distinct being *first*. I am an un-like individual, and nothing else I may be, is even a *close* second.

Hence, I believe that defining oneself in terms of labels or categories that can be applied to others as well, rather than defining oneself with reference to one's specific uniquenesses, diminishes the value of one's person and provides a basis for inflicting pain on oneself or others.

Taking this concept to its rightful conclusion, part of life is explained: Defining oneself in terms of race, ethnicity, gender, religion and the like, is tantamount to explaining oneself in terms of one's shadow. *Definitions are the basis for beliefs and motivations*; therefore, much of human misery can be traced to people defining the substance in terms of the form, the fundamental in terms of the incidental.

Being multidimensional, as are all persons, there are some who are superior to me on one point or another. When considering the total person, however, there is none superior to me. I am not better than others but I am decidedly *advantaged* because I am self-validating and unusually powerful. I am greater than the sum of all aspects of me; I am synergistic.

Though everyone on the planet is unique, most are unique in mere ordinary ways. Each person may be distinct from the next, but almost always, the distinctions are distinctions without differences – differences that matter.

I have immense respect for the person I am. In truth, my greatest need is for me to respect myself, though my first need is for me to love myself. I never neglect either need. So, I respect all that I am, love most of what I am, and anything that I am not – is not important – until proven otherwise.

I am neither arrogant nor haughty; that would bring me close to ordinary. Nor am I conceited; I am simply convinced. I am not intrigued or flattered by my advantages. I am at ease with them. I accept and embrace them as I do my height, my skin color or shoe size.

Naturally then, I am my own knight in brilliant armor, for who could be a better champion for me than I? I am the most important person in my life; by being such, I am of the highest possible value to others as well as to myself. I am at my best when I value myself accordingly.

Be I prince or pauper, I esteem the person I have defined as myself.

Validation

I validate myself to myself as a consequence of being myself.

I do not need anyone or anything outside myself to confirm or validate my worth or value as a person. *External validation is like a mother's milk; it should be needed only in the beginning.*

I do not ever feel blessed or privileged (and neither diminished nor reduced) because of another person – no matter who or what he or she is. Furthermore, it is irrelevant if others do not acknowledge, value or can even recognize my personal greatness. My existence is real, hence my greatness.

It is sufficient that *I* know my worth. Verification and endorsement of my value proceed from within me. I need no co-signer.

What others think, believe or do can be important sometimes, but they are never important enough, however, to undermine the integrity of my identity or personal power. (There is no star about which I orbit, for whose gravitation force is worthy? I orbit about my own star.) I am who I am and know it. I do what I am, to express myself, never to prove myself. I may impress but never with intent.

Taking this concept to its rightful conclusion, part of life is explained: Those who seek or value external validation allow others to define them; the euphoria of the validation never lasts long enough, and like an addict, they will sacrifice their humanity to receive it.

My frame of references is true because I am balanced at the center of my reality. Though not self-contained, I am *self-defined* and that is what drives my self-validation.

Power

The only power worth my struggles is power over myself.

I clearly understand I can have no real power whatsoever over anyone else, except by his or her explicit or implicit permission. Power over others can be a peculiar paradox – a zero-sum game with a pernicious hidden cost; sometimes, the more power I seek over another, the less power I have over myself.

Power over others can lure one into a trap that taxes one's attentions and efforts to maintain it. A person may give you power over himself, for any number of reasons, but there is always a piece of him that resents the submission and it is that piece which hooks the one in power and actually leads him, forcing him to expend his resources to maintain such power. It is like the deluded puppeteer and the puppet. The puppeteer may pull the strings, but the puppet's resistance dictates how, if not also when and where.

Taking this concept to its rightful conclusion, part of life is explained: Power over others, even in small doses, when frustrated or thwarted gives rise to the cruelties that have defined humanity for millennia.

I, on the other hand, am an extremely powerful person because I choose power over myself as the power that matters most to me, and any part of that power I choose to give to another (because of living in an interdependent society) I give with care and deliberation. I calculate the maximum cost I am willing to pay -- or the minimum benefit I am willing to receive – while never forgetting that at anytime, I can choose to take that portion of my power back – also at a cost.

I also declare that I *demand* of myself that *I* be charged with the sole responsibility for my actions and their consequences. I deeply revere my identity and know that I am too powerful to blame anyone else or anything outside myself for the consequences of the choices I make.

In any event, who I have defined myself to be must never be diminished in my eyes; that is a cost I will not pay. I am powerful because I hold my personal humanity in supreme regard and I am not deceived by any power I may be granted over another. *Understanding the nature of power and honoring one's personal power is worth more than the power of one over millions; it is both awesome and profound – it borders on being a god.*

Never again will I trip over who I am and stumble into stupidity.

... And I Am Better For It

In the essay, The Resurrection of Mary Alice's First Child, I mention that I had been in a deeply painful relationship that led to an abrupt upheaval of the nature of my person and all that defined me. To state this situation in less patrician terms and in more plebeian terms: I fell in love with a woman who eventually squatted over me, shit in my face, ripped my heart out and wiped her ass with it.

I endured profound disrespect and eventually ended the relationship. I was in pain being with her and even more pain without her. Along the way, I made a total fool of myself – having no pride – all to no avail. The relationship had choked to death on its own vomit.

No doubt her description of events, especially the aftermath, would differ from the above. Her response, however, to my description of our relationship is irrelevant. What is relevant and most notable is that I am forever deeply grateful and indebted to her; what she put me through (more exactly, what I allowed her to put me through) led to my morphing into who I am. I cannot imagine being on this path to constant improvement without experiencing her selfishness and ruthless disregard for me.

Let it be known that the ugly time in that relationship was one of the darkest periods of my adult life. I plunged into despair. I lost 40 pounds in a matter of weeks. But I did not resort to alcohol or drugs; weeping and sobbing, however, were my consolation and I did so for months. I was a wreck and a shadow of a man who could not imagine surviving. I felt trapped in my own grief.

That relationship, more than any other in my adult life, did more to shape who I am than any other. It constituted a straight line between the person I once was and the person I am continually evolving into today. There was no way I could see the end product and I do not think there was any other way to become that end product.

It is acutely fascinating how one can look up into the darkness in search of light and see nothing but an even darker sky behind which is a bright sun and a warm blue sky. It is a fact worthy of reflection of how hopelessness can choke one's sense of a possibly better tomorrow but with the helping hand of a friend who cares – one does not have to die.

Even more profound is when I look back, I do not recognize, let alone respect, the person I was. I can see that the sky was not that dark and the future was anything other than hopeless. In any event, I am better for it. A fundamental shift began later that year and was well along the way within the two years that followed. I emerged new from the inside out.

Never again will my *identity* and sense of self be contingent on another person. Never again will I value *validation* from another above validation by myself. Never again will *power* over another (e.g., trying to make someone love me) be a focus. Never again will I trip over who I am and stumble into stupidity. Never again will I love and subsequently allow someone to treat me with contempt and disregard. Never because I will never forget.

To be sure, I am still becoming something very different from who I was. One popular dictum of today is, "Whatever doesn't kill you makes you stronger." That is not always true. Sometimes events break you and reduce you to something even less. Whether it makes you stronger or not depends on many things not the least of which is a social infrastructure, such as I had in one man, my best friend.

As an aside, I do not hate my former lover. I can see her and interact with her without even a tinge of what I once felt. My conversion from loving her to feeling neutral toward her is complete. I am a better person because of the pain she inflicted and because I had someone there to see that I survived. To both of them, I salute in almost equal measure.

THE FINALE

... incentives to be good or evil

Humanity: Guilty Or Not Innocent

Because I have arrived here and will someday leave, I am essentially a visiting soul. As a visiting soul who has not only participated in the human drama but has paid painstaking attention to it as an extension of my self-imposed obligation to constantly assess who I am, I have observed an on-going series of activities that could be deemed indictable.

For the moment, let us assume that, as a visiting soul, I plead my case before "God" the Being(s) responsible for the existence of humanity. I plead my case not in prayer, but in this document that will serve as evidence to all those who come after me, that I have appointed myself as judge and jury given that "God" is at best a mere observer and at worst a deserter. I hereby declare that my observations constitute sufficient grounds to consider the adjudication of humanity.

The Inquest:

After a thorough and exhaustive investigation of the history and current behavior of humanity – both with regard to its institutions and individuals -- a formal indictment would be in order and is hereby issued.

The Indictment:

The human race, both as a collective and individually, is hereby charged with crimes against itself, the nature of which include all manner of high crimes and felonies as well as the insidious and the sinister attitudes, beliefs and ideologies upon which its various institutions derive their power and effects.

The Trial:

As judge, I hereby appoint *Carlespie* as the defense attorney and *Carlespie Mary Alice* as the prosecuting attorney.

The Opening Statements:

   The Defense –

   The defense will prove there is a preponderance of moral good in the human race and that any and all of the alleged crimes against itself are perpetrated by the few and in no way diminish the fundamental and ubiquitous virtues that define humanity.

   The Prosecution –

   The prosecution will prove huma
nity to be an egregious threat to itself and has repeatedly, habitually and without compunction proven to be deleterious and malignant. The evidence will clearly show that humanity cannot be trusted to elevate peace, reason, and the welfare and well being of all, above its inherent selfish and malevolent interests.

The Evidence:

There is love and there is hatred.

There is peace and there is war.

There is respect and there is scorn.

There is harmony and there is conflict.

There is truth and there are lies.

There is fairness and there is bigotry.

There is sincerity and there is hypocrisy.

There is selflessness and there is selfishness.

There is sharing and there is greed.

There is honesty and there is duplicity.

There is the scurrilous and there is the sublime.

There is the human and there is the human.

The Closing Arguments:

The Defense –

The prosecution has failed to prove its point beyond a reasonable doubt. Humanity is flawed but it is more decent and good than not. The question that philosophers and theologians have pondered for thousands of years is whether humans are basically good or basically evil. That is the wrong question.

The question should be this: ***Are there more incentives to be good or evil?*** This question acknowledges the fundamental goodness of humans, but it also gives weight to the conditions under which a person (people) exists especially given the abandonment by humanity's Creator. Conditions and the environment are the driving elements that define whether there is good or evil in humans. Therefore, Mr. Juror, you must return a verdict of not guilty.

The Prosecution –

Let the question be as posed by the defense: ***Are there more incentives to be good or evil?*** The evils of humanity are not a function of environment or incentives. If humanity were basically good then no matter the conditions, good would prevail more than it has. There would be some evil but not to the level history has clearly shown – whether "God" is absent or not.

Thus, You must return a verdict of guilty beyond a reasonable doubt because the evidence demands it.

The Verdict:

I, the sole member of the jury, find the defendant, all of humanity, *Guiltless but not Innocent.*

Not Innocent by reason of its own nature being subject to incentives.

Guiltless by reason of the world humanity has created without the help or guidance of its own Creator.

If at least 11 people are inspired

Dancing To The Songs In My Head
(And Not The Ones Played By The DJ)

I am not eccentric or fundamentally contrary. In fact, I willingly – sometimes eagerly – comply with many societal norms, attitudes and beliefs. I often look at this reality through the same lenses, as do many. But often enough and in the ways and at the times that matter most to me, I dance to songs the DJ is not playing. In that regard, I stand out and maybe appear misplaced like the proverbial fly in the ointment.

This book represents some of the songs in my head that are different from the ones played by the DJ (The DJ being society's institutions[1] which perpetuate and propagate their beliefs, attitudes and so forth.) Nonetheless, it has been a rewarding experience tapping on the keyboard watching the words fall out of my mind – words that reflect my ideas and opinions about various aspects of this reality.

In any event, authoring this work has allowed me to challenge and/or shape what I believe. It constitutes a means for those I love to read the pages of my mind and connect even closer to who I am and last of all, it represents another means to honor the memory of my mother, *Mary Alice*. To that end, this book is a success.

The question that springs up at this point relates to how those who are not part of my personal orbit will react. If at least 11[2] of those people are inspired to examine or re-examine what they believe and adopt a position similar to my guiding *ethos*, namely: *There is no idea or belief I so dearly cherish so as to shield it from rigorous scrutiny or thoughtful challenge. There is no idea or belief I esteem so highly that I will not alter it or abandon it* –

---

[1] It is glaringly obvious that the primary institution on which this book has focused is religion. The one thing that drove that focus is the notion that religion claims to derive its authority and its purpose – raison d'etre – from a source superior to humanity. I would have been derelict in my duty as a human if I did not scrutinize that claim.

[2] I chose the number 11 because it is as arbitrary as any other two-digit prime number especially given that the odds of a book rising to the level of "best seller" is far less likely than achieving the sale of 11 books.

sacrifice it in favor of standing even closer to the truth then this book will be successful in more ways than one.

In fact, it is that kind of success that would bring me the kind of joy about which most authors can only fantasize. So, to anyone who picks up this book, I hope you will not blindly dance to the songs played by the DJ but search for songs that ring true and make explainable sense to play in your own head and dance to your heart's delight.

Thank you for your time and attention.

A Dirge For Inamorata
(For The Last Time)

I did not know that when we *danced* together,
It would be for the last time

I did not know that when you *whispered* those erotic words,
It would be for the last time

I did not know that when we *made* fiery and bewitching love,
It would be for the last time

I did not know that on that day when we *dreamed* of our future,
It would be for the last time

I did not know that when you *wrote* to me about your love,
It would be for the last time

I did not know that when we *kissed* good-bye before you left,
It would be for the last time

I did not know that when we *spoke* three times that day,
It would be for the last time

Too soon the last time, my inamorata ... too soon

I thought our hearts would beat in rhythm together for always

But for everything there will be a last time,
Later or sooner – there will be

>a last smile
>a last tear
>
>a last breath
>a last everything

The last time belongs to yesterday
The last time belongs to memories
>until my last time

There is no idea or belief I so dearly cherish so as to shield it...

About The Author

First, to matters of tertiary importance: I was awarded a full-three-year academic scholarship to Cranbrook High School in Bloomfield Hills, Michigan. Sometime afterwards, I earned an academic scholarship to Wayne State University where I procured a Bachelor of Science degree in Business Administration (Finance and Business Economics) with "High Distinction." Later, I earned a Master's degree in Business Administration, also from Wayne State University.

Now to matters of primary importance: I am indeed my mother's son. My name is Carlespie Mary Alice McKinney, and I am Mary Alice's first of seven children – three boys and four girls – born into the African-American experience in the 1950's. I was as much my mother's confidante as I was her oldest child. For 12 years we suffered her husband's raw brutality – she far more than I – where finally, he made sure I would be the audience to her murder.

Through a series of life-altering events I underwent a critical metamorphosis facilitated by incessant contemplation and introspection. By the time I reached my mid-forties, all the major components of who I am today had been put in place – I emerged as a synergistic human. Nonetheless, my growth as a person trapped inside the mind of a human visiting Prison Earth continues. That being stated, there are two prime directives to which I firmly and fervently adhere – the first of which is as follows:

There is no idea or belief I so dearly cherish so as to shield it from rigorous scrutiny or thoughtful challenge. There is no idea or belief I esteem so highly that I will not alter it or abandon it – sacrifice it in favor of standing even closer to the truth.

Part of my self-imposed mission as a human is to honor what is true even if it means rejecting an idea or notion I once cherished.

My second directive is to honor the self I am above all others so I am best able to honor others. Stating the second directive another way:

... naturally then, I am my own knight in brilliant armor, for who could be a better champion for me than I?

Nonetheless, having observed and experienced the conditions of the human drama, I suffer from a type of quiet and simmering state of relentless pain. The unkindnesses and the cruelties humans inflict on each other choke my heart. I want to know the "whys," especially why humans are allowed to continue to perpetuate their interminable inhumanities. The holy books, prophets, teachers and other religious leaders and philosophers provide answers that are at best specious and vacuous and at worst, utterly parlous.

To that end (and for other reasons too), I stumbled into becoming a deist. But my heart weeps for I sense my time trapped inside the mind of this person visiting Prison Earth is all too close to its end. So I can only wish that my sons, and my "baby girl," along with my grandchildren and all the few others I love can escape the agony that arises from not knowing the "whys," either because they believe they already know or they do not deem it important that they do not know.

Suggested Reading

Adler, M. J. (1981). *Six great ideas*. New York: Touchstone.

Allen, J., Als, H., Lewis, J., & Litwack, L. F. (2007). *Without sanctuary*. Santa Fe: Twin Palms Publishers.

Asimov, I. (1968). *Science, numbers and I*. New York: Ace Publishing Corporation.

Barnes, D., Burgdorf, A., & Wenck, L. S. (1987). *Critical thinking*. Austin TX: Steck-Vaughn Company.

Berne, E. (1964). *Games people play*. New York: Grove Press.

Blackburn, S. (1999). *Think*. Oxford: Oxford University Press.

Blatner, D. (1997). *The joy of π*. New York: Walker and Company.

Book of Mormon: Another testament of Jesus Christ. (1981). Salt Lake City: The Church of Jesus Christ of Latter-day Saints.

Brooks, M. (2009). *13 things that don't make sense*. New York: Vintage Books.

Cameron, J. (1982). *A time of terror: A survivor's story*. Baltimore: Black Classic Press.

Campbell, R., & Sowden, L. (Eds). (1985). *Paradoxes of rationality and cooperation: Prisoner's dilemma and Newcomb's problem*. Vancouver, Canada: The University of British Columbia Press.

Dawkins, R., (2009). *The greatest show on earth: The evidence for evolution*. New York: Free Press.

Dhammapada: A new translation of the Buddhist classic. (2006). (E. Fronsdal, Trans.). Boston: Shambhala Publications.

Egner, R. E. (1958). *Bertrand Russell's best*. New York: The New American Library.

Flemings, H. (2003). *A philosophical scientific and theological defense for the notion that a God exists*. Lanham, MD: University Press of America.

Franz, R. (1983). *Crisis of conscience.* Atlanta: Commentary Press.

Gamow, G. (1965). *One two three ... infinity: Facts and speculations of science.* New York: The Viking Press & Bantam Book.

Ginzburg, R. (1988). *100 years of lynchings.* Baltimore: Black Classic Press.

Gracian, B. (C Maurer. Trans.). (1991). *The art of worldly wisdom.* New York: Doubleday.

Harris, S. (2006). *Letter to a christian nation.* New York: Alfred A. Knopf.

Hitchens, C. (2007). *god is not great.* New York: Twelve Hachette Book Group.

Holy Bible: New international version. (1984). Nashville: Holman Bible Publishers.

Holy Vedas. (P.S. Vidyalankar, Eds.). (1983). Dehli, India: Clarion Books.

Kiersky, J. H. & Caste, N. J. (1995). *Thinking critically.* St. Paul: West Publishing Company.

Kipfer, B. A. (2007). *Consider this ... questions that make you think.* New York: Random House.

Kirby, G. R., & Goodpaster, J. R. (2007). *Thinking.* Upper Saddle River NJ: Pearson Prentice Hall.

Koran, the meaning of the glorious. (n.d.). (M. M. Pickthall, Trans.). New York: The New American Library.

Lakoff, G. & Johnson, M. (1999). *Philosophy in the flesh.* New York: Basic Books.

Last days of Socrates. (1969). (H. Tredennick, Trans.). New York: Penguin Classics.

Livingston, G. (2004). *Too soon old, tool late smart.* New York: Marlowe & Company.

Magee, B. (1998). *The story of thought*. Great Britain: Dorling Kindersley Publishing.

McFarlane, E. & Saywell, J. (1995). *The book of if: Questions for the games of life and love*. New York: Quality Paperback Book Club.

Meyer, S. C. (2009). *Signature in the cell: DNA and the evidence for intelligent design*. New York: HarperOne Publishers.

Miller, R. K. (1998). *The Informed Argument*. Orlando: Harcourt College Publishers.

Mlodinow, L. (2008). *The drunkard's walk: How randomness rules our lives*. New York: Pantheon Books.

O'Brien, J. A. (1942). *God can we find him?* Glen Rock NJ: Paulist Press.

Ornstein, R. (1995). *The roots of the self*. New York: Harper San Francisco.

Pinker, S. (2007). *The language instinct*. New York: Harper Perennial Modern Classics.

Pinker, S. (2007). *The stuff of thoughts*. New York: Penguin Group.

Rogers, J.A. (1957). *From "Superman" to man*. Mattituck, NY: Amereon House.

Rosenthal, J. S. (2005). *Struck by lightning: The curious world of probabilities*. Toronto: HarperCollins Publishers.

Schick, T., & Vaughn, L. (1995). *How to think about weird things: Critical thinking for a new age*. Mountain View, CA: Mayfield Publishing Company.

Shenkman, R. (2008). *Just how stupid are we?: Facing the truth about the American voter*. New York: Basic Books.

Siu, R.G.H. (1979). *The craft of power*. New York: John Wiley & Sons.

Sri Guru Granth Sahib. (1985). (G.S. Talib, Trans.). South Asia Books.

Sutphen, D. (1991). *The oracle within.* New York: Pocket Books.

Talmud, New edition of the Babylonian. (v.5-6). (1896-1903). (M.L. Rodkinson, Trans.). Cornell University Library.

Tao Te Ching: A new English vesion. (2006). (L-Tzu & S. Mitchell, Trans.). New York: Harper & Row.

Tannen, D. (1986). *That's not what I meant.* New York: Ballantine Books.

White, A. D. (1965). *A history of the warfare of science with theology in Christendom.* New York: The Free Press.

Wysong, R.L. (1976). *Creation-the evolution controversy.* East Lansing MI: Inquiry Press.

Youngson, R. (1998). *Scientific blunders: A brief history of how wrong scientists can sometimes be.* New York: Carroll & Graf Publishers.

Zinn, Howard. (2003). *A people's history of the United States: 1492 – Present.* New York: Harper-Collins Publisher

References

Age of consent, (n.d.). Retrieved August 2, 2009, from http://www.webistry.net/jan/consent.html

Bismark, O. (n.d.) Retrieved June 24, 2009, from http://en.wikiquote.org/wiki/Otto_von_Bismarck

Bonaparte, N. (n.d.), Retrieved June 24, 2009, from http://www.quotedb.com/quotes/290

Boy, 12, kills man who attacked his mom (2008, April 2). Retrieved from http://www.wtop.com/?nid=25&sid=138022

Breaking Election Promise OK: Judge (January, 30 2005). Calgary Herald.

Brooks, M. (2009). *13 things that don't make sense.* New York: Vintage Books.

Cutler, A., Lynch, M., et al. (n.d.). The Sambia, Retrieved July 11, 2009, from http://people.stthomasu.ca/~belyea/2003 Sambian.htm

Dawkins, R., (2009). *The greatest show on earth; The evidence for evolution.* New York: Free Press.

Diogenes (n.d.). Retrieved June 26, 2009, from http://www.in2greece.com/English/historymyth/history/ancient/diogenes.thm

Einstein, A. (n.d.). Retrieved June 26, 2009, from http://www.Brainyquote.com/quotes/authors/a/albert_einstein_6.html

Goldman, R. Why do kids kill? (2008, November 12). ABC News Internet Ventures.

Hitler, A. (n.d.). Retrieved June 24, 2009, from http://www.allgreatquotes.com/adolf_hitler_quotes5.shtml

Hitler, A. (n.d.). Retrieved June 24, 2009, from http://www.allgreatquotes.com/adolf_hitler_quotes7.shtml

Hitler, A. (n.d.). Retrieved June 28, 2009, from http://www.allgreatquotes.com/adolf_hitler_quotes.shtml

Hitler, A. (n.d.). Retrieved June 24, 2009, from http://www.brainyquote.com/quotes/quotes/a/adolfhitle385640.html

Holy Bible: New International Version. (1984). Nashville: Holman Bible Publishers.

Hubbard, E. (n.d.). Retrieved June 26, 2009, from http://www.quotationspage.com/quote/285.html

Huie, W.B. (January 1956). The shocking story of approved killing in Mississippi. *Look Magazine.*

Hunt, A. Police: Man kills wife, injures son, then shoots self. (2007, November 25) *Detroit Free Press.* Retrieved from http://www.freep.com/apps/pbcs.dll/article?AID=20071125/NEWS/71125019/1048/SPORTS06

Lavoie, D. (2002, June 14). Religious sect member convicted of murder in starvation of son. *The Boston Globe.*

Le Bon, G. (1879). Retrieved from http://jenbayne.wordpress.Com//2009/10/29/are-gender-differences-all-in-the-head-ask-the-rat/

Letter To Horace Greeley, 1862, retrieved from http://showcase.net/web/creative/Lincoln/speeches/greeley.htm

Lincoln, A. (n.d.). Retrieved June 26, 2009, from http://thinkexist.com/quotation/nearly_all_men_can_stand_adversity-but_if_you/10078html

Mann, T. (n.d.). Retrieved June 26, 2009, from http://www.Brainyquote.com/quotes/quotes/t/thomasmann382425.html

McClellan, S. (2008). *What happened: Inside the Bush White House and Washington's culture of deception.* Philadelphia: PublicAffairs.

Monks fight at Jerusalem's Church Of The Holy Sepulchre (n.d.). Retrieved June 27, 2009. from http//www.novinite.Com/view_news_php?id=98742

Napoleon on the art of war. (1999). (J. Luvaas, Trans.). New York: Free Press.

Napoleonic guide. (n.d.). Retrieved June 26, 2009, from http://www.napoleonguide.com/maxim_himself.htm

Pasteur, L. (n.d.). Retrieved July 1, 2009, from http://www.Historylearningsite.co.uk/louis_pasteur.htm

Pasteur, L. Deep cove crier. (December 1997). Retrieved July 1, 2009, from http://www3.telus.net/st_simons/cr9712.htm

Petrarch (n.d.). Retrieved July 1, 2009, from http://thinkexist.com/quotation/rarely_do_great_beauty_and_great_virtue_dwell/169031.html

Planck, M. http://www.people.ubr.com/historical-figures/by-first-name/m/max-planck/max-planck-quotes/a-new-scientific.aspx

Pope, A. (1709). An essay on criticism.

Rosenthal, J. (2005). *Struck by lightning ... The curious world of probabilities.* Toronto:. HarperCollins Publishers.

Sagan, C. (1987). *Parade.* The fine art of baloney detection.

Shakespeare. *Henry VI.*

Shakespeare. *Julius Caesar.*

Shakespeare. *Romeo and Juliet.*

Sharon, A. (n.d.). Retrieved June 27, 2009, from http://en.wikipedia.org/wiki/Ariel_Sharon

Shaw, G.B. Retrieved July1, 2009, from http://www.brainyquote.com/quotes/authors/g/george_bernard_shaw_2.html

Shine, K.N. (2003, June 18). DNA tests exonerate man. *Detroit Free Press,* pp. 1B, 8B.

Sinclair, N., Esparza, S., & Mrozowski, J. (2007, December 5). Fund set up for 7-year old 'hero' who saved mom. *Detroit News.* Retrieved from, http://www.detnews.com/apps/pbcs.dll/article?AID=2007712050466.

Siu, R.G.H. (1979). *The craft of power.* New York: John Wiley & Sons.

Slavin, B. (2002, April 25). Shaken Saudis take hard look at society. *USA Today.*

Stern, B. (1927). Social factors in medical progress. New York: Columbia University Press.

Stevenson, A. (n.d.). Retrieved June 24, 2009, from http://www.quotesandpoem.com/quotes/listquotes/author/adial-stevenson/3

Stevenson. A. Retrieved June 24, 2009, from http://en.wikiquote.org/wiki/Adlai_Stevenson

Stevenson.A. (n.d.). Retrieved June 24, 2009, from http://thinkexist.com/quote/with/keyword/adlai_stevenson/

Thomas, W. (n.d.). Retrieved June 26, 2009, from http://www.gaia.com/quotes/w_i_thomas

Tubman, H. (n.d.). Retrieved June 24, 2009, from http://www.brainyquote.com/quotes/authors/h/harriet_tubman.html

Voltaire. (n.d.). Retrieved June 26, 2009, from http://www.brainyquote.com/quotes/authors/v/voltaire_5.html

Voltaire. (n.d.). Retrieved June 27, 2009, from http://www.famousquotesandauthors.com/authors/voltaire_quotes.html

Voltaire. (n.d.). Retrieved June 26, 2009, from http://www.quotationspage.com/quote/33103.html

Voltaire. (n.d.). Retrieved June 27, 2009, from http://thinkexist.com/quotation/if_you_wish_to_converse_with_me-deine_your/175628.html

Youngson, Robert. (1998). Scientific blunders: *A brief history of how wrong scientists can sometimes be.* New York: Carroll & Graf Publishers.

INDEX

3 Choices, 28
11 Turns, i
20 Things, 1
1600 Pennsylvania, 222
4654 days, 233

A.
Abell 1835 IR1916, 192
abortion, 84
    hypocrisy, 85
academic scholarship, 264
adroit, vi, 74
advice, 7-9, 21
affirmative action, 41
Africa, 212
African-American(Black) 2, 7, 20,
    21, 23, 25, 120, 135,
    140, 143, 147
    light v dark, 137, 143
    "shades" of color, 140
    lynchings, 148, 150
    "talking White," 153
African slaves, 31
age of consent, 113
agnostics, 175
alacrity, 94
Allah, 107, 109, 207
Alexander the Great, 99
Amin, I., 110
Amun Ra, 207
ancestors, 25, 255
Antonius, Marcus, 11
aphorisms (mindless), 218-219
aphrodisiacs, 3
apostate, i
apothegm, 255
apotheosize, 21, 99, 238
apple-orange, 18-19, 244-245
arduous, 157
Aristotle, 50
arguments, 52
Askew, F. & C., vii
atheist, 175
Auntie Sara, 97
Auntie Tubman, 142

B.
Baal, 177, 207, 216
Babel, Tower of, 55
babes, 209
"Baby Girl,",v, 39
baleful, 24, 97
baneful, 161
basic credo (my), 9, 68, 139,
    162, 178, 278, 281

battles (choosing), 87
beauty, 2, 50
being right, 67
beliefs, 138, 159
bemused, 35
benighted, 161
Bibbs, G., vii
Bible, 196, 218
    interpretation, 196
    Matthew (6:14), 74
    Judges (6:31, 32), 216
Bismark, O., 17
    elections, 17
blessed, 212
blood (thicker than water), 37
Bonaparte, N., 16
    Stupidity in politics, 16
    being contradicted, 162
    torture, 16
Book of Mormon, 218
Booker T & The M.G.'s, 253
bravado, 120
Brittish Royal Family, 25
Bryant, R., 109
Buddha, 116
Bush, G., 23
butterflies, 238

C.
Caesar, Julius, 11
callipygian, 9
Cambridge, MA, 120
capital offenses, 80
capital punishment, 78
celebrity, 99
"celemourn," 253
    birthday, 253
    death-day, 253
character, 45
charm, 50
children follow parents, 18
Christian principles, 3
Church ... Holy Sepulcher, 214
churlish, 87
Civil Rights Act, 121, 145
Civil War, 23, 142
class, 1
closed mind, 70
cogitated, 163
cogent, 23
cognitive dissonance, 21, 70, 159,
    189
coincidence, 218
collectivism, 125
colored, 143
Columbia, 91

Communication, 55
confluence, 115
congruent, 159
conpunction, 150
context of discipline, 83
conviction of innocent, 69
corporal punishment, 82
corporate America, 33
cost-benefit calculation, 59
cowardice, 252
Cranbrook High School, I, 264, 281
Cranes, 264
Craft, C., vii
creationists, 179
crimes against humanity, 28
critical thinking, 176
Crow, 265
Crowley, J., 120
cruelty, 82

D.
D.J., 278
dailies, 43
dark skin, 2, 137, 143
Dagon, 207
Dawkins, R., 183
death, 91
    ordinary, 91
Declaration of Independence, 63
deist, ii, 170, 174-178, 226
deleterious, 24, 130
Democrats, 33
Descarte, 175
DéToi, v
Devil, 205, 239
dictum, 273
different fruit same tree, 18
Diogenes, 66, 99
discipline, 82
Disjointed States of America, 141
diversity, 126
DNA, I, 37, 69, 70, 181
DNR, 63, 85
domestic violence, I, 20, 128, 232, 233, 236, 241, 242, 243
    helpless, 232
    reasons, 129-130
doubt (the advantage of), 30
doxology, 198
dragon-slayer, 88
dutiful steward, 102

E.
Earhart, A., 26
editor, ix
Einstein, A., 35

    quote about stupidity, 35
elixir, 6
Emancipation Proclamation, 60
Emerson, R., 50
epiphany, ii, 247
eschew, 52
esoteric, 197
est is totus illic est, 226
eternal punishment, 227
ethos, i, 52, 100, 115, 197
every thing happens ..., 106
evolution, 2, 176, 179-183
excoriating, 148
experience-teacher, 4

F.
factious, 197
facts, 159
facts of life, 7
faith, 177, 179, 183, 207
fallacious, 53, 198
Father's Day, 39
feckless, 8
feculent, 151, 198, 254
fellatio, 98
female, 131
Five Senses, v
Flemings, H., vi, 174
flummoxed, 133
fool others, self, 23
"forgainst," iii
forgiveness, 74
Four Songs, v
friendship, 10, 12
    with opposite sex, 14
fulcrum, 113, 135, 162

G.
Gates, H., 120
gargantuan, 101
gauche, 147
Genesis, 55
genital mutilation, 128
germane, 127
Ghislaine, v
Gideon, 216
Ginzburg, R., 148
gluteophilic, 9
"God," vi, 1, 29, 46, 89, 117, 169, 171, 184
    bless, 53, 54
    defending, 215
    forgiving, 74
    if I were, 193
    image of humans, 90

gender, 173, 184
    maintaining image, 217
    playing or being, 221
    questions for, 223-225
    thanking, 207
    what I believe, 169, 171
Goldie, 256
"good hair," 143
Good Samaritan, 102
Greeley, H., 59
Green Onions, 253

H.
harakiri, 128
heaven, 185, 205
hell, 185, 206
hellion, 4
Henry VI, 123
Henry, P., 63
hero, 101
    definition, 102
heterodox, 127
heterogeneity, 125
heterosexualistic, 113, 132
high school reunion, 266
Hiroshima, 79
Hitler, A., 16, 53, 80
holocaust, 151
holy sites, 214
homicides, 84
    categories, 84
    codify, 86
    youth offenders, 249
homogeneity, 125
homophobic, 113, 128, 132, 161
Horizon Program, 264
hypocrisy, 132
hypothetical question, 51
Hubbard, E., 35
    quote about stupidity, 35
humanhood, 132
humanity, 275
    on trial, 275-277
Hume, 175
hummingbirds, 238
Humpty Dumpty, 246

I.
identity, 269
idiotropic, I, 164
image of humans, 90
imagine, 89
    "God," 89, 184
imperious, ix, 201
"In God We Trust," 153
in toto, 127
inamorata, 226, 258, 282+
inane, 153

individualism, 125
inimical, 12
infatuation, 93
intransigent, 12
introspection, 43
invidious, 65
irony, 39

J.
Jehovah, 109, 207
Jehovah's Witness, I, 156, 174, 245
Jesus, 66, 95, 109, 116, 207
Jews, 151
jihad, 123
Jim Crow Laws, 149
Joash, 216
Johnson, C., 256
jujitsu, 73

K.
Kante, 175
Karma, 109, 110
King, Jr., M.L., 137
knight, 99, 281
knights, 88
Koa Boo Boo, 108, 177
Koran, 218

L.
lachrymose, 91, 267
Lady Luck, 106
lawyers, 123
LeBon, G., 30
Lee, E., vii, 264, 266
LeGé, v
Leslie, L., vii
Lincoln, A., 59, 76
locked up mind, 71
Locke, 175
Locus of Identity, 130
Look Magazine, 109
love, 93
    unconditional, 93
    your enemies, 95
Luciano, "L," 110
lust, 93
lying, 111

M.
Madoff, 194
magnanimous, 45, 201
maleficent, 171
males, 132
malem in se, 59
mama, 231
    eulogy, 238
    her murder, 234

husband's name, 254
   obituary, 237
Mann, P., 105
Mary Alice, iii, v, 254
   her murder, 234
martial arts, 83
"Massa," 137
masculinity, 132
   counterfeit, 134
masturbation, 187, 219
Matysse, v
maxim, 53, 218
meaning of life, 163
Mecca, 199
McClellan, S., 23
McEady, M., vi
McGaugh, S., 71
McKinney, A., vii
McKinney, C., 50, 163, 239
   biological father, 255
   childhood, 233
   identity, 268
   in shock, 234
   name change, 257-260
      reaction to, 261
   power, 270
   regrets, 235, 238
   resurrection, 268, 272
   source of name, 256
   put on trial, 248-252
   validation, 269
McKinney, M.A., 239
   her words, 250
men (impersonators), 132
ménage a trois, 33
Meyer, S., 182
Milam, J., 109
miscreants, 201
misogyny, 130
missive, 7
modest dress, 21
Mohammed, 116
Molech, 177, 207
money, 1, 7, 153, 205
monks, 214
   Armenian, 214
   Greek Orthodox, 214
morality, 59
motives, 45, 47, 59, 61
   intrinsic, 47
   extrinsic, 47
movies, 43
Moynihan (Senator), 66
murder, 86, 246

N.
"N" word, 147-152
Nagasaki, 79
Neely, C., vi
Negro, 143
New Age, 74, 109
New Guinea, 98
nocent, 65
nomenclature, 101

O.
Obama, B., 120, 145, 253
objurgated, 136
obligations of humans, 163, 165
O'Dell, 239, 244
opprobrious, 102
opinion v. intellect, 35
opposites attract, 13
Our Own Doings, 171

P.
pain of love, 6
passion v. intellect, 35
Pasteur, L., 71
patriarchal, 129
Patrick, 266
pattern of behavior, 120
pedantic, ix
pedigree, 26
pejorative, 102
perfidious, 146
perfunctory, 261
perspicacious, 135
Petrarch, 50
phlegmatic, 258
Pilate, Pontius, 66
plebeian, 272
pogrom, 111, 161
politics, 16, 33, 123
Pollyannish, 165
pontificate, 155
"poor white trash," 148
Pope, 60
Pope, A., 74
posit, 164, 180
Pot, P., 80, 110
power, 76, 132, 196, 270
placebo effect, 191
placid, 258
Planck, Max, 145
prayer, 172, 176, 193, 209,
   power of, 236
Prison Earth, iii, iv, 1, 7, 20, 22,
   65, 91, 108, 185, 193,
   220, 253, 282
probability, 180
problem-solving, 72
procellous, 135

proclivities, 164
propagate, 278
proscribe, 60, 62, 133, 184
privileged, 131
prostitute, 33, 85
puerile, 157
pugnacious, 16

Q.
quality of life, 63

R.
racial profiling, 120
racism, 120, 121, 135, 140,
    145, 161
    reason, 135
    legacy, 135
    reinforced, 136
random chance, 106, 115
rape, 114
reality v. perception, 105
reap ... sow, 109
reasons for this book, iii
Reed-Avery, H, vii
relatives, 37
religion, 2, 172, 187, 188, 193
    control, 190
    different ones, 201
    divide, 189
    evolution of, 203
    reductio ..., 199
    revelation of, 203
    source, 191
    trick, 205
reminiscing, 118
Republicans, 33
resilience, 246
resipiscence, 157
Richmond, C., 257
Robidoux, J., 199
roller-go-round, iv
Roman principle, 161
Romeo and Juliet, 123
Rosenthal, J., 180
Rubin, V., 71

S.
salacious, 114
salient, iv
Sambian, 97, 98
Samuels, C.J., ix
sanctity of life, 63, 80
Sarbanes-Oxley Act, 60
Satan, 185, 199
sciolism, 198
search for intelligent life, 20
sexual abuse (priests), 60

Stackhouse, D., v
Sagan, C., 17
    being bamboozled, 17
self-defined, 270
self-knowing, 164
self-perceptive, 164
self-preservation, 31, 103
sententious, 96
set-points, 164
seppuku, 128
Sept. 11-hijackers, 205
sex, 113
sexism, 128
sexual harassment, 132-133
Shakespeare, W., 11, 123
Sharon, A., 214
Shaw, G., 51
Shintoist, 116
Shiva, 107, 116
siblings, 244-245, 254
silence, 155
Siu, R.G.H., 76, 82, 196
slave mentality, 137
slavery, 59
slippery slope, 64
Spanish Inquisition, 149
spanking, 82
Spinoza, B., 175
sports, 41
Stackhouse, D., v
Stalin, J., 80, 110
Starr, D., vii
Stevenson, A., 16
stupidity, 1, 21, 35-36, 153
sudden death, 22
suicide, 62
summer 1961, 118
swastika, 152
sychophantic, 21, 100
synergistic, iii, 75, 164-165, 269

T.
Taeug, C., vi
tail wagging the dog, 5
tail of two friends, 14
teachers, 4, 41
temerity, 237
tertiary, 132, 281
theists, 175
Theresa, 245
Thomas, E., vii
Thomas, Jr., J, v
Thomas, W., 105
Thompson, D., vii
three beautiful words, 157
Till, E., 109
time 180

timing and consequences, 65, 193
timorous, iii, 142
too much alike, 12
Torah, 218
traumatize, 246
travails, 127
truckle, 99
truculent, iii
truth, vi, 66, 67
Tubman, H., 23, 26, 137, 142

U.
"Uncle Alfred,",141
"Uncle Jacksons,"140
"Uncle Jay-Jay,",141
"Uncle Thomases,"141
unctuous, 99
Underground Railroad, 23, 142
unfair fight, 66
unit cohesion, 126
Unitied States, 3
United States of White America, 120, 121, 135
un-witting bait, 244

V.
vagaries, 188
validation, 269, 273
valor, 88
vampires, 38
Venecia, 239, 244
Vietnam War, 156
visceral, 75, 133
Vishnu, 109, 207
Voltaire (Arouet, F.M.), 30
    communication, 57, 145
    define terms, 82
    quote about beauty, 50
    quote about certainty, 30
    quote about money, 153
    quote about opinions, 66

voters, 34

W.
Walden, D., vii, 264
water, 37
Wayne State University, 281
West, R., 256
Whimsical Chance, 171
White Americans, 2, 120, 135, 148
    Southern, 149
White terrorism, 148
why humans exist, 163
Williams, T., vii

Wilson, J., 253
Workings of Others, 171
worship, 172, 176
Wyniemko, K, 69

Y.
Yahweh, 109
yesterday,118
"yestermorrow," 266

Z.
zero-sum game, 66
Zeus, 177, 207

www.ingramcontent.com/pod-product-compliance
Lightning Source LLC
Chambersburg PA
CBHW070554100426
42744CB00006B/272